HATE CRIMES

To my parents, Lawrence and Elizabeth Herek, and to Jack.

GMH

To Dace Stone, and to the staff, board of directors, volunteers, and members of the National Gay & Lesbian Task Force.

KTB

We both dedicate this book to all of those who are working to end violence against lesbians and gay men.

GMH and KTB

HATE CRIMES is under
the general editorship of
Jon R. Conte, Ph.D.

HATE CRIMES

Confronting Violence
Against Lesbians and Gay Men

Edited by

Gregory M. Herek
Kevin T. Berrill

 SAGE Publications
International Educational and Professional Publisher
Newbury Park   London   New Delhi

For information address:

SAGE Publications, Inc.
2455 Teller Road
Newbury Park, California 91320
E-mail: order@sagepub.com

SAGE Publications Ltd.
6 Bonhill Street
London EC2A 4PU
United Kingdom

SAGE Publications India Pvt. Ltd.
M-32 Market
Greater Kailash I
New Delhi 110 048 India

Printed in the United States of America

Library of Congress Cataloging-in-Publication Data

Main entry under title:

Hate crimes: confronting violence against lesbians and gay men /
    edited by Gregory M. Herek, Kevin T. Berrill.
        p.   cm.
    Includes bibliographical references and index.
    ISBN 0-8039-4541-8.—ISBN 0-8039-4542-6 (pbk.)
    1. Gays—United States—Crimes against. 2. Hate crimes—United
States. I. Herek, Gregory M. II. Berrill, Kevin T.
HV6250.4.H66H38   1992
364.1'555'08664—dc20   91-34912

99 10 9 8 7 6 5

Sage Production Editor: Diane S. Foster

Contents

PART V: Implications for Policy

Foreword

In recent years, the number of reported attacks against Americans because of their race, religion, sexual orientation, or ethnic origin has increased dramatically. These hate crimes are carried out by organized groups as well as by individuals. They are intended to harm their victims and also to send a message of intimidation and fear to entire communities of people. The fact that such offenses still occur in the United States is an indication that we must be vigilant to protect the democratic values in which we take such great pride.

In 1865 the Ku Klux Klan formed and began attacking and intimidating African Americans. Its members used terrorism as a weapon to reestablish the old plantation social and economic order. The Klan's efforts were designed to prevent African Americans from exercising their constitutional rights to vote and hold office.

Today the targets of the Klan and other hate groups such as White Aryan Resistance and the Skinheads also include gay men and women, religious groups, and other minorities. Although some of their members use more sophisticated methods, they continue to rely on hate crimes as their principal weapon of intimidation. They have declared war on the U.S. government and the principles of equality and democracy that it represents.

Hate crimes are extraordinary in nature and require a special governmental response. As a starting point, we need to understand the dimensions of the problem. For this reason, I introduced in 1988 the Hate Crimes Statistics Act, which requires the Department of Justice to collect and publish annual statistics on crimes that manifest prejudice based on race, religion, sexual orientation, and ethnic origin. The bill was passed by both houses in the 101st Congress and finally signed by President Bush on April 23, 1990, as Public Law 101-275.

The Hate Crimes Statistics Act generated controversy in part because it included "sexual orientation" as a category upon which hate crimes are often based. This was in recognition of the rising tide of anti-gay violence that has been documented by the National Gay & Lesbian Task Force and such local groups as San Francisco's Community United Against Violence and the New York City Gay and Lesbian Anti-Violence Project.

Before the Hate Crimes Statistics Act, no federal statute specifically addressed anti-gay violence. Nor do current federal laws protect the rights of gay men and lesbians from discrimination in employment, housing, or services. Consequently, federal law enforcement response to anti-gay violence was virtually nonexistent until 1990. At the local level, law enforcement has historically been deficient. Although some agencies are now sincerely trying to do a better job in responding to this violence, in most areas of the country, the issue is treated as insignificant at best. At worst, the victims are blamed as though they brought the violence on themselves.

It was against this backdrop that I, acting in my role as then-chairman of the House Judiciary Subcommittee on Criminal Justice, convened the first congressional hearings on anti-gay violence on October 9, 1986. The testimony provided at those hearings clearly documented the problem of anti-gay violence, the importance of research into its scope and sources, and the immediate need for action to respond to it and prevent it.

The editors of this volume, Dr. Herek and Mr. Berrill, both testified at those hearings. Since then, they have been active in efforts to increase our understanding of this serious problem and to help formulate effective responses to it. The papers they have collected here represent an important milestone, the first anthology devoted exclusively to serious discussion of what is known about anti-gay prejudice and violence. It is a most thorough and thoughtful book, one that should be read by all Americans who wish to understand the specific dimensions of anti-gay violence and the general problem of hate crimes in our society. It will be especially useful to law enforcement personnel, legislators, and policymakers.

Whether based on sexual orientation, race, religion, or ethnicity, bigotry and the violence it inspires pose a grave threat to the peace and harmony of our communities. The need to alert Americans to this threat is great. We need especially to educate our youth about tolerance and about appreciating the benefits that we enjoy as a result of our culture's rich diversity of peoples, beliefs, and ways of living. This ground-breaking book sounds an alarm and provides tools for understanding the dimensions of hate violence. It deserves your careful study.

THE HONORABLE JOHN CONYERS, JR.
U.S. HOUSE OF REPRESENTATIVES

Introduction

Violence against lesbians and gay men is not a new problem. People who call themselves gay or whose sexual partner is of their own gender have long been subjected to physical brutality. Historically, such violence has often represented official state policies, as in thirteenth-century Europe, where the crime of sodomy was punishable by castration, torture, and death (Boswell, 1980). Similar laws in the American colonies mandated the death penalty, castration, or mutilation as early as the 1600s (Katz, 1976). In the twentieth century, between 5,000 and 15,000 of those forced to wear the pink triangle, which identified them as homosexual, are believed to have died behind the barbed wire of Nazi camps (Adam, 1987; Plant, 1986).

Private citizens also have perpetrated anti-gay violence. In the United States in the twentieth century, police often have looked the other way while young men preyed on gay people outside bars and in other public settings. And lesbians and gay men have often been harassed and brutalized by their relatives, co-workers, and schoolmates. The stigma attached to being gay usually prevented them from reporting their victimization, while public officials and law enforcement personnel typically remained indifferent to the problem.

Indeed, the victims themselves often have been blamed. For example, following the murder of a gay man in Miami in 1954, local newspapers "demand[ed] that homosexuals be punished for tempting 'normals' to commit such deeds" (Taylor, 1982, quoted in Adam, 1987). Lacking the safety of numbers and community, being assaulted has been a price one paid for being visible. It is not surprising, therefore, that the vast majority of gay men and women opted for invisibility as a way to avoid stigma and violence (see also Comstock, 1991; D'Emilio, 1983).

But many gay people are no longer willing to remain hidden. Since World War II and with even greater intensity since the 1969 Stonewall rebellion, lesbians and gay men have become increasingly visible in public life. They have organized for equality and challenged long-standing stereotypes. They have created an unprecedented community infrastructure, one that is still growing and helping to foster significant social and political gains. And, in the course of coming out as a community, they have gained respect from others and have increased their own self-esteem (see, for example, Bérubé, 1990; D'Emilio, 1983).

These gains have been achieved at a price. By coming out, lesbians and gay men also make themselves easier targets for those who hate and wish to harm them. In the last decade, as lesbians and gay men became more visible than ever before in American society, an unprecedented number of attacks against them were reported. During that same decade, the AIDS epidemic hit the United States, inflicting personal losses on gay people that resembled those of wartime. Tens of thousands of Americans died, most of them gay or bisexual men, a disproportionate number of them African American or Hispanic. With AIDS came an epidemic of stigma directed at those who were diagnosed and those who were suspected of being infected with the human immunodeficiency virus (HIV). AIDS was used to rationalize prejudice, discrimination, and violence against gay men and lesbians.

The widespread anti-gay violence of the 1980s coincided with a rising number of reported attacks against religious, racial, and ethnic minorities and women. Police departments and advocacy groups have documented thousands of racist, sexist, and anti-Semitic attacks, including episodes of murder, arson, bombings, assault, cross burnings, vandalism, and harassment.[1] Many of the perpetrators have also engaged in anti-gay violence. In 1983, for example, members of a neo-Nazi group who torched a Jewish community center in Indiana also firebombed a gay Christian church in Missouri (Berrill, 1986). The Klansman who lynched Michael Donald, a heterosexual Black man, in Mobile, Alabama, in 1981 had previously kidnapped and beaten a gay man (Segrest & Zeskind, 1989).

Every such incident carries a message to the victim and the entire community of which he or she is a part. Each anti-gay attack is, in effect, a punishment for stepping outside culturally accepted norms and a warning to all gay and lesbian people to stay in "their place," the invisibility and self-hatred of the closet. But in recent years, as the community's consciousness about hate crimes and its unwillingness to tolerate them has grown, anti-gay attacks increasingly have failed to enforce the cultural codes of silence and invisibility. Instead, new organizations have been formed in the past decade through which gay people have encouraged each other to speak out about their experiences of violence.

These trends were dramatized in 1978 when Harvey Milk, San Francisco's first openly gay supervisor, was assassinated by fellow supervisor Dan White, a law-and-order conservative who epitomized the "old" San Francisco that opposed the burgeoning lesbian and gay community. Many observers felt that White's light prison sentence[2] reflected the low value placed on the lives of gay people by the citizens of that old San Francisco. But part of Harvey Milk's legacy was a new way of responding to anti-gay violence. Anticipating that he might someday be a target for assassination, Milk left several tape recordings in which he called upon gay people to respond to his death with increased visibility. He pleaded, "If a bullet should enter my brain, let that bullet destroy every closet door" (Shilts, 1982, p. 372).

Many have heeded his call. Rather than retreating or hiding or accepting attacks as inevitable, lesbians and gay men have gotten angry and gotten organized. They have created organizations that can act collectively to confront violence and help those who are victimized. In San Francisco, the Community United Against Violence was formed soon after Milk's death. In other communities across the United States, lesbians and gay men similarly have established programs that provide counseling and advocacy for victims, sensitize and work with police and prosecutors, and educate the public about the causes and consequences of anti-gay violence. They have launched street patrols, documented anti-gay violence, initiated antiviolence projects, built coalitions with other groups to oppose hate violence, and lobbied for hate crime laws. They have participated in public forums, rallies, demonstrations, civil disobedience, and other political actions.

At the national level, efforts against anti-gay violence commenced with the establishment in 1982 of the Anti-Violence Project of the National Gay Task Force (NGTF), which, in 1986, changed its name to the National Gay & Lesbian Task Force (NGLTF). Early Task Force attempts to enlist government support usually met with a wall of indifference and ignorance. In 1983, for example, the NGTF contacted the National Institute of Justice (NIJ), the research arm of the Department of Justice, to secure assistance in addressing the problem. An NIJ official asked NGTF's Jeff Levi, "Is there violence against gays?"

Nevertheless, progress was made. The Democratic party's 1984 national platform included a plank condemning anti-gay violence. Lesbian and gay groups participated in congressional hearings in 1983 on police abuse. The NGLTF and other groups successfully conducted victimization studies, all of which documented the extent of the problem. Armed with statistical data and anecdotal reports, the NGLTF asked the Honorable John Conyers (D-MI) to convene a special hearing of his Criminal Justice Subcommittee of the House Committee on the Judiciary to examine the problem of anti-gay violence. On October 9, 1986, the subcommittee heard testimony from law enforcement personnel, community activists, academics, and victims of anti-gay violence.

In important respects, the current volume had its genesis in those hearings. By 1986 the two editors had corresponded with each other and exchanged information. Berrill had directed the NGLTF Anti-Violence Project since its inception, compiled annual reports on anti-gay violence around the country, lobbied government officials, made numerous public appearances, and assisted numerous local groups in organizing against violence. In 1984 he coordinated and cowrote the NGTF's first major survey on anti-gay violence (NGTF, 1984) and in 1985 began issuing annual reports based on information collected from local groups across the country.

Herek had written his doctoral dissertation on anti-gay prejudice, had begun to publish academic papers on the topic, had conducted a survey to document anti-gay prejudice at Yale University (where he was a faculty member), and had recently become chairperson of the Committee on Lesbian and Gay Concerns (CLGC) of the American Psychological Association (APA). Working with CLGC staff liaison Carol Burroughs and APA lobbyist Bill Bailey, Herek had worked to raise the issue of anti-gay violence as a problem that the APA should address, following its 1975 commitment to "remove the stigma long associated with a homosexual orientation" (APA, 1975).

Both of us testified at the 1986 hearings, Berrill on behalf of the NGLTF and Herek for the APA.[3] The hearings, we felt, represented a tremendous step forward in identifying anti-gay violence as an important issue at the national level. After the hearings, we faced the question of what to do next. We both recall a late-evening supper with Bill Bailey in a small cafe near Washington's Dupont Circle in 1986. As we discussed goals, the issue of documentation emerged as a priority. We all felt that official documentation of the problem of anti-gay violence was needed to foster an adequate government response. We believed that beginning to document anti-gay hate crimes would be a concrete, positive step that the federal government realistically might take in the near future. We also decided to lobby the National Institute of Mental Health (NIMH) and the National Institute of Justice (NIJ) to urge them to identify anti-gay violence as an important problem to be targeted for research funding.

Berrill pursued these goals through the NGLTF, Herek and Bailey through the APA. We focused our initial efforts on a House bill from the previous congressional session that would mandate collection of statistics on hate crimes based on race, ethnicity, and religion. That bill had failed to achieve passage before the 99th Congress ended. We felt that adding "sexual orientation" to the categories of violence included in the bill would be both significant and feasible.

Berrill and Bailey helped to organize a meeting for representatives from several lesbian and gay organizations and other concerned groups to discuss how the Hate Crimes Statistics Act could best be rewritten to include sexual orientation. Concerns were raised about victims' privacy (which previously was not addressed in the bill), and appropriate language was drafted to protect the confidentiality of gay women and men who reported hate crimes.

The revised version of the bill was introduced in the 100th Congress as H.R. 3193 (by Representative Conyers) and S. 702 (by Senator Simon). With the addition of "sexual orientation," the legislation suddenly became very controversial. The coalition of groups supporting the new bill had to overcome strong initial opposition from some members of Congress. A considerable amount of lobbying and grass-roots organizing was necessary to get constituents to persuade their congressional representatives not to delete "sexual orientation" from the bill in committee. These efforts paid off, however, and the bill was voted out of committee in the House in October 1987.

Around this time, our individual involvements with the ever-growing coalition of groups working to pass the bill changed. Gregory Herek's term as chairperson of the Committee on Lesbian and Gay Concerns ended. Organizational changes were occurring at both the NGLTF and the APA. Kevin Berrill turned over primary responsibility for lobbying to NGLTF Legislative Director Peri Jude Radecic. Bill Bailey turned over lobbying for the bill to other members of the APA staff: Clinton Anderson, Larry Rickards, and Greg Wilmoth.

The House version of the bill passed by a 383-29 margin, thanks largely to intensive lobbying by a coalition of civil rights, religious, professional, and law enforcement groups.[4] The Senate version was reported favorably out of the Judiciary Committee. Its passage by the full Senate, however, was blocked by Senator Jesse Helms (R-NC).

In the 101st Congress, the Hate Crime Statistics Act was reintroduced as H.R. 1048 and S. 419. Once again, it passed the House by a wide margin (368-47) but was delayed in the Senate, primarily by Mr. Helms (for more details, see Cohen, 1989; "Congress Bill on Hate," 1988). Finally, on February 8, 1990, the Senate voted on an amendment to the bill offered by Mr. Helms. The amendment would have expressed the "sense of the Senate" that sodomy laws should be enforced, that the federal government should not prohibit discrimination on the basis of sexual orientation, and that "school curricula should not condone homosexuality as an acceptable lifestyle in American society." Helms's amendment was defeated by a vote of 77-19. The Senate then approved the act by a vote of 92-4. President Bush signed the Hate Crime Statistics Act (Public Law 101-275, 104 Stat. 140) into law on April 23, 1990, at a public ceremony attended by gay and lesbian activists, including Berrill. That ceremony marked the enactment of the first federal law ever to include a "sexual orientation" provision and the first time that lesbian and gay activists ever were invited to a White House event.

Meanwhile, the National Institute of Justice (NIJ) and the National Institute of Mental Health (NIMH) responded to lobbying efforts by the NGLTF, the APA, and other members of the coalition that had supported the Hate Crimes Statistics Act. The NIJ sponsored a 1987 report on the response of the criminal justice system to bias crime. According to the landmark report, "the most frequent victims of hate violence today are Blacks, Hispanics, Southeast Asians, Jews, and gays and lesbians. Homosexuals are probably the most frequent victims" (Finn & McNeil, 1987, p. 2).

The NIMH sponsored a research workshop on violence against lesbians and gay men. The workshop, which was co-chaired by Herek and Berrill, brought together an interdisciplinary group of researchers, clinicians, and community workers to develop an agenda for research on anti-gay violence and other hate crimes. The final report of the workshop comprised a dozen papers that were published in a special issue of the *Journal of Interpersonal Violence* (1990, volume 5, number 3). Those papers constitute the core of this volume.

To them we have added new theoretical and empirical papers as well as several first-person accounts by survivors of anti-gay violence. Some chapters are fairly technical and will not be easily accessible to the lay reader. Others may seem too heavily laden with advocacy for the scientist or researcher. We do not necessarily agree with everything that is said in the chapters that follow. We feel, however, that they offer a variety of perspectives and approaches for understanding the problem of violence against lesbians and gay men and working to end it. We hope that the volume will serve as a source book for academic researchers, policymakers, activists, and members of the gay and lesbian community.

The congressional hearings, passage of the Hate Crimes Statistics Act, initiatives by NIMH and NIJ, and this volume all have involved a mixture of science and advocacy, scholarship and politics. Sometimes these different perspectives have easily complemented each other. At other times, a clear tension has existed between them. The dialectic between politics and scholarship has been an integral part of our collaboration as editors. We each feel that we have benefited greatly from the other's perspectives, insights, and questions. We are certain that the book has been made better by our constant efforts to evaluate data and theory with the critical eye of the scientist while simultaneously posing the activist's question of how the results will affect the lesbian and gay community. We believe that the activist-academic collaboration provides a powerful model for dealing not only with anti-gay violence but with many problems faced by lesbians and gay men and members of other minority groups.

We view this book not as the definitive final word on the subject but as a beginning. We recognize its limitations. It addresses the problem of anti-gay violence only in the United States.[5] Its chapters tend to focus more on Whites than people of color, more on men than women, and more on middle-class adults than on the poor, the elderly, and youth. To a large extent, these limitations reflect the state of scholarship on hate crimes against lesbians and gay men. They also no doubt reflect our own limitations as editors in finding more materials to describe the experiences of diverse groups. We hope that others will overcome these limitations in future works, that they will build upon this volume to create a comprehensive body of literature on how violence and hate crimes affect all sectors of the lesbian and gay male community. In this spirit, we welcome the publication of Gary Comstock's (1991) book as this volume goes to press, and we look forward to many more books and articles in the area.

This book is published as the decade of the 1990s begins. If past is indeed prologue, lesbians and gay men are likely to experience continued gains on the one hand and increased violent backlash on the other. But, whereas backlash once stifled gay expression and visibility, the emergence of gay and lesbian communities has made it possible not only to withstand and counter such attacks but to emerge from them stronger and more determined to survive, endure, and prosper. We hope that this book will contribute to that struggle.

As with any book of this sort, many people and groups contributed to its completion. We are grateful to all of them. In particular, we wish to acknowledge and thank Ecford Voit of the National Institute of Mental Health; Jon Conte, editor of the

Journal of Interpersonal Violence; and Terry Hendrix of Sage Publications. Kevin Berrill expresses his thanks to the organizations that supported the Anti-Violence Project, which made possible his work on the volume: the National Gay & Lesbian Task Force Policy Institute, the Public Welfare Foundation, the Threshold Foundation, the Joyce Mertz-Gilmore Foundation, and the Ms. Foundation. We both wish to thank Nancy Capitanio and Theresa Reid for their generous and skillful assistance throughout the project. We also thank Bob Gravel, Kathy Sarris, and Ed Hassell, for bravely sharing their experiences of victimization with the Criminal Justice Subcommittee of the U.S. House of Representatives. Their testimony is reprinted in this volume. Finally, we thank Bill Bailey and John Gorman.

NOTES

1. These include the Anti-Defamation League (1991), the Center for Democratic Renewal (Lutz, 1987), the Klanwatch project of the Southern Poverty Law Center (1989), the National Abortion Federation (1991), and the National Institute Against Prejudice and Violence (1990).

2. White was convicted of two counts of voluntary manslaughter and received a sentence of seven years and eight months. He was paroled six years later in 1985 (Jennings, 1979; Shilts, 1982; "Slayer of Coast Mayor," 1985).

3. Two other contributors to this book, Joyce Hunter and David Wertheimer, also testified (Committee on the Judiciary, 1986).

4. Among the groups in the coalition were the American Civil Liberties Union, American Jewish Committee, American Jewish Congress, American Psychological Association, Anti-Defamation League, Center for Democratic Renewal, National Association for the Advancement of Colored People (NAACP), People for the American Way, and Police Executive Research Forum.

5. In this regard, see the *Pink Book* (1988) and van den Boogard (1989).

REFERENCES

Adam, B. D. (1987). *The rise of a gay and lesbian movement.* Boston: Twayne.

American Psychological Association (APA). (1975). Minutes of the Council of Representatives. *American Psychologist, 30,* 633.

Anti-Defamation League of B'nai Brith. (1991). *Audit of anti-Semitic incidents.* New York: Author.

Berrill, K. (1986). *Anti-gay violence: Causes, consequences, responses.* Washington, DC: National Gay & Lesbian Task Force.

Bérubé, A. (1990). *Coming out under fire: The history of gay men and women in World War II.* New York: Free Press.

Boswell, J. (1980). *Christianity, social tolerance, and homosexuality.* Chicago: University of Chicago Press.

Cohen, G. (1989, October 31). Hate crimes bill stalled by Helms' opposition. *San Francisco Examiner,* p. A10.

Committee on the Judiciary. (1986). *Anti-gay violence: Hearing before the Subcommittee on Criminal Justice of the Committee on the Judiciary, House of Representatives* (Serial No. 132). Washington, DC: Government Printing Office.

Comstock, G. (1991). *Violence against lesbians and gay men.* New York: Columbia University Press.

Congress bill on hate and violent acts gains. (1988, May 22). *New York Times,* p. 18.

D'Emilio, J. (1983). *Sexual politics, sexual communities: The making of a homosexual minority in the United States, 1940-1970.* Chicago: University of Chicago Press.

Finn, P., & McNeil, T. (1987). *The response of the criminal justice system to bias crime: An exploratory review.* (Available from Abt Associates, Inc., 55 Wheeler Street, Cambridge, MA 02138-1168)

Jennings, D. (1979, May 22). It's voluntary manslaughter—maximum penalty eight years. *San Francisco Chronicle,* pp. A1, A18.

Katz, J. (1976). *Gay American history.* New York: Crowell.

Lutz, C. (1987). *They don't all wear sheets.* New York: National Council of Churches. (Available from the Center for Democratic Renewal, P.O. Box 50469, Atlanta, GA 30302)

National Abortion Federation. (1991). *Incidents of violence & disruption against abortion providers.* (Available from the National Abortion Federation, 1436 U Street NW, Washington, DC 20009)

National Gay Task Force (NGTF). (1984). *Anti-gay/lesbian victimization: A study by the National Gay Task Force in cooperation with gay and lesbian organizations in eight U.S. cities.* Washington, DC: Author. (Available from the National Gay & Lesbian Task Force, 1734 14th Street NW, Washington, DC 20009)

National Institute Against Prejudice and Violence. (1990). *Forum,* 5(1).

Pink Book Editing Team. (Eds.). (1988). *Second ILGA pink book: A global view of lesbian and gay liberation and oppression.* Utrecht, the Netherlands: Interfacultaire Werkgroep Homostudies.

Plant, R. (1986). *The pink triangle.* New York: Holt.

Segrest, M., & Zeskind, L. (1989). *Quarantines and death: The far right's homophobic agenda.* Atlanta, GA: Center for Democratic Renewal.

Shilts, R. (1982). *The mayor of Castro Street: The life and times of Harvey Milk.* New York: St. Martin's.

Slayer of coast mayor is free after six years. (1985, January 7). *New York Times,* p. A15.

Southern Poverty Law Center. (1989). *Hate violence and White supremacy: A decade in review.* Montgomery, AL: Author.

Taylor, C. (1982). Folk taxonomy and justice in Dade County, Florida, 1954. *Anthropological Research Group on Homosexuality Newsletter,* 4(1-2), 9.

van den Boogard, H. (1989). Blood furious underneath the skins . . .: On anti-homosexual violence: Its nature and the needs of the victims. In *Homosexuality, which homosexuality? International conference on gay and lesbian studies* (pp. 49-60). London: GMP.

SURVIVOR'S STORY

Eight Bullets

Claudia Brenner

The first bullet: When the first bullet hit me, my arm exploded. My brain could not make the connections fast enough to realize I had been shot. I saw a lot of blood on the green tarp on which we lay and thought for a split second about earthquakes and volcanoes. But they don't make you bleed. Rebecca knew. She asked me where I had been shot. We had encountered a stranger earlier that day who had a gun. We both knew who was shooting us. Perhaps a second passed.

The second bullet: When the second bullet hit my neck I started to scream with all my strength. Somehow the second bullet was even more unbelievable than the first.

The third bullet: The third bullet came and I now know hit the other side of my neck. By then I had lost track of what was happening or where we were except that I was in great danger and it was not stopping.

The fourth bullet: I now know a fourth bullet hit me in the face. Rebecca told me to get down, close to the ground.

The fifth bullet: The fifth bullet hit the top of my head. I believe Rebecca saw that even lying flat I was vulnerable and told me to run behind a tree.

The sixth bullet: The sixth bullet hit Rebecca in the back of her head as she rose to run for the tree.

The seventh bullet: The seventh bullet hit Rebecca's back as she ran. It exploded her liver and caused her to die.

The eighth bullet missed.

It is not surprising that Stephen Roy Carr believed us both dead. He shot to kill. The neck. The head. The back. A single bolt action rifle that he loaded, shot, and unloaded eight times. Surely he believed us both dead or he would have used more of the 27 rounds of ammunition he left in his haste to get away.

He shot from where he was hidden in the woods 85 feet away, after he stalked us, hunted us, spied on us. Later his lawyer tried to assert that our sexuality provoked him.

He shot us because he identified us as lesbians. He was a stranger with whom we had no connection.

He shot us and left us for dead.

It was May 13, 1988, the second day of a three-day backpacking trip on the Appalachian Trail in south central Pennsylvania. Rebecca had driven up from Blacksburg, Virginia, where she was finishing her last semester of a master's program in business at Virginia Tech. She was becoming a great success in the academic world, having papers accepted at conferences in her field and receiving numerous offers for placements in Ph.D. programs. These achievements were a surprise to her, though not to those who loved her. She was not yet accustomed to academic recognition. Rebecca Wight was 28 years old, of Puerto Rican/Iranian/Anglo heritage. She had grown up in a variety of countries around the world; her father was a diplomat with the U.S. government.

A painful divorce and the subsequent death of her mother left Rebecca, the oldest of three sisters, with tremendous survival skills, ambition, and hope—though not always with the confidence and discipline she wished for. She was a self-taught feminist who had known lesbianism was an option for herself. Her relationship with me was her first acknowledged lesbian love, a reality that, I think, she celebrated with mixed emotions. In Virginia she was cautious about public expressions of affection, fearful of rejection from her conservative academic community.

At the time of our trip, I was 31 years old, a White, Jewish lesbian who had come out in college in the late 1970s. I was firmly embedded in a strong women's community in Ithaca, New York, and was seasoned to the political and emotional realities of lesbianism in "progressive" America. I was committed to liberation and willing to take some risks, though also aware of the need for discretion in a homophobic culture. In May 1988, I was temporarily based in Ithaca, where I was scrambling to earn money to go back to Virginia Tech to finish graduate school in architecture.

My relationship with Rebecca had been interrupted by my acceptance of a fellowship abroad to do research for my thesis. I had returned from Israel in February and we were in the midst of figuring out long-distance love. We had seen each other two weeks earlier, when I was in Virginia. We were feeling close and wonderful. Our plan had been to hike for a few days and then drive to Washington, D.C., to celebrate the birthday of Rebecca's youngest sister. The weather was fine, with the delightful May sunshine and warmth. Compared with the rock climbing and hang gliding of Rebecca's past, the trip was simple and designed for a few pleasant days.

We had no premonition, no warning that the world as we knew it was about to be irreparably shattered. There was only life as we all are accustomed to expect. The days before had been filled with overheated car engines, school and money pressures, long-distance phone calls, and occasional stomachaches. Even our two brief exchanges with the stranger on the trail, though disturbing, had seemed of little consequence. Early in the morning he wanted cigarettes; later he asked if we were lost. We never saw him again. We thought he was a strange character, a "creep," but we had no clues that he was planning to murder us. No clue that, after we saw him continue south on the trail, as we headed east on a side trail, he would circle back around to ensure that our paths intersected once again, this time with him hidden. From that position, on a glorious sunny Friday afternoon, he lay with his rifle. After he watched us make love and have fun, he exploded our world with his hate and his bullets.

We could not have known that this tall, thin, unkempt, gangly man could so lack respect for human life as to shoot to kill. *Murder* had not yet become a word in my vocabulary. I had been sheltered from such horrendous realities, whether by economic privilege, by race, or by living in the United States. Anti-gay murder was just a concept without names or faces. Anti-gay violence was a problem of harassment, not a matter of life and death.

During the moments of the shooting, Rebecca's ability to think and function was astonishing. I know that in the next few minutes, the last of her life, she saved my life. Her thinking and instructions got me out of his range and behind the tree. We both made it behind the tree, and the shooting stopped. Rebecca slumped against the tree trunk, needing its support. She was fading, losing her vision and her ability to communicate in this world. In my panic and disbelief, I asked her over and over again what to do. Already starting to lose consciousness, she looked at me and told me quite simply and calmly, "Claudia, stop the bleeding." At that moment, a transition happened. I began to stop my intense bleeding. My brain started to function again, very clearly. Rebecca very definitely let go and began to die.

I could not have articulated it, but deep inside I began to realize how badly wounded she was and that she would not be able to walk. I knew we desperately needed help. I knew that only three people knew of the shooting: He who had done it, who would surely tell no one that two women lay dying in the woods; Rebecca, who could no longer stand or speak; and me. I went for help.

Somehow, knowing that the situation was urgent, I forced myself to leave Rebecca's side. I never saw her again. If I had stayed, I surely would have died as well.

I walked in terror, shock, and ripping pain, never knowing if he would appear. I walked to get help for Rebecca, with a survival instinct that I don't understand. I followed a map. Although it was a very long way, sometimes uphill on an unkept trail, I didn't stop. I know now that it was nearly four miles, and it took several hours. Darkness came. Finally, I reached a road. Two young men stopped their car to my flashlight signal, and took me to Shippensburg, Pennsylvania, the closest town with any police and emergency help. The State Police responded immediately with the search that found Rebecca's body later that night. Simultaneously, I was taken by helicopter to Hershey Medical Center, where I had emergency surgery. Miraculously, I survived the five bullet wounds with no permanent debilitating conditions. The surgeons and many others on the medical staff told me repeatedly how close I had come to death: Four of the bullets hit within a fraction of an inch from fatality.

During the next two weeks, the State Police conducted an intensive investigation that led to the capture of Stephen Roy Carr. Later, the district attorney of Adams County successfully prosecuted the murderer, but not before his defense attorney sought to inflame the case with his assertion of provocation. Carr was convicted of first-degree murder in October of 1988 and later sentenced to life in prison with no possibility of parole.

Perhaps the only antidote to the horror of the shooting has been the response. Whether legal, medical, emotional, personal, or distant, it has been filled with human compassion and generosity. From the moment I awoke from the surgery, I was helped 24 hours a day with the shock, pain, terror, and grief. My every need was cared for, an effort that required extraordinary love and commitment on the part of my chosen family, my closest friends, my parents, and my community. Help and support came from every direction and continue even now.

I remember distinctly, as I walked alone on the trail after the shooting, how intensely silent were the normal forest sounds after the explosions of the gunshots. I wondered if the birds were communicating about the horror they had witnessed that afternoon. Less than a week later, thunderstorms covered our campsite with water, washing away the blood, cleaning the area of the violence. Although the gunshots have for the most part quieted in my mind; though my wounds have healed; though I now speak widely of the homophobia that destroyed and stole the life of a lover, a sister, a daughter, a friend; I will always walk with an awareness of the tragedy I knew on that silent trail.

PART I

AN OVERVIEW OF THE PROBLEM

Anti-Gay Violence and Victimization in the United States: An Overview

KEVIN T. BERRILL

Since the birth of the modern gay liberation movement in the 1960s, a large body of data on anti-gay violence and other victimization has developed. Thousands of episodes—including defamation, harassment, intimidation, assault, murder, vandalism, and other abuse—have been reported to police departments and local and national organizations (Berrill, 1986; NGLTF, 1986, 1987, 1988, 1989, 1990; NGLTF Policy Institute, 1991). Many thousands more incidents have gone unreported (see Chapter 18 of this volume by Berrill & Herek). Numerous empirical studies, many of them unpublished, also have shown the problem of anti-gay violence to be widespread.[1]

The first national study focusing exclusively on anti-gay violence was conducted by the National Gay & Lesbian Task Force (NGLTF, 1984). The study sampled 1,420 gay men and 654 lesbians (n = 2,074) in eight U.S. cities: Boston, New York, Atlanta,

AUTHOR'S NOTE: I thank Gregory M. Herek and Steven K. Aurand for their valuable assistance in the research and writing of this chapter. I also thank all those who have contributed to the growing body of research on anti-gay violence.

19

St. Louis, Denver, Dallas, Los Angeles, and Seattle. Among those surveyed, 19% reported having been punched, hit, kicked, or beaten at least once in their lives because of their sexual orientation; 44% had been threatened with physical violence. In addition, 94% had experienced some type of victimization (including being verbally abused, physically assaulted, abused by police, assaulted with a weapon, having property vandalized, being spat upon, being chased or followed, or being pelted with objects), and 84% knew other gay or lesbian individuals who had been victimized because of their sexual orientation.

Many respondents had been multiply victimized. For example, 92% of those who were the targets of anti-gay epithets noted that they had experienced such harassment "more than once" or "many times." More than two thirds (68%) of those who had been threatened with violence and nearly half (47%) of those who had been physically assaulted reported multiple experiences of such episodes.

The threat of anti-gay violence had a major impact on the attitudes and behavior of those surveyed by the NGLTF: 83% of the men and women believed that they might be victimized in the future, and 62% said that they feared for their safety. Also, 45% reported having modified their behavior to reduce the risk of attack. For example, they took a self-defense class, avoided certain locations, or avoided physical contact with friends or lovers in public places.

Other surveys of anti-gay violence and harassment, representing nine U.S. cities, nine states, and six regional or national samples, are reported in Tables 1.1, 1.2, and 1.3. Although sample characteristics, geographic locations, and sampling strategies varied considerably, all of the surveys found harassment and violence to be widespread.[2] Of those that reported rates of specific types of victimization, the median proportion of respondents who were verbally harassed was 80%; 44% were threatened with violence; 33% had been chased or followed; 25% were pelted with objects; 19% experienced vandalism; 17% were physically assaulted; 13% were spat upon; and 9% experienced an assault with an object or weapon. Many of the lesbians and gay men who were surveyed also reported that they fear anti-gay harassment and violence and that they anticipate such victimization in the future. In the studies that asked about these concerns, the

text continued page 24

TABLE 1.1 Summary of Seven Anti-Gay Violence/Victimization Surveys (1988-1991)

Type of Victimization	A N = 234 (M = 150; F = 84) %	B N = 1,363 (M = 796; F = 561 UNK = 6) %	C N = 234 (M = 113; F = 121) %	D N = 291 (M = 166; F = 125) %	E N = 721 (M = 461; F = 260) %	F N = 542 (M = 314; F = 228) %	G N = 395 (M = unk; F = unk) %
Verbal abuse	79	84	91	—	87	—	—
Threats of violence	45	45	—	—	48	37	—
Property violence	22	14	27	16	18	—	—
Targets of objects	—	25	28	21	27	25	—
Followed or chased	38	34	41	32	31	—	13
Spat upon		15	12	7	15		
Punched, hit, kicked	24	20	24	18	19	17	9
Weapon assault	9	7	7	7	9	10	—
Victimized by police	—	16	30	—	22	—	—
Sexual assault	—	9	—	8	6	—	5
Victimized in school[a]	—	—	—	—	49	—	—
Familial verbal abuse	—	—	—	—	22	24	—
Familial physical abuse	—	—	—	—	5	8	—
Any familial abuse	—	—	—	—	23	—	—
Fear for safety	—	—	—	—	—	—	—
Expect future harassment	—	—	—	—	—	—	—
Know others victimized	—	—	94	—	—	—	56

NOTE: A = Utah (Aaron, 1991); B = Massachusetts (LeBlanc, 1991); C = 36 states, DC, and Canada (Platt, 1990); D = 31 states and the District of Columbia (Comstock, 1989); E = Pennsylvania (Gross, Aurand, & Adessa, 1988; data cited derived through secondary analysis of original report); F = Baltimore, Maryland (Morgen & Grossman, 1988); G = District of Columbia (District of Columbia Lesbian and Gay Anti-Violence Task Force, 1988).
a. Victimization in high school or junior high school.

TABLE 1.2 Summary of Six Anti-Gay Violence/Victimization Surveys (1984-1987)

Type of Victimization	H N = 133 (M = 58; F = 75) %	I N = 734 (M = 323; F = 411) %	J N = 167 (M = 87; F = 80) %	K N = 213 (M = 138; F = 75) %	L N = 323 (M = 176; F = 147) %	M N = 2,074 (M = 1,420; F = 654) %
Verbal abuse	81	58	80	83	84	86
Threats of violence	36	24	31	47	45	44
Property vandalized	19	12	10	20	20	19
Targets of objects	21	—	22	21	26	27
Followed or chased	32	14	25	37	38	35
Spat upon	—	—	11	13	11	14
Punched, hit, kicked	16	11	10	23	16	19
Weapon assault	5	—	4	10	9	9
Victimized by police	8	8	20	24	14[a]	20
Sexual assault	14	—	5	—	—	—
Victimized in school[b]	—	—	33	38	37[b]	37
Familial verbal abuse	41	—	19	—	38	34
Familial physical abuse	—	—	4	—	—	7
Any familial abuse	—	—	19	—	—	—
Fear for safety	79	—	51	70	—	62
Expect future harassment	76	—	—	88	77	83
Knows others victimized	89	—	—	85	85	84

NOTE: H = Vermont (Vermonters for Lesbian and Gay Rights, 1987); I = Alaska (Identity, Inc., 1986; percentages reflect victimization in Alaska only); J = Philadelphia (Aurand, Adessa, & Bush, 1985); K = Wisconsin (Wisconsin Governor's Council on Lesbian and Gay Issues, 1985); L = Maine (Steinman & Aurand, 1985); M = eight U.S. Cities: Boston, New York, Atlanta, St. Louis, Denver, Dallas, Los Angeles, and Seattle (National Gay & Lesbian Task Force, 1984).
a. Percentage for Maine (Steinman & Aurand, 1985) represents only verbal abuse by police.
b. Victimization in high school or junior high school. Percentage for Maine (Steinman & Aurand, 1985) represents victimization in high school only.

TABLE 1.3 Other Victimization Studies

Author/Date	Sample Size	Sample	Findings
Jay & Young (1977)	N = 5,400 4,400 males 1,000 females	National	Verbal abuse: males 77% females 71%
			Physical abuse: males 27% females 14%
Bell & Weinberg (1978)	N = 977 684 males 293 females	San Francisco Bay Area	Robbed or assaulted: males 35% females 3%
Bradford & Ryan (1987)	N = 1,917 1,917 females	National	Verbally harassed: 52% Physically assaulted: 6%
McKirnan & Peterson (1987)	N = 3,404 2,655 males 749 females	Chicago Metropolitan Area	Verbal abuse: males 67% females 60%
			Physical attack: males 20% females 8%
Peebles, Tunstall, & Eberhardt (1985)	N = 506 326 males 180 females	Richmond, VA	Ever been attacked or abused: males 35% females 28%
New York State Lesbian & Gay Lobby (1985)	N = 380 (n's for males and females not indicated)	New York State	Verbally abused: 75% Physically attacked: 21%
New Jersey Lesbian & Gay Coalition (1984)	N = 362 256 males 104 females 2 unspecified	New Jersey	Experienced physical violence: 17%
Mayor's Office of Policy Management (1983)	N = 1,340 1,082 males 254 females 4 unspecified	Boston	Verbal abuse: 76% Physical attack: 24% Vandalism/robbery: 21% Sexual assault: 3%

continued

TABLE 1.3 Continued

Minneapolis Gay Community Services (1979; as reported in Anderson, 1982)	N = 289 (n's for males and females not indicated)	Minneapolis	Verbal harassment: 72% Physically assaulted: 23% Sexually assaulted: 67%
Gay and Lesbian Community Action Council (1990)	N = 1,864 876 males 988 females	Minneapolis/ St. Paul metropolitan area	Physical abuse: 11% Police mistreatment: 12% Emotional abuse: 39% Sexual abuse: 7%
Seattle Commission for Lesbians and Gays (1991)	N = 1,291 657 males 626 females 8 unspecified	Seattle metropolitan area	Physically attacked: 16% Police verbal abuse: 6% Familial verbal abuse: 16% Verbal abuse by strangers: 64%
Teichner Associates ("Results of Poll," 1989)	N = 400 287 males 113 females	National	Physically abused or assaulted (ever): 12% Physically abused or assaulted (in the past year): 7%
Mayors Advisory Committee on Lesbian and Gay Issues	N = 400 237 males 167 females 3 unspecified	New Orleans	Verbally harassed: 64% Physically assaulted: 21% Treats of violence: 26% Police verbal abuse: 14% Police physical abuse: 7%

median proportion reporting that they feared for their safety was 66%; a median proportion of 80% expected to be the target of anti-gay violence or harassment in the future.[3]

Whereas the data discussed above are drawn from surveys of victims, information on homicides cannot be obtained through such a method. Consequently, little is known about the prevalence of anti-gay homicide. Altogether, 62 homicides involving gay victims were reported to the NGLTF by local organizations for the year 1989 (NGLTF, 1990). Of these, 15 were classified as unambiguously anti-gay by local groups or police. The remaining 47 murders were identified as "gay related" (i.e., killings in which the victim's sexual orientation appeared to have been a relevant factor but the motivation was uncertain and anti-gay prejudice was not clearly manifest). Many of these and other homicides documented in recent years appeared to have been sex related. Some showed signs of having been committed by serial murderers. The number of anti-gay or gay-related murders reported to the NGLTF was 70 in 1988, 64 in 1987, 80 in 1986, and 20 in 1985 (NGLTF, 1990). These figures are believed to sharply underestimate the magnitude of the problem.

Anti-gay murders are often marked by extreme brutality. According to a study by Miller and Humphreys (1980, p. 179): "An intense rage is present in nearly all homicide cases involving gay male victims. A striking feature . . . is their gruesome, often vicious nature. Seldom is the homosexual victim simply shot. He is more apt to be stabbed a dozen or more times, mutilated and strangled."

Recalling victims of murder and other attacks that she has seen, Melissa Mertz, director of Victim Services at Bellevue Hospital in New York City, observed that "attacks against gay men were the most heinous and brutal I encountered. They frequently involved torture, cutting, mutilation, and beating, and showed the absolute intent to rub out the human being because of his [sexual] preference" (M. Mertz, personal communication, March 12, 1986).

VARIATIONS IN VICTIMIZATION

Gender Differences

In the NGLTF study and in other studies, gender differences in rates of victimization are evident (see Tables 1.3 and 1.4). Males generally experienced greater levels of anti-gay verbal harassment (by nonfamily members), threats, victimization in school and by police, and most types of physical violence and intimidation (including weapon assaults and being pelted with objects, spat upon, and followed or chased). Lesbians, on the other hand, generally experienced higher rates of verbal harass-

text continued page 28

TABLE 1.4 Percentages of Victimization Experienced by Lesbians and Gay Men

	Rates of Victimization (percentages)															
	1		2A		2B		3		4		5		6		7	
Type of Victimization	M	F	M	F	M	F	M	F	M	F	M	F	M	F	M	F
Verbal abuse	90	78	92	81	90	77	—	—	85	74	—	—	87	69	86	82
Threats of physical violence	49	34	62	32	51	26	—	—	39	22	45	29	56	30	54	35
Property vandalized	20	14	19	12	21	19	16	16	10	10	—	—	29	14	16	11
Target of objects	33	16	41	13	24	11	27	14	34	9	26	23	—	—	30	19
Followed or chased	37	31	43	23	26	19	36	28	28	21	—	—	49	20	39	29
Spat upon	14	13	19	12	17	6	8	5	16	6	—	—	—	—	19	11
Punched, hit or kicked	24	9	24	7	29	6	24	10	16	4	18	15	33	11	29	10
Assaulted with weapon	11	5	12	5	11	3	11	2	6	1	9	11	15	2	10	4
Familial verbal abuse	32	38	18	25	22	28	—	—	16	22	19	29	—	—	—	—
Familial physical abuse	8	6	4	4	8	5	—	—	5	2	6	10	—	—	—	—

Category	1 M	1 F	2A M	2A F	2B M	2B F	3 M	3 F	4 M	4 F	5 M	5 F	6 M	6 F	7 M	7 F
Any familial abuse	—	—	19	25	22	29	—	—	16	22	—	—	—	—	—	—
Victimization by police	23	13	26	15	31	8	—	—	24	16	—	—	—	—	20	11
Victimization in junior high	—	—	51	13	50	12	—	—	31	6	—	—	—	—	—	—
Victimization in high school	—	—	51	19	59	21	—	—	41	12	—	—	—	—	—	—
Victimization in college	—	—	28	21	33	37	—	10	26	20	—	—	—	—	—	—
Sexual assault	—	—	6	3	9	4	—	5	5	4	—	—	—	—	12	6
Fear for safety	58	70	—	—	—	—	—	—	48	59	—	—	—	—	—	—
Expectation of harassment	81	87	—	—	—	—	—	—	—	—	—	—	—	—	—	—
Modified behavior	39	57	—	—	—	—	—	—	—	—	—	—	—	—	—	—

NOTE: 1 = NGLTF (1984); N = 1,420 males, 654 females. 2A = Gross et al. (1988), Philadelphia; N = 291 males, 146 females. 2B = Gross et al. (1988), Pennsylvania (except Philadelphia); N = 170 males, 114 females. 3 = Comstock (1989); N = 166 males, 125 females. 4 = Aurand et al. (1985); N = 87 males, 80 females. 5 = Morgan and Grossman (1988); N = 314 males, 228 females. 6 = Aaron (1991); N = 150 males, 82 females. 7 = LeBlanc (1991); N = 796 males, 561 females.

ment by family members and reported greater fear of anti-gay violence. In two surveys that measured discrimination, lesbians also were found to have encountered significantly more discrimination than gay men (Aurand, Adessa, & Bush, 1985; Gross, Aurand, & Adessa, 1988). Both gay men and lesbians appear to suffer comparable rates of familial physical abuse. With respect to settings where attacks occurred, Comstock (1989) found that the gay men in his sample were more likely to be victimized in school or in public *gay*-identified areas (outside gay bars and businesses or in gay cruising areas), whereas lesbians tended to experience victimization in *non-gay*-identified public settings and in the home.

Gender differences in rates of victimization may result from several factors. First, men in the United States are more likely than women to suffer violent crime (Bureau of Justice Statistics, 1989).[4] Second, the generally higher visibility of gay men may make them more vulnerable to violence. Even a cursory examination of such sources as the *Gayellow Pages* (Green, 1988), for example, reveals that gay male establishments—such as bars, businesses, and other organizations—are far more numerous than those serving lesbians. This suggests that gay men have more opportunities to go to public gay-identified contexts than do lesbians, which presumably increases their risk for anti-gay violence (Harry, 1982). Third, gay men may tend to recognize their sexual orientation earlier than do lesbians (Aurand et al., 1985; Gross et al., 1988).[5] If gay men, on average, have been "out" about their sexual orientation for a longer period of their lives than have lesbians, they also would have had more opportunities, on average, to encounter anti-gay violence and harassment.

Fourth, lesbians may be more likely than gay men to have modified their own behavior out of fear for their personal safety. For example, they may avoid certain locations or affectionate physical contact with lovers or same-sex friends (NGLTF, 1984; Chapter 3 of this volume by von Schulthess). Such self-imposed limits and the fear that motivates them are themselves a serious form of victimization. Finally, anti-lesbian violence may be difficult to distinguish from more general violence against women. According to preliminary research by von Schulthess (Chapter 3), attacks against lesbians exist on a continuum from exclusively antiwoman to exclusively anti-gay. Without explicit verbal indication by the perpetrator, lesbian victims may not know whether an incident is sexist or heterosexist or both.

Racial/Ethnic Differences

To date, only two studies have examined racial and ethnic differences in rates of victimization. Both have found lesbians and gay men of color to be at increased risk for violent attack because of their sexual orientation. Using responses to questionnaires (n = 291) that were mailed to lesbian and gay groups across the United States and distributed at two gay conferences, Comstock (1989) found that lesbians and gay men of color (n = 68) were more likely than White respondents (n = 223) to report having been chased or followed (43% as compared with 29%), pelted with objects (31% compared with 17%), or physically assaulted (21% compared with 18%). He also found that gay people of color were more likely than White gays to be victimized in gay- or lesbian-identified areas (such as gay neighborhoods or outside gay establishments). Race was unrelated to experiencing vandalism/arson and being spat upon.

Among 400 San Francisco women who were surveyed at gay and lesbian community events and establishments (Chapter 3, von Schulthess), lesbians of color (n = 69) were more likely than White lesbians (n = 327) to report having experienced physical violence, threats, vandalism, or rape. White lesbians reported greater rates of verbal assault.

Most of the lesbians and gay men of color in both studies were Black or Latino/a. Their higher levels of victimization therefore may well be associated with the higher risk of violent crime faced generally by Blacks and Hispanics in the United States (Bureau of Justice Statistics, 1989). Additional research with larger and more representative samples of lesbians and gay men clearly is needed to assess the relationship between membership in minority racial and ethnic groups and the risk of anti-gay violence.

PERPETRATORS

Most of what is known about the perpetrators of anti-gay violence is based on anecdotal information, surveys of victims, and reports by victims to gay community-based victim assistance organizations such as San Francisco's Community United Against Violence (CUAV). The general profile of a "gay-basher" that emerges from CUAV data is a young male, often acting together with other young males, all of whom are strangers to the victim(s) (Lu, 1991). When CUAV clients who were victimized in 1990 could give the approximate age of their assailants, 418 of the perpetrators (54%) were identified as age 21 or under. Among the 920 perpetrators whose gender was known, 92% were males. Of the 390 incidents in which victims could count the number of perpetrators, 57% involved multiple perpetrators. Of the 801 perpetrators whose race could be determined by victims, 40% were White, 30% were Black, 23% were Latino, and 5% were Asian/Pacific Islander (the remaining 2% were classified as "other"). It should be recognized that these data are somewhat limited in their generalizability because they come primarily from males victimized in public settings, such as on the street.

A similar profile emerges in a study of anti-gay violence by Le-Blanc (1991; $n = 1,363$) in which respondents who had been victimized gave detailed information on the most recent or most serious attack against them by strangers or acquaintances. Out of 661 episodes in which respondents could identify the gender of the perpetrators, 92% were perpetrated by males. In the remaining incidents, 4% were perpetrated by females and 4% involved both male and female assailants. Of the 637 attacks where the race of the perpetrators was identified, 80% of the perpetrators were White, 16% were Black, 4% were Hispanic, and less than 1% were Asian. Among the 587 respondents who were attacked by strangers, most said that their assailants were adolescents (42%) or in their twenties (45%). The remainder reported the age of the perpetrators as 10 years or younger (2%) or 30 years or older (11%). Out of 646 individuals who gave information about the number of perpetrators, only 22% were attacked by a single individual. Another 22% were attacked by two persons, 20% by three persons, 17% by four persons, and 19% by five or more persons.

In a survey by Comstock (1991; $n = 294$), victims of 117 anti-gay physical assaults identified most assailants to be young, White males. In contrast to LeBlanc's (1991) study, in which the great majority (78%) of incidents involved more than one perpetrator, slightly less than half (48%) of the incidents in Comstock's study involved multiple perpetrators.

Hate Group Activity

The majority of hate crimes against lesbian and gay people do not appear to be committed by individuals who are affiliated with organized hate groups (i.e., groups that exist to promote hostility and violence toward individuals because of their racial, religious, or sexual identity or political ideology; NGLTF, 1990). Nevertheless, many offenders may be encouraged by the rhetoric of hate groups (Finn & McNeil, 1987). Moreover, anti-gay violence by hate groups appears to be increasing. According to the Atlanta-based Center for Democratic Renewal (formerly the National Anti-Klan Network), Ku Klux Klan and neo-Nazi groups have increasingly targeted gay and lesbian people for physical attack and intimidation (Lutz, 1987). In a recent report, the Klanwatch Project of the Southern Poverty Law Center (1987, p. 5) also acknowledged that "anti-gay sentiment is exploited by white supremacists to organize the bigoted. Neo-Nazis, Skinheads, Identity followers, white robed cross burners and talk show circuit 'racialists' may be divided over tactics, but they agree on who their enemies are. And gays, like Blacks and Jews, are categorically hated."

In recent years, anti-gay activity by extremist groups has included the firebombing of a gay Christian church in Missouri by a member of the neo-Nazi group known as The Order, the execution-style murders of three gay men in North Carolina by individuals linked to the White Patriot party, the attempted bombing of a gay and lesbian dance club by members of the Aryan Nation, increasing attacks by neo-Nazi Skinheads, and the national dissemination of anti-gay propaganda via computer bulletin boards by affiliates of the Aryan Nation. "Queers" are also among those singled out for extermination in a White Patriot party "Declaration of War" against "enemies of the White race" (NGLTF, 1989; NGLTF Policy Institute, 1991). In 1989 organizations in 19 communities across the United States reported anti-gay activity by hate groups to the NGLTF. Attacks by Skinheads were by far the most numerous and brutal of all hate group incidents documented (NGLTF, 1990).

Police Abuse

In theory, law enforcement officials are responsible for protecting lesbians and gay men from anti-gay crimes. Some police officers, however, view such crimes as harmless pranks or as an acceptable form of behavior (Finn & McNeil, 1987). Still others are themselves perpetrators of anti-gay harassment and violence. In the studies described in Tables 1.1, 1.2, and 1.3, the median proportion of lesbians and gay men who reported some form of victimization by police because of their sexual orientation was 20%. Nationwide, there have been numerous documented cases of police verbal and physical abuse, entrapment, blackmail, unequal enforcement of the law, and deliberate mishandling of anti-gay violence cases (Committee on the Judiciary, 1983; Harry, 1982; Humphreys, 1970/1975; NGLTF, 1986, 1987, 1988, 1989, 1990; NGLTF Policy Institute, 1991). Examples of anti-gay police abuse during the past decade include a brutal assault upon several Latina lesbians in New York City in which one woman was knocked unconscious (NGLTF, 1987); a beating of a Los Angeles gay motorist that resulted in broken bones, lacerations, and nerve damage (NGLTF, 1990); and a raid on a Manhattan bar patronized by Black and Latino gay men that injured patrons and destroyed the bar's interior (Committee on the Judiciary, 1983).

SETTINGS FOR VICTIMIZATION

Anti-gay violence is often viewed solely in terms of street crimes committed by strangers. It also occurs in other settings, however—including schools and colleges, the home, and prisons and jails—where the victim may be acquainted or even intimate with the perpetrator.

Victimization in Schools and Colleges

Although diversity and pluralism ideally should be cherished values in the academic environment, anti-gay prejudice and violence are serious problems at many colleges and universities. In 1989 alone, a total of 1,329 anti-gay episodes were reported to the NGLTF by lesbian and gay student groups on just 40 college

TABLE 1.5 Summary of Victimization Studies Conducted at Yale, Rutgers, Pennsylvania State, and Oberlin

	Rates of Victimization (percentages)			
Type of Victimization	Yale (N = 166)	Rutgers (N = 118)	Pennsylvania State (N = 125)	Oberlin (N = 111)
Verbal insults	65	55	76	40
Overheard anti-gay remarks	98	90	—	84
Threats of physical violence	25	16	26	—
Property damaged/ destroyed	10	6	17	5
Objects thrown	19	12	12	5
Followed or chased	25	18	22	14
Spat upon	3	1	5	5
Assaulted/wounded with a weapon	1	2	1	1
Punched, hit, kicked, beaten	5	4	5	3
Sexually harassed/ assaulted	12	8	—	18
Anticipate future victimization	92	86	94	—
Fear for safety	57	35	64	—
Know others who have been victimized	76	57	66	—
Nonreporting of at least one incident	90	88	94	90

SOURCE: Yale, Rutgers, Pennsylvania State, and Oberlin data are from Herek (1986), Cavin (1987), D'Augelli (1989), and Norris (1990), respectively.

campuses (NGLTF, 1990). The overwhelming majority of the incidents (1,304, or 98%) involved harassment, intimidation, or vandalism (see Chapter 16 by Berrill).

In studies of anti-gay violence and harassment at Yale (Herek, 1986), Rutgers (Cavin, 1987), Pennsylvania State (D'Augelli, 1989), and Oberlin (Norris, 1990), between 3% and 5% of the respondents had been punched, hit, kicked, or beaten at some point in their college careers; 16% to 26% had been threatened with physical violence, and 40% to 76% had been verbally harassed (see Table 1.5). Similar rates of victimization have been documented on other campuses.

Among gay, lesbian, and bisexual students surveyed at the University of Massachusetts (n = 174), 45% had been verbally threatened or harassed, and 21% had been physically confronted or assaulted (Yeskel, 1985). Rates of such abuse at the University of Illinois (n = 92) were 58% and 15%, respectively (O'Shaughnessey, 1987). At the University of Oregon, 54% of sexual minority students reported experiencing verbal harassment or threats; 86% had viewed anti-gay graffiti, 96% had overheard anti-gay jokes, and 61% feared for their personal safety (Task Force on Lesbian and Gay Concerns, 1990).[6]

Studies undertaken by the state of New York (Governor's Task Force on Bias-Related Violence, 1988) and Pennsylvania State University (Campus Environment Team, 1988) also confirmed the wide scope of anti-gay episodes on college campuses. According to the Governor's Task Force (1988, p. 56), "Many campuses in New York experience anti-gay/lesbian incidents and even more have anti-gay/lesbian feelings. In the face of this, most have no organizational support and few have experimented with promising policies to alleviate this problem." Moreover, "while evidence shows serious problems for many groups [on New York State campuses], the most severe hostilities are directed at lesbians and gay men" (p. ES6). At Pennsylvania State University, gay men and lesbians were found to be the most frequent victims of "direct acts of intolerance" reported to campus authorities in 1988. Of 30 such incidents reported to the Office of Student life, 21 involved gay students as victims (Campus Environment Team, 1988).

It appears that anti-gay violence and harassment are also widespread at the high school and junior high school levels. Between 33% and 49% of the respondents in studies conducted in Maine (Steinman & Aurand, 1985), Wisconsin (Wisconsin Governor's Council, 1985), Philadelphia (Aurand et al., 1985), Pennsylvania (Gross et al., 1988), and eight U.S. cities (NGLTF, 1984) had experienced harassment, threats, and/or violence while in high school or junior high school (see Table 1.1, row 11). According to the Governor's Task Force (1988), teenagers surveyed about their biases against a variety of minorities reacted more negatively to gay people than to any other group.[7] The report described this aversion as "alarming" and concluded that gay men and lesbians "are perceived as legitimate targets that can be openly attacked"

(p. 97). The report noted that teenagers' written comments about gays were "often openly vicious" and that "a number of students threatened violence against gays" (p. 84).

Violence in the Home

The home is another context in which anti-gay violence and harassment occur. In surveys measuring rates of anti-gay abuse by relatives, between 16% and 41% of the respondents had experienced verbal insults or intimidation by relatives and 4% to 8% had encountered physical violence as well (see Table 1.1, rows 12, 13, and 14; also Seattle Commission, Table 2; see also Chapter 4 of this volume by Hunter).

The extremes of anti-gay domestic violence were revealed in a recent trial in Chicago for the murder of a 4-year-old boy by his mother and her live-in boyfriend. During the summer of 1987, the boy was starved, burned, stuck with pins and needles, beaten with various implements, scalded with steaming water, tied up and hung upside down, and gagged for hours because he was perceived to be homosexual. His brother was also tortured for the same reason. The boy was eventually killed by a blow to his head ("Story of Boy's Torture," 1990).

Violence in Prisons and Jails

Nowhere is anti-gay violence more trivialized and more inescapable than in prisons and jails. Research on male rape in prisons suggests that homosexual inmates are disproportionately the victims of sexual assaults. Typically, the perpetrators are heterosexual men (Wooden & Parker, 1982). Letters to the NGLTF and other organizations by gay prisoners describe widespread beatings, rapes, verbal harassment, and other abuse of those who are gay or HIV-positive, or perceived to be so. The consequence for many gay inmates is unrelenting fear, isolation, humiliation, and violence. Moreover, such attacks are often ignored and even encouraged by prison officials. According to one inmate writing to the NGLTF, "Nothing is ever did [*sic*] to anyone for raping a homosexual here in prison. It is actually as if it is legal to rape and assault homosexuals. So, it is a life of

TABLE 1.6 Anti-Gay Episodes Reported to the National Gay & Lesbian Task Force: 1985 to 1989

	1985	1986	1987	1988	1989
Verbal harassment or threats of violence	859	3,473	5,463	5,548	5,353
Physical assaults or objects thrown	445	732	835	885	795
Bomb threats	9	50	26	54	82
Vandalism	216	191	338	449	385
Police abuse	—	160	155	205	330
Police harassment	238	250	62	—	—
Arson/bombings	5	10	4	9	11
Homicides	20	80	64	70	62
Other	250	—	61	28	13
Total	2,042	4,946	7,008	7,248	7,031

being . . . constantly threatened, raped, assaulted and be [sic] degraded" (NGLTF, 1988, pp. 22, 23).

TRENDS IN ANTI-GAY VIOLENCE

Although the pervasiveness of anti-gay violence has been clearly demonstrated, questions remain about whether attacks are on the upswing. During the 1980s, lesbian and gay community organizations documented a dramatic increase in episodes ranging from harassment to homicide. The number of anti-gay incidents reported by local groups to the National Gay & Lesbian Task Force increased from 2,042 in 1985 to 7,031 in 1989 (see Table 1.6).[8] Lack of systematic data collection throughout most of the United States and underreporting by victims, however, prevent an accurate measurement of the full extent of the problem. This, in conjunction with changes in the number of groups reporting to the NGLTF each year, has made it difficult to gauge how the national scope of the problem has changed over time. Although the number of tabulated incidents has more than tripled in a five-year period, it is unclear to what extent this increase reflects greater victimization or improved documentation by local groups across the country.

Several gay victim assistance agencies and police departments also have documented an increase in anti-gay violence reports in recent years, an indication that the problem may be growing in some locales. For example, between 1987 and 1991, the New York City Gay and Lesbian Anti-Violence Project experienced more than a fivefold rise in its bias incident caseload (from 117 to 592; Reyes, 1992).

During 1991 alone, recorded anti-gay episodes increased substantially in five major urban areas—Boston, Chicago, Minneapolis/St. Paul, New York City, and San Francisco—that span the U.S. (NGLTF Policy Institute, 1992). In comparison with 1990, attacks reported to gay and lesbian victim service agencies rose by 6% in Chicago, 11% in San Francisco, 17% in New York City, 42% in Boston, and 202% in Minneapolis/St. Paul. Altogether, 1,822 incidents were documented in the five metropolitan areas, a 31% increase over 1990 and a 161% increase since 1988, the year that several of the victim assistance programs were established. Although police in the five cities recorded only 362 anti-gay crimes in 1991, this figure is 41% higher than the number documented in 1990.

Greater reporting by victims and other factors may account for some of the rise in reports in 1991, but the magnitude of the increases in every city suggests there was a growth in actual levels of violence. Given that cities as geographically diverse as these recorded increases during 1991, it is likely that many other U.S. communities also experienced a similar upswing.

Survey data provide still more evidence that anti-gay violence is increasing, at least in certain areas. According to a longitudinal study of gay men in New York City, the proportion of respondents who experienced some form of anti-gay violence increased from 9% in 1985 to 14% in 1990. During this period, rates of victimization fluctuated, dropping as low as 7% in 1986 and rising as high as 17% in 1988 (see Chapter 2 by Dean, Wu, & Martin).

In Philadelphia, gay men and lesbians surveyed in 1986-1987 (Gross et al., 1988) experienced criminal violence at approximately *twice the rate* of those surveyed in 1983-1984 (Aurand et al., 1985). Whereas 10% of the lesbians and 24% of the gay men surveyed in Philadelphia had been victims of criminal violence in a 12-month period spanning 1983-1984, 20% of the lesbians and 46% of the gay men surveyed in that city during 1986-1987 had experienced criminal violence in the 12 months prior to completing the survey. The authors attribute the increase partly to having obtained a more representative sample in the later study and partly to an actual rise in levels of victimization during the three-year period.

AIDS and Anti-Gay Violence

All evidence suggests that AIDS has negatively affected the cultural climate in which anti-gay violence occurs. According to the Presidential Commission on the Human Immunodeficiency Virus Epidemic (1988, p. 140), "Increasing violence against those perceived to carry HIV, so-called 'hate crimes,' are a serious problem. The Commission has heard reports in which gay men in particular have been victims of violent acts that are indicative of a society that is not reacting rationally to the epidemic."

Survey data confirm the conclusion that AIDS has contributed to the problem of anti-gay violence. In Gross et al.'s (1988) study of anti-gay violence in Pennsylvania (n = 721), 13% of the gay men and 1% of the lesbian women reported that they had experienced violence or harassment that was AIDS related (such as being called a "plague-carrying faggot" during an attack). In the Morgen and Grossman (1988) study of anti-gay violence in Baltimore (n = 542), 7% of the males and 6% of the females had encountered "AIDS-associated" harassment or violence in a single year. According to a mail-in survey by Platt (1990) of gay men and lesbians in 36 states, the District of Columbia, and Canada (n = 234), 15% of those who had been verbally or physically attacked reported that the perpetrator(s) had made reference to AIDS.

Asked whether fear and hatred associated with AIDS had fostered anti-gay harassment and violence in their communities, approximately two thirds of the groups reporting incidents to the NGLTF for the year 1989 answered affirmatively (NGLTF, 1990). Of the 7,031 anti-gay episodes reported to the NGLTF in 1989, 15% (1,078) were classified by local groups as "AIDS related" (i.e., incidents that involved verbal reference to AIDS by perpetrators or were directed against persons with AIDS). The proportion of AIDS-related incidents in previous years was 17% (1,259) in 1988,

15% (1,042) in 1987, 14% (681) in 1986, and 8% (173) in 1985 (NGLTF, 1986, 1987, 1988, 1989). The actual extent of AIDS-related episodes is probably underestimated because most organizations reporting to the NGLTF did not routinely note whether AIDS was a factor in the incidents they documented.

Although newspaper headlines assert that attacks on homosexuals have been provoked by the fear of AIDS ("AIDS Epidemic Fuels Attacks on Gays," 1988; Johnson, 1987), AIDS is probably less a cause of anti-gay sentiment than it is a new focus and justification for expressions of anti-gay prejudice (Herek & Glunt, 1988). Such prejudice is hardly a new phenomenon (see Chapter 5 by Herek). What is new, however, is the visibility of lesbian and gay people in American society as a result of AIDS. Since the onset of the epidemic, there has been a dramatic and unprecedented increase in media attention to gay and lesbian issues. Such coverage, along with growing political activism within the gay community as a result of AIDS, may have simultaneously increased public acceptance and exposed gay men and lesbians to greater risk of violence.

LIMITATIONS OF EXISTING DATA

A major limitation of all prevalence studies of anti-gay violence conducted to date is that they have been based on nonrepresentative samples. Many lesbians and gay men, fearing hostility and discrimination because of their sexual orientation, conceal their gay identities to some degree. To reach such a hidden population, researchers have found it most feasible to conduct surveys at gay/lesbian-identified settings. With the exception of the national telephone survey by Teichner Associates ("Results of Poll," 1989), all prevalence studies discussed in this chapter gathered data by distributing questionnaires at group meetings or events, at gay establishments (such as bars or community centers), or through gay publications and mailing lists.

Such convenience samples do not include an adequate representation of the lesbian and gay male population of the United States. Gay publications, meetings, events, and institutions are frequently avoided by, or are inaccessible to, lesbian and gay people who are closeted, disabled, economically disadvantaged, elderly or very young, members of racial minority groups, or living in rural settings. Indeed, in most surveys that provided demographic data, a disproportionate number of those sampled were White, male, highly educated, and of middle income.

Another limitation of some studies is that they reached only those motivated to complete a questionnaire on violence or discrimination. In some cases, respondents were self-selected, such as when they answered a mail-in survey or volunteered to complete a questionnaire at a gay establishment or group meeting. Finally, most if not all existing research has overlooked violence against heterosexuals who were perceived to be gay or who were supportive of lesbian and gay rights. Many such attacks, including murders, have been documented by local groups across the nation (Lu, 1991; NGLTF, 1986, 1988).

Because of these limitations, the actual extent of anti-gay violence and other victimization is unclear now and will remain so until additional research has been conducted using more representative samples. It is clear, however, that anti-gay violence is widespread. Even if no attempt is made to generalize from the samples described in this chapter, the sheer number of incidents reported in these studies is staggering.

CONCLUSION

Although more research is needed to better understand the scope and nature of anti-gay violence and victimization, there is ample evidence to show that the problem is severe. Indeed, the quantitative and qualitative data gathered thus far are a frightening testament to the human cost of anti-gay bigotry. What no measurement of the problem can adequately convey, however, is the fear and anguish experienced not only by the survivors but also by the communities of which they are a part. The response that is urgently needed now, in addition to greater study of the problem, is for public officials, educators, clergy, and all people of conscience to acknowledge, condemn, and counter anti-gay prejudice and violence.

NOTES

1. This chapter does not address the problem of suicide among lesbian and gay people. Although suicide is, by definition, self-inflicted, it can be viewed as yet another form of anti-gay violence when it occurs, as it frequently does, because of self-hatred resulting from anti-gay prejudice in society (U.S. Department of Health and Human Services, 1989; Morgen & Grossman, 1988; also Chapter 4 by Hunter).

2. Because of the differences in sampling method, sample composition, and methods used to calculate results, comparisons among the different surveys should be made with caution. For a discussion of methodological considerations, see Chapter 17 of this volume.

3. This discussion does not include surveys that were limited to measuring rates of victimization on college campuses.

4. According to the annual crime survey conducted by the Bureau of Justice Statistics (1989), 36.3 males (age 12 and over) per 1,000 as compared with 21.6 females (age 12 and over) per 1,000 suffered criminal violence in 1987.

5. According to a study of lesbians and gay men in Philadelphia by Aurand et al. (1985), lesbians reported that they first recognized their sexual orientation at age 21.7, compared with an average age of 15.8 for males. Among gay and lesbian people surveyed in Pennsylvania (Gross et al., 1988), females first recognized their sexual orientation at an average age of 20.6, whereas males did so at age 15.4. A study of gay people in the San Francisco Bay Area yielded a similar age difference. Bell, Weinberg, and Hammersmith (1981, p. 83) reported that 57% of the 569 White gay males and 67% of the 110 Black gay males in their sample had labeled themselves as "homosexual" before age 18. In contrast, 44% of the 224 White lesbians and 49% of the 61 Black lesbians had labeled themselves by age 18.

6. Some anti-gay violence studies that included questions about victimization on campus reported lower rates of such abuse (Aurand et al., 1985; Gross et al., 1988; Morgen & Grossman, 1988). In contrast to the previously cited studies with samples made up of self-identified lesbian, gay, or bisexual persons, these studies included a large number of individuals who did not recognize their sexual orientation during their college years. Presumably, such samples should show lower rates of homophobic victimization on campus than those composed entirely of gay-identified individuals. In fact, this was the case.

7. Among the high school and junior high school students surveyed by the Governor's Task Force on Bias-Related Violence (1988, p. 84; $n = 2,823$), only 12% believed it would be "good" or "very good" to have a gay person move into their neighborhood, and only 37% thought it would be acceptable. In contrast, between 50% and 60% of the respondents said it would be "good" or "very good" to have neighbors of different racial or ethnic backgrounds, and approximately 90% thought having such neighbors was at least acceptable.

8. Unlike previous annual reports, the NGLTF Policy Institute report on anti-gay violence in 1990 and 1991 did not feature a tally of incidents documented nationwide. This change came about because many local organizations lacked the resources to systematically document anti-gay episodes and report to

the NGLTF on an annual basis. Consequently, the NGLTF's national figures sharply underrepresented the national scope of the problem and could not measure national trends in levels of violence. Despite these limitations, previous NGLTF reports demonstrated that acts of anti-gay violence occur in great numbers across the country and provided an undeniable body of evidence that demanded official measures to counteract the problem.

In examining anti-gay violence in 1990 and 1991, the NGLTF Policy Institute focused on several U.S. major metropolitan areas—including Boston, Chicago, Minneapolis/St. Paul, New York City, and San Francisco—where victim assistance agencies monitor anti-gay violence and where police track such crimes. Although neither local groups nor police claim their violence data reflect all or even most anti-gay incidents that occur locally, the consistent and ongoing nature of their monitoring efforts made it possible to examine annual trends in reporting by victims. Such trends provide an important indication of whether anti-gay violence and other victimization is increasing or decreasing in these cities and perhaps elsewhere across the country.

REFERENCES

Aaron, M. (1991). *Anti-gay and lesbian violence in Utah: Reported incidents and results of 1990 survey conducted by the Anti-Violence Project of the Gay and Lesbian Community Action Council of Utah.* Salt Lake City: Gay and Lesbian Community Action Council of Utah.

AIDS epidemic fuels attacks on gays. (1988, June 8). *New York Post*, p. 3.

Anderson, C. L. (1982). Males as sexual assault victims: Multiple levels of trauma. *Journal of Homosexuality, 7,* 145-162.

Aurand, S. K., Adessa, R., & Bush, C. (1985). *Violence and discrimination against Philadelphia lesbian and gay people.* (Available from the Philadelphia Lesbian and Gay Task Force, 1501 Cherry Street, Philadelphia, PA 19102)

Bell, A. P., & Weinberg, M. S. (1978). *Homosexualities: A study of diversity among men and women.* New York: Simon & Schuster.

Bell, A. P., Weinberg, M. S., & Hammersmith, S. K. (1981). *Sexual preference: Its development in men and women. Statistical appendix.* Bloomington: Indiana University Press.

Berrill, K. T. (1986). Anti-gay violence: Causes, consequences, responses. Washington, DC: National Gay & Lesbian Task Force.

Bradford, J. B., & Ryan, C. C. (1987). *National lesbian health care survey: Mental health implications.* Unpublished manuscript.

Bureau of Justice Statistics. (1989). *Criminal victimization in the U.S.: 1987* (Ref. No. NCJ-115524). Washington, DC: U.S. Department of Justice.

Campus Environment Team, Pennsylvania State University. (1988). *Campus climate and acts of intolerance.* Unpublished manuscript.

Cavin, S. (1987). *Rutgers sexual orientation survey: A report on the experiences of the lesbian, gay and bisexual members of the Rutgers community.* Unpublished manuscript.

Committee on the Judiciary. (1983). *Police misconduct: Hearing before the Subcommittee on Criminal Justice of the Committee on the Judiciary* (Serial No. 98-50). Washington, DC: Government Printing Office.

Comstock, G. D. (1989). Victims of anti-gay/lesbian violence. *Journal of Interpersonal Violence, 4,* 101-106.

Comstock, G. D. (1991). *Violence against lesbians and gay men.* New York: Columbia University Press.

D'Augelli, A. R. (1989). Lesbians' and gay men's experiences of discrimination and harassment in a university community. *American Journal of Community Psychology, 17,* 317-321.

District of Columbia Lesbian and Gay Anti-Violence Task Force. (1988). *Violence against lesbians and gay men in the Washington metropolitan area.* (Available from the DC Lesbian and Gay Anti-Violence Task Force, 1734 14th Street N.W., Washington, DC 20009)

Finn, P., & McNeil, T. (1987). *The response of the criminal justice system to bias crime: An exploratory review* (Available from Abt Associates, Inc., 55 Wheeler Street, Cambridge, MA 02138-1168)

Gay and Lesbian Community Action Council. (1990). *Out and counted, a survey of the Twin Cities gay and lesbian community.* (Available from the GLCAC, Sabathani Center, Suite 204, 310 East 38th Street, Minneapolis, MN 55049)

Governor's Task Force on Bias-Related Violence. (1988). *Final report.* (Available from the Division on Human Rights, 55 W. 125th Street, New York, NY 10027)

Green, F. (Ed.). (1988). *Gayellow Pages* (17th ed.). New York: Renaissance House.

Gross, L., Aurand, S., & Adessa, R. (1988). *Violence and discrimination against lesbian and gay people in Philadelphia and the Commonwealth of Pennsylvania.* (Available from the Philadelphia Lesbian & Gay Task Force, 1501 Cherry Street, Philadelphia, PA 19102)

Harry, J. (1982). Derivative deviance: The cases of extortion, fag-bashing and the shakedown of gay men. *Criminology, 19,* 546-564.

Herek, G. M. (1989). Hate crimes against lesbians and gay men: Issues for research and policy. *American Psychologist, 44,* 948-955.

Herek, G. M. (1990). Illness, stigma, and AIDS. In P. Costa & G. R. VandenBos (Eds.), *Psychological aspects of serious illness* (pp. 103-150). Washington, DC: American Psychological Association.

Herek, G. M. (1986). *Documenting prejudice on campus: The Yale Sexual Orientation Survey.* Unpublished manuscript.

Herek, G. M., & Glunt, E. K. (1988). An epidemic of stigma: Public reactions to AIDS. *American Psychologist, 43,* 886-891.

Humphreys, L. (1975). *Tearoom trade: Impersonal sex in public places* (enlarged ed.). Chicago: Aldine. (Original work published 1970)

Identity, Inc. (1986). *One in ten: A profile of Alaska's lesbian and gay community.* Anchorage: Author.

Jay, K., & Young, A. (1977). *The gay report.* New York: Summit.

Johnson, D. (1987, April 24). Fear of AIDS stirs new attacks against gays. *New York Times.*

LeBlanc, S. (1991). *8 in 10: A special report of the Victim Recovery Program of the Fenway Community Health Center.* Boston: Author. (Available from the Fenway Community Health Center, 7 Haviland Street, Boston, MA 02115)

Lu, M. (1991). *1990 statistical analysis, Community United Against Violence.* Unpublished manuscript.

Lutz, C. (1987). *They don't all wear sheets.* New York: National Council of Churches. (Available from the Center for Democratic Renewal, P.O. Box 50469, Atlanta, GA 30302)

Mayor's Advisory Committee on Lesbian and Gay Issues. (1991). *Exposing hatred: A report on the victimization of lesbian and gay people in New Orleans.* Available from the Louisiana Lesbian and Gay Political Caucus, P.O. Box 53075, New Orleans, LA 70153.

Mayor's Office of Policy Management. (1983). *The Boston project: A profile of Boston's gay and lesbian community* (Preliminary report of findings). Boston: Office of the Mayor.

McKirnan, D. J., & Peterson, P. L. (1987, March 12). Social indicators: Psychological attitudes, and discrimination and anti-gay violence. *Windy City Times,* p. 2.

Miller, B., & Humphreys, L. (1980). Lifestyles and violence: Homosexual victims of assault and murder. *Qualitative Sociology, 3*(3), 169-185.

Morgen, K. B., & Grossman, J. L. (1988). *The prevalence of anti-gay/lesbian victimization in Baltimore.* Unpublished manuscript.

National Gay & Lesbian Task Force (NGLTF). (1984). *Anti-gay/lesbian victimization: A study by the National Gay Task Force in cooperation with gay and lesbian organizations in eight U.S. cities.* Washington, DC: Author. (Copies of this and other NGLTF reports [in subsequent references, see "Available from the NGLTF"] may be obtained from the NGLTF, 1734 14th Street N.W., Washington, DC 20009)

National Gay & Lesbian Task Force. (1986). *Anti-gay violence and victimization in 1985.* Washington, DC: Author. (Available from the NGLTF)

National Gay & Lesbian Task Force. (1987). *Anti-gay violence, victimization and defamation in 1986.* Washington, DC: Author. (Available from the NGLTF)

National Gay & Lesbian Task Force. (1988). *Anti-gay violence, victimization and defamation in 1987.* Washington, DC: Author. (Available from the NGLTF)

National Gay & Lesbian Task Force. (1989). *Anti-gay violence, victimization and defamation in 1988.* Washington, DC: Author. (Available from the NGLTF)

National Gay & Lesbian Task Force. (1990). *Anti-gay violence, victimization and defamation in 1989.* Washington, DC: Author. (Available from the NGLTF)

National Gay & Lesbian Task Force Policy Institute. (1992). *Anti-gay/lesbian violence, victimization and defamation in 1991.* Washington, DC: Author. (Available from the NGLTF)

New Jersey Lesbian & Gay Coalition (NJLGC). (1984). *Summary of Discrimination Survey.* (Available from the NJLGC, P.O. Box 1431, New Brunswick, NJ 08903)

New York State Lesbian & Gay Lobby. (1985). *Information collected from questionnaire "16 questions".* Unpublished summary.

Norris, W. (1990). *The report of the general faculty of Oberlin College by the ad hoc committee on lesbian, gay and bisexual concerns.* Unpublished manuscript. (Available from William Norris, Department of Sociology, King Building #305, Oberlin College, Oberlin, OH 44704-1095)

O'Shaughnessey, M. E. (1987). *Chancellor's campus-wide task force on sexual orientation: Final report.* Unpublished manuscript.

Peebles, E. H., Tunstall, W. W., & Eberhardt, E. E. (1985). *A survey of perceptions of civil opportunity among gays and lesbians in Richmond, Virginia.* Richmond, VA: Research Task Force (with technical assistance from the Commission on Human Relations).

Platt, L. (1990). [Unpublished data]. Graduate School of the City University of New York, Program in Social/Personality Psychology.

Presidential Commission on the Human Immunodeficiency Virus Epidemic. (1988). *Final report.* (Available from the National AIDS Program, Public Health Service, Department of Health and Human Services, 200 Independence Avenue S.W., Washington, DC 20201)

Results of poll. (1989, June 6). *San Francisco Examiner,* p. A-19.

Reyes, N. (Ed). (1992). *New York City Gay and Lesbian Anti-Violence Project 1991 Annual Report.* Available from the New York City Gay and Lesbian Anti-Violence Project, 208 West 13th Street, New York, NY 10011.

Seattle Commission for Lesbians and Gays. (1991). *A survey of the Seattle area lesbian and gay community: Identity and issues.* (Available from the Seattle Commission for Lesbians and Gays, c/o Office for Women's Rights, 700 3rd Avenue, Room 940, Seattle, WA 98104)

Southern Poverty Law Center. (1987). Gay-bashing prevalent among hate crimes. *Klanwatch Intelligence Report,* p. 5. (Available from the Southern Poverty Law Center, 400 Washington Avenue, Montgomery, AL 36104)

Steinman, R., & Aurand, S. K. (1985). *Discrimination and violence survey of gay people in Maine.* (Summary available from the NGLTF)

Story of boy's torture rocks courtroom. (1990, February 18). *St. Louis Post-Dispatch,* p. 72G.

Task Force on Lesbian and Gay Concerns. (1990). *Creating safety, valuing diversity: Lesbians and gay men in the university.* (Available from the Department of Public Safety, 1319 E. 15th Street, University of Oregon, Eugene, OR 97403)

U.S. Department of Health and Human Services. (1989). *Report of the secretary's task force on youth suicide.* Washington, DC: Government Printing Office.

Vermonters for Lesbian and Gay Rights. (1987). *Discrimination and violence survey of lesbians and gay men in Vermont.* Unpublished summary.

Wisconsin Governor's Council on Lesbian and Gay Issues. (1985). *Violence survey final report.* (Available from the NGLTF)

Wooden, W. S., & Parker, J. (1982). *Men behind bars: Sexual exploitation in prison.* New York: Da Capo.

Yeskel, F. (1985). *The consequences of being gay: A report on the quality of life for lesbian, gay and bisexual students at the University of Massachusetts at Amherst.* (Available from the Office of Gay, Lesbian and Bisexual Concerns, Crampton House S.W., University of Massachusetts, Amherst, MA 01003)

2

Trends in Violence and Discrimination Against Gay Men in New York City: 1984 to 1990

LAURA DEAN
SHANYU WU
JOHN L. MARTIN

The purpose of this chapter is to examine the direction of trends over time in the proportion of the gay male population victimized by others through acts of personal violence or acts of discrimination. Statistics reported by many community groups give the clear impression that more gay men than ever before are experiencing anti-gay prejudice and hate crimes in their communities (see Chapter 1). Other larger studies confirm these trends. For example, the most recent report on anti-gay violence by the National Gay & Lesbian Task Force (NGLTF, 1991) indicates

AUTHORS' NOTE: This research was supported by grant R01 MH39557 from the National Institute of Mental Health and by the New York City Department of Public Health. Part of this work was also supported by Research Scientist Development Award K02 MH00779. A portion of this chapter was prepared while the third author was a Fellow at the Center for Advanced Study in the Behavioral Sciences. We are grateful for the financial support for this fellowship provided by the John D. & Catherine T. MacArthur Foundation. This work would not have been possible without the cooperation and trust of the gay community of New York City and the patience and generosity of the study participants over many years.

that rates of verbal and physical assaults increased by an average of 42% in six geographically diverse urban areas of the United States. New York City's rate of increase was estimated at a staggering 65%. Additional support corroborating these increasing trends may be found in Herek (1989) and in a report published by the New York City Commission on Human Rights (1986).

Currently available data relevant to prevalence and incidence of anti-gay victims and events are primarily derived from passive surveillance systems (e.g., New York City Gay and Lesbian Anti-Violence Project, 1990), which depend on police records and individuals' willingness to report such events to local authorities or agencies. Interpretation of the data is difficult because surveillance systems of this type are vulnerable to a number of biases that can artificially increase or decrease rates of reporting crimes and acts of aggression or can act in both directions simultaneously. It is generally well documented (D'Emilio, 1983, for example) that rates of anti-gay hate crimes historically have been underreported for many years, due to the stigma surrounding homosexuality and fear of revealing one's sexual preference to the police or other authorities (see also Chapter 18 by Berrill & Herek). The advent in some communities of victim advocacy groups staffed by gay people and designed to provide a safe place to report hate crimes has certainly helped to correct the problem of underreporting due to fear and embarrassment. Coincident with the growth of these advocacy groups, however, have come (a) the AIDS epidemic, (b) greater public awareness of homosexuality, and (c) increased media coverage of anti-gay violence events. For gay men and other victims of anti-gay hate crimes, the combination of these events in the 1980s has led to a heightened awareness that such crimes do in fact occur and with (presumed) greater frequency than anyone had imagined. In addition, the events of the 1980s appear to have led increasing numbers of gay men to conclude that (a) there was no reason *not* to report hate crimes; (b) in fact, there are potential benefits to be gained for the community by reporting such crimes; and (c) it is one's civic duty to report the occurrence of anti-gay hate crimes if anything is to be done to curtail them. Thus the rise in rates of anti-gay hate crimes during the decade of the 1980s may be due more to an increased willingness by the gay population to report these events than to a true increase in their occurrence (see also Chapter 1 by Berrill and Chapter 15 by Herek).

We have attempted to address this question directly through the use of a longitudinal study, which employed standardized measures at each data collection point and involved active attempts to contact and reinterview all individuals initially enrolled. As Herek and Berrill (Chapter 17) note, these methods are essential to begin to develop estimates of the true rate and direction of anti-gay prejudice. Data derived from longitudinal studies of select cohorts, however, also have a number of inherent interpretation problems. Specifically, three main influences must be considered in analyzing trends over time. They are usually referred to as *age effects, history* or *period effects,* and *cohort effects* (Riley, Johnson, & Foner, 1972, pp. 27-90).

Simply put, age effects refer to the relationship between a person's age and the likelihood of an event; period or history effects refer to the relationship between the passage of time and the likelihood of an event; and cohort effects refer to the relationship between the time or generation into which a person is born and the likelihood of an event. It is generally recognized that the three effects cannot be estimated simultaneously because they are logically confounded, each effect being a linear function of the other two (Baltes, 1968; Glen, 1975). (See Baltes & Nesselroade, 1970; Fienberg & Mason, 1979; and Glen, 1975, for discussions of the problem.) We can begin to disentangle these effects, however, by making specific comparisons that hold constant, or control for, at least one of the three factors.

In this chapter, we attempt to examine trends over time (a history effect) in the incidence of anti-gay violence and discrimination while also considering the potential role of aging and cohort effects in determining these trends. This represents our initial attempt to examine our data for these effects, and thus our approach is purely descriptive. We employ no tests of significance and do not attempt to model patterns in the data.

METHODS

The Interview

The data used in this analysis were collected as part of the Longitudinal AIDS Impact Project, which began in 1984 and is currently ongoing at the Columbia University AIDS Research Unit in New York City. Analytic and descriptive summaries of these data may be found elsewhere (Martin, 1986, 1987, 1988; Martin, Dean, Garcia, & Hall, 1989; Martin, Garcia, & Beatrice, 1989). A major aim of this project has been to describe and analyze the psychological adaptation processes used by individuals and groups in the gay community as they cope with the AIDS epidemic. Using retrospective and prospective study designs, as well as structured face-to-face interviews for data collection, a wide range of information has been gathered on physical and mental health, social network characteristics, personality factors, coping efforts, stressful life events, AIDS-related bereavement, and anti-gay prejudice. Data have been collected annually since 1985. The time period covered by most of the questions in the interview encompassed the 12 months prior to the day of the interview.

Study Participants

The 1985 cohort. Our first sample was recruited in early 1985 through several methods. These included (a) stratified probability sampling (Kish, 1965) of members of gay male organizations in New York City; (b) "targeted" or "applied" sampling methods (Sudman, 1976), such as face-to-face recruitment at specific times and locations (e.g., the 1985 Gay Pride Festival in New York City) to broaden the scope of the sampling base; and (c) personal referral or "snowball" sampling (Biernacki & Waldorf, 1981) to gain access to gay networks not directly accessible to us as researchers. A complete description of these sampling methods and the resulting components of the sample may be found in Martin and Dean (1990). For this discussion, it is important to note that the sampling methods we employed resulted in a broad cross section of the male homosexual community living throughout New York City in 1985. Infection with human immunodeficiency virus (HIV, the cause of AIDS) was not considered as a criterion for entry into, or exclusion from, the study. Because, however, this was originally conceived as a study of the impact of AIDS on people at risk, men who had already received a diagnosis of AIDS from a physician as of the time of recruitment were excluded from the sample.

A total of 851 individuals were enrolled of whom 746 were interviewed at baseline in 1985. The remaining 105 respondents who were enrolled but not interviewed in 1985 have been employed as a "waiting list" control group and were interviewed for the first time in 1986. Such a control group permitted assessment of the effects of being intensively interviewed on a number of outcomes of interest to us, such as sexual behavior and psychological distress. We have found no interview effects on any of the rates of prejudice reported here. The use of a waiting list control group had the effect of increasing the sample size from wave 1 to wave 2 in cross-sectional analyses. Increasing the number of respondents by 105 drawn from the waiting list, while decreasing the sample by 80 (attrition from wave 1 to wave 2), resulted in a net increase from 746 at wave 1 to 771 at wave 2. This cohort of men has been interviewed annually since their recruitment, providing a total observation period of six years, from 1984 to 1990.

Because this is a longitudinal study involving repeated assessments of a sample originally drawn in 1985, it was necessary to evaluate the effects of attrition on the estimates provided. Our largest attrition occurred between wave 1 (1985) and wave 2 (1986); approximately 10% of the 746 respondents enrolled dropped out of the study. Since then, our attrition rate for all reasons including death has remained stable at approximately 5% per year.

Given our interest in examining age effects in this cohort, Table 2.1 shows the redistribution of the sample across three age categories as a function of aging. It clearly illustrates a limitation inherent in studies that employ a "closed" cohort, such as the one we are describing here: The number of individuals in the youngest age group diminished over time as these persons matured into the next age group. The aging pattern shown in Table 2.1 indicates that our ability to produce stable estimates decreases sharply over time in the youngest age group. That is, when the cohort was recruited in 1985, there were 159 men aged 18 to 29; as of 1989 the size of this age group had shrunk to 36, none of whom were younger than 25. By 1990 only 25 men were 29 years of age or younger. Thus we have no information from our original 1985 cohort that is informative with respect to the rates of violence and discrimination among gay men aged 18 to 24 in 1989 or 1990.

TABLE 2.1 Number (and Percentage) of Respondents in Each Age Group During Six Years of Observation

| | Year of Interview | | | | | |
Age Group	1985 (746)	1986 (771)	1987 (741)	1988 (701)	1989 (655)	1990 (592)
18-29	169 (23%)	121 (16%)	91 (12%)	56 (8%)	36 (5%)	25 (4%)
30-45	489 (66%)	542 (70%)	538 (73%)	526 (75%)	494 (75%)	434 (73%)
46 or older	88 (12%)	108 (14%)	112 (15%)	119 (17%)	125 (19%)	136 (23%)

NOTE: Columns add to 100%.

The 1990 cohort. To study and compare the most recent generation of gay men with their aging counterparts, it was necessary to recruit a new cohort, aged 18 to 23, in 1990. We attempted to conduct the sampling of these men in exactly the same way as the 1985 cohort was sampled. Unfortunately, we were not able to recruit a random sample from the organization sampling frame, because the organizations included in the frame did not have memberships with sufficient numbers of young gay men. Thus we relied most heavily on snowball sampling and face-to-face recruitment methods. A complete description of these methods is forthcoming (Dean & Martin, 1991). A total of 174 gay men aged 18 to 23 were recruited and interviewed in a six-month period in 1990, coincident with the sixth wave of interviews conducted with the 1985 cohort. Several of these young men turned 24 between the time they were recruited and time they were interviewed. Thus the age range of the 1990 cohort is actually 18 to 24.

Characteristics of the two cohorts. Table 2.2 provides a descriptive picture of the two gay male cohorts we have available for study. Six years of data are shown for the 1985 cohort while only a single year of data is available for the 1990 cohort. It can be seen that, at the start of the study in 1985, the sample ranged in age from 19 to 72 (*mean* = 35.7, SD = 8.5). Of the total, 37% were coupled with a lover; the group was primarily White (87%) and college educated (82%), with a median income of $25,000 in

TABLE 2.2 Demographic Characteristics of Two Cohorts of New York City Gay Men

Characteristic	1985	1986	1985 Cohort 1987	1988	1989	1990	1990 Cohort 1990
Age	36	37	38	39	40	41	21
(mean & range)	19-75	20-75	21-76	22-77	23-78	24-76	18-24
Race							
(% Black/Hispanic)	13%	12%	12%	11%	10%	10%	38%
Lover status							
(% coupled)	37%	41%	43%	45%	46%	45%	15%
Closetedness							
(% half in)	20%	16%	15%	14%	14%	13%	22%
Knowledge of HIV status							
(% informed)	7%	21%	34%	46%	57%	71%	45%
ARC or AIDS[a]							
(% diagnosed)	2%	4%	6%	6%	7%	8%	0%
Deceased							
(cumulative %)	—	<1%	2%	4%	7%	10%	—

a. No respondent was diagnosed with AIDS in 1985.

1984. By 1990 the original sample had aged by six years; a slightly larger proportion were coupled; and many more men had been informed of their HIV antibody status.

The 1990 cohort of young gay men differs markedly in a number of ways from the older cohort: They are, on average, 20 years younger; nearly four times as many (38%) are Black or Hispanic; only one third as many (15%) are coupled with a lover; and less than half (45%) have been tested and informed of their HIV infection status.

Measures

Our measures of the experience of anti-gay prejudice were divided into those involving acts of violence and those involving acts of discrimination. The data reported here describe the percentage of the sample who experienced at least one event of anti-gay violence or anti-gay discrimination within one-year intervals, from 1984 to 1990. This approach generates the most conservative estimate of the occurrence of these events because it does not consider multiple violence or prejudice events experienced by the same person within a given year.

Anti-gay violence. Anti-gay violence was measured by asking, "In the past year have you been the victim of anti-gay violence. . . . I mean, was an attempt made to harm you or were you harmed because you are gay." This was the only definition or clarification given of the term *violence.* If the respondent answered in the affirmative, he was asked, "What happened?" Interviewers were trained to probe to encourage the subject to describe the event that occurred in concrete terms. If the respondent gave only a vague description, such as "people say things all the time," the interviewer asked him to focus on one event and describe it. Interviewers were asked to write the respondent's description verbatim in the interviewer booklet.

A content analyses of the violence events has been conducted only for the first two waves of data. Each event was classified into one of three levels: Level 1 included verbal abuse and threats; Level 2 included having objects hurled, being spat on, and the like; Level 3 included being physically assaulted. Each event was classified into the highest level possible. For 1985 (wave 1), 39% of all violence events were categorized as Level 1, 30% were categorized as Level 2, and the remaining 31% were categorized as Level 3. For 1986 (wave 2), 49% of all violence events were categorized as Level 1, 22% were Level 2, and 29% were Level 3 events. The majority of events were not reported to the police: In 1987 (the first year we asked the question), 13% of all violence events had been reported to the police. This figure remained stable at 13%-14% from 1988 through 1990. We did not ask whether events had been reported to community agencies.

Anti-gay and anti-AIDS discrimination. The second question used to assess prejudice events was this: "In the past year, have you been discriminated against in any way because of being gay or because of fear of AIDS?" Again, if the respondent answered yes, then the interviewer asked "What happened?" and probed to get a concrete description. These answers were then written into the questionnaire and the event was classified by the interviewer into precoded content areas. Interviewers were asked to make a determination, with the subject's help (if not obvious from the description), of whether the act of discrimination was simply because the subject was gay or if it also had something to do with AIDS.

In both 1985 and 1986, the majority (70%) of all discrimination events were classified by respondents as being related to their homosexuality as opposed to some type of fear about AIDS. The figures shifted toward a balanced distribution (50/50) in 1987 and 1988. In 1989 and 1990, however, they once again approached their original distributions of 70% gay related and 30% AIDS related.

In response to both questions about violence and discrimination, some subjects reported that they had been victimized in some way (for example, not being hired for a job) but were not sure if it was because of their being gay. In those cases, interviewers were asked to circle the response code "don't know." These events were not counted as anti-gay prejudice events. If a respondent was robbed at gunpoint and there was no reason to believe it had anything to do with his being homosexual, then it was not counted as anti-gay violence. In the case of someone being approached in a gay setting where it seemed the perpetrator was looking for a gay victim, however, the incident was counted under anti-gay violence.

Our questions about violence and discrimination give us only a partial view of some of the prejudice that gay men experience. They do not allow for or include institutionalized anti-gay bias, unless the subject could describe a specific incident in which he was denied a common privilege or excluded from something. For instance, if a man said that he is excluded (in general) from getting legally married, we did not count it; however, if he told us that he applied for a marriage license and was turned down, we did count it.

Our method also does not take into account things like anti-gay graffiti, which is widespread and which none of the subjects going about his daily life in New York City could avoid, or jokes made by comedians about gay people in general. With the onset of the epidemic, such messages have become even more brutal than in previous eras. Only when an individual was directly targeted for these types of violence, however, did we count them as episodes.

It should also be noted that, at this stage, our analysis does not allow for a sharp distinction between what is classified as violence and what is classified as discrimination. This ambiguity is particularly applicable to the classification of verbal abuse. If they recalled the abuse, most victims of this event classified it as anti-gay violence. Some, however, felt more strongly that it represented discrimination and chose that category rather than the violence category. To reduce the effects of these types of ambiguities on our estimates of anti-gay prejudice, the data we present show separate rates for (a) violence, (b) discrimination, and (c) the two combined into a general category of anti-gay prejudice (i.e., one or both occurred in a particular time period).

The Analysis

All analyses presented here were conducted in three ways: (a) as cross-sectional analyses using all available respondents at each data point; (b) as a panel analysis, using only subjects who had been interviewed at all six time periods; and (c) as a "progressive" or series of panel analyses at each time point, which included only respondents who had complete data through a given interview. The different approaches resulted in figures that did not vary systematically. The magnitude of the differences never exceeded one to two percentage points. Thus we concluded that attrition from the study was not biased with respect to the likelihood of experiencing anti-gay prejudice. In addition, we were thus free to employ all available data at each time point to generate the most stable estimates possible.

RESULTS

Historical effects. We first examined rates of violence and discrimination to evaluate historical trends over time, from 1984 to 1990, for the total sample. Table 2.3 shows these figures for each cross section of the 1985 cohort. Looking first at the incidence of anti-gay violence, the results shown in the first row of Table 2.3 suggest a sharp increase in the number of persons experiencing these events during the four-year period from 1984 to 1988: The rate nearly doubles from 9% in the 1985 interview (which includes violence experienced in 1984) to 17% in the 1988 interview (which includes violence in 1987). In the 1989 and 1990

TABLE 2.3 Annual Percentage (and Number) of Respondents Reporting at Least One Incident of Antigay Violence or Discrimination

Type of Event	Year of Interview					
	1985 (746)	1986 (771)	1987 (741)	1988 (701)	1989 (655)	1990 (592)
Violence	9% (64)	7% (52)	12% (91)	17% (120)	12% (79)	14% (84)
Discrimination	15% (115)	15% (116)	16% (116)	12% (84)	10% (66)	10% (60)
Violence or discrimination	21% (154)	20% (151)	25% (187)	26% (180)	20% (128)	21% (126)

interviews, however, there appears to be a decrease in the rate of violence events to a level midway between the low of 7% in 1985 and the high of 17% in 1988.

Looking now at the second row in Table 2.3, it appears that there has been a downward trend in the number of individuals experiencing events classified as anti-gay discrimination. From 1984 to 1987, reports of discrimination were stable at approximately 15% per year. This figure declined steadily by one third to 10% in 1989 and 1990.

The third row of Table 2.3 combines rates of violence events with discrimination events to derive an estimate of the numbers of gay men who experienced one or the other (or both) types of prejudice on an annual basis. The trends shown here are quite consistent, approximately 20%, at the beginning (1985 and 1986) and the end (1989 and 1990) of the six years of observation. There was a clear elevation, however, in 1987 and 1988, to approximately 25%.

Examination of the combined rates of the two types of prejudice events also is of interest because it provides a way of assessing the extent of overlap between groups of individuals experiencing violence and discrimination. Should we find a high degree of overlap between those reporting violence and those reporting discrimination, it would suggest that there may be something about these individuals that places them at especially high risk for these types of events. Contrary to this idea, however, Table 2.3 shows that the experience of *both* violence and

TABLE 2.4 Annual Percentage of Respondents Reporting at Least One Incident of Anti-Gay Violence or Discrimination Broken Down by Age

| | Year of Interview | | | | | |
| | 1985 | 1986 | 1987 | 1988 | 1989 | 1990 |
Age Group	(746)	(771)	(741)	(701)	(655)	(592)
Violence:						
18-29	11%	14%	22%	28%	14%	4%
30-45	9%	6%	12%	17%	13%	16%
46 or older	2%	2%	6%	10%	6%	10%
Discrimination:						
18-29	18%	17%	12%	12%	8%	8%
30-45	16%	16%	18%	12%	12%	11%
46 or older	8%	13%	8%	13%	8%	9%
Violence or discrimination:						
18-29	24%	27%	30%	37%	19%	12%
30-45	22%	20%	27%	26%	21%	24%
46 or older	8%	9%	12%	18%	14%	15%

discrimination within the same-year period is relatively rare in this sample. For example, 25 respondents were victims of both violence and discrimination in 1985; this represents 3% of the total sample (N = 746) and 16% of the portion of the sample that reported at least one prejudice event that year (N = 154).

Age effects. Based on Table 2.3, it appears that the percentage of gay men who were victims of anti-gay violence fluctuated around 12% over time. Table 2.3 also demonstrates a fairly steady decline in the percentage reporting one or more anti-gay or anti-AIDS discrimination events. While these patterns may be due to historical, contextual, or ecological events, they also may reflect the possibility that older men are less likely to experience violence and discrimination. Because the sample is aging, this alternative explanation should be examined. To determine whether the risk of prejudice events changes as a function of age, we divided the 1985 sample into three age groups and allowed respondents to mature into older age groups as we examined the data over time (see Table 2.1). We then examined the historical trends in violence and discrimination across the three age groups. These results are shown in Table 2.4.

Looking first at the incidence of violence events in the top panel of Table 2.4, there is a clear and consistent difference between the three age groups through 1988: Younger gay men were the victims of anti-gay violence consistently more often than older gay men. This trend disappeared in 1989 and 1990, as the sample aged.

Looking next at the middle panel of Table 2.4, which shows the annual incidence of discrimination events, it appears that age is a less influential variable with respect to this type of prejudice. The primary discernible differences in rates of discrimination appear to be between the two younger age groups (18 to 45) and the oldest age group (46 or older). As with violence, the trend is in the direction of younger men being at higher risk compared with older men, at least until 1988.

Combining reports of at least one violence event or one discrimination event, shown in the third panel of Table 2.4, we again see a stable and consistent age difference through 1988: In each of the first four years of observation, men aged 18 to 29 were more likely than men aged 30 or older to experience anti-gay violence or discrimination. Similarly, men aged 30 to 45 were more likely than men aged 46 or older to experience anti-gay violence or discrimination.

One possible conclusion to draw from Table 2.4 is that the inverse relationship between age and the likelihood of anti-gay prejudice disappeared by 1990. An alternative explanation, however, is that, because of the aging of the original cohort, we simply had no respondents aged 18 to 24 in 1990. Given this progressive truncation in age range, an adequate age contrast over time cannot be made based only on the 1985 cohort.

An appropriate age comparison requires that we introduce data from the 1990 sample of gay men, aged 18 to 24, and compare their rates of prejudice with the rates of the other three age groups for 1990, shown in Table 2.4. For the new cohort, these rates were 32% for anti-gay violence, 17% for anti-gay or anti-AIDS discrimination, and 46% for either type of prejudice. Comparison of these percentages with the corresponding percentages in the last column of Table 2.4 indicates a strong and consistent inverse age effect: The youngest men were the most likely to experience anti-gay prejudice. This finding suggests that the diminishing inverse age effect shown in Table 2.4 is an artifact due to the aging of the 1985 cohort.

TABLE 2.5 Comparison of Two Birth Cohorts, Aged 18 to 24, on the Incidence of Anti-Gay Violence and Discrimination

			Year of Interview			
Birth Cohort	*1985*	*1986*	*1987*	*1988*	*1989*	*1990*
Violence:						
1961-1966 (N = 41)	5%	9%	19%	24%	12%	4%
	(2/41)	(3/34)	(6/32)	(7/29)	(3/26)	(1/24)
1967-1972 (N = 174)	NA	NA	NA	NA	NA	32%
						(55/174)
Discrimination:						
1961-1966 (N = 41)	5%	9%	3%	7%	4%	4%
	(2/41)	(3/34)	(1/32)	(2/29)	(1/26)	(1/24)
1967-1972 (N = 174)	NA	NA	NA	NA	NA	17%
						(30/174)
Violence or discrimination:						
1961-1966 (N = 41)	7%	18%	22%	31%	12%	8%
	(3/41)	(6/34)	(7/32)	(9/29)	(3/26)	(2/24)
1967-1972 (N = 174)	NA	NA	NA	NA	NA	46%
						(71/174)

NOTE: NA = data not available. Decreasing numbers in the older birth cohort reflect annual attrition rates for this age group.

Cohort effects. By introducing the 1990 cohort, we provide the basis for comparing age-matched generations to determine whether being a particular age at different times in history influences the likelihood of experiencing anti-gay prejudice. To make this comparison, we selected the 41 men from the 1985 sample who were 18 to 24 years old at the time of study enrollment. This group represents the 1961-1966 birth cohort. The 1990 sample of 174 men, also aged 18 to 24, represents the 1967-1972 birth cohort. A comparison of these two generations is shown in Table 2.5.

The most striking feature of Table 2.5 is the generational difference between the two age-matched birth cohorts in their rates of reported prejudice experiences. Whereas the picture is consistent for both violence and discrimination considered separately, the most dramatic illustration of a cohort (and history) effect is shown in the third panel of Table 2.5. Focusing on violence and discrimination combined, 7% of gay men aged 18 to 24 reported at least one incident of prejudice in 1985. Six years later, this percentage increased by more than a

TABLE 2.6 Percentage of 1985 Cohort (N = 851) Broken Down by Number
of Years in Which Anti-Gay Violence or Discrimination Was
Reported

Type of Prejudice	Number of Years (percentage)					
	0	1	2	3	4	5+
Violence	68	17	8	4	2	< 1
Discrimination	62	22	10	4	2	1
Violence or discrimination	50	22	13	7	4	2

factor of six: 46% of gay men aged 18 to 24 reported at least one
such incident in 1990.

Summary of six years of observation. Before discussing these results, it will be useful to summarize the incidence of violence and
discrimination during the entire six years of observation. Using all
available data from the 1985 cohort, Table 2.6 shows the number of
years (from 1984 to 1990) during which at least one incident of violence, discrimination, or either type of prejudice occurred.

The first row in Table 2.6 shows that 32% of the sample reported at least one anti-gay violence incident in one or more
years of this study; 15% experienced at least one such incident in
two or more years of the study. The statistics are similar for discrimination events: 38% of the sample reported at least one incident in one or more years in which they were discriminated
against due to being homosexual or due to fear of AIDS; 17% reported experiencing at least one discrimination event in two or
more years of the study. Combining violence and discrimination
into a single category, the last line in Table 2.6 indicates that,
during the course of six years, from 1984 to 1990, half of the
sample experienced at least one incident of anti-gay prejudice;
26% experienced such events in two or more years.

DISCUSSION

The results presented here can be summarized as follows.
First, anti-gay violence increased substantially to 17% in 1988

from less than 10% in 1985 and 1986. It subsequently declined to 14% in 1990. In contrast, a clear downward trend over time was observed for the incidence of anti-gay discrimination. At the start of the observation period, 15% of the sample reported at least one occurrence of discrimination; at the end of the observation period, this number had decreased to 10%.[1] Combining both violence and discrimination into a single category of prejudicial acts, the evidence suggests that a steady annual rate of approximately 20% of the gay male population represented by this sample were victims of these acts. There is also evidence of a substantial, time-limited increase to 25% of that population during 1987 and 1988.

These estimates apply only to the generation of men we sampled in 1985. Examining that group more carefully by plotting historical trends within three age groups revealed that the risk of experiencing anti-gay violence was substantially elevated for younger gay men (aged 18 to 29) compared with older gay men. This age effect is clear through 1988, from which point we no longer are able to make statements about gay men aged 18 to 24 based on the 1985 cohort. When we include data on 18- to 24-year-old gay men collected in 1990, however, we see a strong age effect: In 1990 32% of gay men in the youngest age group experienced at least one incident of anti-gay violence. This percentage is more than three times higher than the percentages for any other age group in 1990. In fact, it is the highest rate of reporting of anti-gay violence for any age group at any time point during the entire study. These data strongly support the conclusion that, compared with older gay men, younger gay men have been and continue to be at substantially higher risk of experiencing anti-gay violence.

The relationship between anti-gay or anti-AIDS discrimination and age is less clear. The evidence presented here suggests that gay men aged 46 or older tended to be at less risk of experiencing discrimination compared with younger gay men, at least from 1984 to 1987. From 1988 onward, there seems to be little clear relationship between age and discrimination, based on the aging 1985 cohort. This conclusion must be modified, however, when we consider the data for 18- to 24-year-old men sampled in 1990. Consistent with the data on violence, the highest percentage (17%) of discrimination can be found in the youngest group of gay men in the most recent time period available.

Combining violence and discrimination into a single category of prejudice events, and considering both the 1985 and the 1990 cohort, the evidence of an age effect is substantial and compelling: Nearly half (46%) of the 18- to 24-year-old men in the 1990 cohort experienced at least one prejudice event compared with 12%-24% of men in all other adult age groups during the same time period. Again, the clear conclusion to be drawn from these data is that younger gay men have been and continue to be more likely to experience acts of anti-gay prejudice compared with older gay men.

Not only do these findings support the claim of an age effect, they also provide clear evidence that the generation or cohort into which a gay man was born strongly influences his likelihood of experiencing anti-gay prejudice. Of men aged 18 to 24 in 1985, 5% experienced at least one incident of anti-gay violence; six years later, this figure increased to 32% for the same age group. Although less dramatic, the pattern is the same for anti-gay and anti-AIDS discrimination. Finally, combining violence and discrimination into a general category of prejudice events, we found that 7% of 18- to 24-year-old men experienced at least one incident of prejudice in 1985; that figure rose to 46% in 1990 for the same age group.

Overall, these data suggest that anti-gay violence and discrimination affect a relatively stable portion of the gay male population from year to year. In addition, the findings also suggest that aging has a protective effect with respect to the likelihood of experiencing anti-gay prejudice: Fewer older gay men experience these events compared with younger gay men. On the other hand, it appears that the world is becoming a more dangerous place for young gay men as they mature into adulthood. Whether this increased danger is due to increased hostility directed toward members of the gay community from heterosexual segments of society, or whether the new generation of gay men is more willing to challenge, confront, and report those who might perpetrate prejudicial events, is unclear at this time. It is not unreasonable to assume that the net changes reported here are due to a combination of both types of forces.

NOTE

1. It is interesting to note that the New York City Council passed an ordinance in 1987 that prohibited discrimination on the basis of sexual orientation.

REFERENCES

Baltes, P. B. (1968). Longitudinal and cross sectional sequences in the study of age and generation effects. *Human Development, 11*, 145-171.

Baltes, P. B., & Nesselroade, J. R. (1970). Multivariate longitudinal and cross sectional sequences for analyzing ontogenetic and generational change: A methodological note. *Developmental Psychology, 2*, 163-188.

Biernacki, P., & Waldorf, D. (1981). Snowball sampling: Problems and techniques of chain referral sampling. *Sociological Methods and Research, 10*, 141-163.

Dean, L., & Martin, J. L. (1991). *Problems in the development of community sample of gay men aged 18 to 23.* Unpublished manuscript.

D'Emilio, J. (1982). *Sexual politics, sexual communities: The making of a homosexual minority in the United States, 1940-1970.* Chicago: University of Chicago Press.

Fienberg, S. E., & Mason, W. M. (1979). Identification and estimation of age-period-cohort models in the analysis of discrete archival data. In K. F. Schuessler (Ed.), *Sociological methodology* (pp. 1-67). San Francisco: Jossey-Bass.

Glen, N. D. (1975). Cohort analysts' futile quest: Statistical attempts to separate age, period and cohort effects. *American Sociological Review, 41*, 900-903.

Herek, G. M. (1989). Hate crimes against lesbians and gay men: Issues for research and policy. *American Psychologist, 44*(6), 948-955.

Kish, L. (1965). *Survey sampling.* New York: John Wiley.

Martin, J. L. (1986). AIDS risk reduction recommendations and sexual behavior patterns among gay men: A multifactorial categorical approach to assessing change. *Health Education Quarterly, 13*(4), 347-358.

Martin, J. L. (1987). The impact of AIDS on gay male sexual behavior patterns in New York City. *American Journal of Public Health, 77*(5), 578-581.

Martin, J. L. (1988). Psychological consequences of AIDS-related bereavement among gay men. *Journal of Consulting and Clinical Psychology, 56*, 856-862.

Martin, J. L., & Dean, L. (1990). Development of a community sample of gay men for an epidemiologic study of AIDS. *American Behavioral Scientist, 33*(5), 546-561.

Martin, J. L., Dean, L., Garcia, M. A., & Hall, W. (1989). The impact of AIDS on a gay community: Changes in sexual behavior, substance use, and mental health. *American Journal of Community Psychology, 17*, 269-293.

Martin, J. L., Garcia, M. A., & Beatrice, S. (1989). Sexual behavior changes and HIV antibody in a cohort of New York City gay men. *American Journal of Public Health, 79*, 501-503.

National Gay & Lesbian Task Force. (1991). *Anti-gay/lesbian violence, victimization & defamation in 1990.* Washington, DC: Author.

New York City Commission on Human Rights. (1986). *Report on discrimination against people with AIDS.* New York: Author.
New York City Gay and Lesbian Anti-Violence Project. (1990). *Annual report.* New York: Author.
Riley, M. W., Johnson, J., & Foner, A. (1972). *Aging and society: Vol. 3. A sociology of age stratification.* Beverly Hills: Sage.
Sudman, S. (1976). *Applied sampling.* New York: Academic Press.

3

Violence in the Streets: Anti-Lesbian Assault and Harassment in San Francisco

BEATRICE von SCHULTHESS

On November 10, 1990, a male driver hit a car outside Club Q (a gay and lesbian bar in San Francisco). He got out of his own automobile and confronted the lesbian occupants of the car he'd struck, shouting "What the fuck are you looking at, you dyke bitches? There's no damage, get back in your car." The man then drove a short distance and was involved in another confrontation in which he struck another woman in the mouth. In his ensuing confrontation with patrons leaving the club, he injured seven other women, two of them seriously (Conkin, 1990, p. 1).

This incident is only one example of the many acts of violence committed against lesbians in the United States (see Chapter 1). For lesbians, such violence only intensifies the sense of intimidation that they already experience daily as women.

Despite growing national interest in violence against lesbians and gay men, few empirical studies have focused specifically on

AUTHOR'S NOTE: I wish to acknowledge the help of the staff of Community United Against Violence in San Francisco throughout the research process. Special thanks are due to Jill Tregor and former staff member Lester Olmstead-Rose.

violence against lesbians. When lesbians have been included in research samples, their experiences often have been described primarily in comparison with those of gay men rather than in their
own right (Aurand, Addessa, & Bush, 1985; Comstock, 1989; Gross,
Aurand, & Addessa, 1988; National Gay & Lesbian Task Force,
1984). The goals of the study described in this chapter were to
document the nature and extent of violence against lesbians in San
Francisco and to develop a better understanding of the unique features of anti-lesbian violence. This chapter reports preliminary results from a study conducted in 1989 and 1990.

METHOD

Sample

The sample consisted of 400 self-identified lesbian and bisexual women in San Francisco. The overwhelming majority were
lesbians (371 or 94%), with a small number of bisexuals (25 or
6%).[1] Most of the women were White (327 or 82%); the remainder were Black (22 or 6%), Latina (19 or 5%), Asian (7 or 2%),
Native American (7 or 2%), or self-described as "other," which
frequently meant a combination of two of the above categories
(14 or 4%). Most of those surveyed (307 or 78%) were between 20
and 35 years of age; the remainder were younger than 20 (2 or
0.5%), between 36 and 45 years (73 or 18%), between 46 and 55
years (11 or 3%), or over 55 (2 or 0.5%). All of the respondents
lived or worked in San Francisco.

The Survey Instrument

The survey instrument was a self-administered two-page
questionnaire (see Appendix, pp. 73-74). Respondents who indicated that they had experienced some sort of anti-lesbian violence were asked to provide information about the type of
assault, the location of the incident, the injuries they suffered
and medical treatment they received, other assistance they received, and whether they reported the incident to the police.
Demographic information (age, race, sexual identity, neighborhood of residence) was collected for all respondents.

Procedure

During the one-year period starting in fall 1989, surveys were collected from 402 women using two different recruitment methods.[2] Over half (208 or 52%) of the surveys were collected by me or a female research assistant who approached respondents individually at local community events such as the Lesbian/Gay Freedom Day Parade and the Castro Street Fair. Potential respondents were told that the purpose of the survey was to document the extent of violence against lesbians in San Francisco. They also were told that the researcher was a graduate student working with Community United Against Violence (CUAV), a local agency that provides education, counseling, and advocacy services for the lesbian and gay community. Although an exact count was not made of the number of women who refused to complete the questionnaire, neither I nor the research assistant encountered a significant number of refusals. The high response rate was probably due to several factors. First, the survey outreach was conducted at lesbian and gay events, where the women in attendance were likely to be highly motivated to participate as a way of helping to stop anti-lesbian violence. Second, the research assistant and I stood near or in the CUAV booth, which may have enhanced our legitimacy among potential respondents. Third, the fact that the survey focused solely on lesbians created interest among potential participants, many of whom commented that they had never seen a survey for or on lesbians.

The remaining 48% of the completed surveys were obtained through a local women's bookstore and a community center. Stacks of questionnaires were left at each location and a sealed box was provided where respondents could deposit completed questionnaires. Although not all of the questionnaires distributed at these sites were returned, a response rate cannot be calculated because no initial tabulation was made of the number of surveys left at each location.

The Interview

The last item on the survey explained that the researcher wished to conduct follow-up in-depth interviews and requested that the respondent give her name, address, and telephone number if she was interested in participating. Those who provided this information were promised complete confidentiality. Of the women who filled out the survey, 75 (19%) indicated that they would be willing to be interviewed. Seven of them have been interviewed since February of 1990. The semistructured interviews, which lasted between 90 minutes and 3 hours, were conducted at the CUAV offices. Each woman was asked a series of open-ended questions about her experiences with anti-lesbian violence. The questions were designed to elicit discussion about the circumstances, situations, and issues surrounding the incidents indicated on each respondent's survey as well as her knowledge of and experiences with social service agencies in San Francisco. The interviews were audiotaped and later transcribed. Interview notes were coded so that no names or identifying information appeared on the transcription.

RESULTS AND DISCUSSION

The Survey

The survey results paint an alarming picture of violence against the lesbians in this sample. Of the 400 respondents, 334 (84%) reported experiencing anti-lesbian verbal harassment at some point in their lives; two thirds of these women had experienced anti-lesbian verbal harassment within the last year. These were not isolated events: An overwhelming majority of the women who had experienced some sort of verbal harassment (216 or 86%) reported more than one incident within the last 12 months.

In addition, 226 (57%) of the respondents reported that they had experienced the threat of violence or actual violence because of their sexual orientation. Of these, 161 (40% of the sample) had been threatened with physical violence; 134 (33%) had been chased or followed; 110 (27%) had had objects thrown at them; and 48 (12%) had been punched, hit, kicked, or beaten (see Table 3.1). Of the women who were involved in some sort of incident, 36 (16%) suffered injuries ranging from bruises and a black eye to internal injuries and knife wounds.

Only 34 (15%) of those who had been victimized reported the incident to the police, and approximately the same number called any sort of social service agency. The most frequent reason

TABLE 3.1 Types of Violence Experienced by Respondents

Have people ever done any of the following to you because of their perception of your sexual orientation? (check all that apply)

Type of Violence	Past Year	Lifetime
Threatened with physical violence	40	161 (40%)
Thrown objects at you	39	110 (27%)
Chased or followed you	49	134 (33%)
Punched, hit, kicked, or beat you	6	48 (12%)
Assaulted/wounded you with a weapon	2	11 (3%)
Set fire to or vandalized your property	18	40 (10%)
Sexually assaulted/raped you	3	23 (6%)
Robbed you	10	27 (7%)

NOTE: The "Lifetime" column includes experiences within the previous year plus events that occurred earlier. A total of 226 women experienced violence or were threatened with violence. Women reporting verbal abuse but not violence or the threat of violence are not included in this table.

cited by survey respondents for not reporting an incident (whether verbal or physical) was that they did not perceive it as "serious enough." One of the women who was interviewed explained, "No, I've never reported an incident. It never seemed . . . I was never attacked physically, so it never seemed important, you know, an assault or anything."

Of those who desired emotional support or counseling, 35 (16%) felt that it was not available to them. Because heterosexism pervades the criminal justice system as well as many legal and social service agencies, many lesbians justifiably fear that they will be further traumatized if they report an attack (see Chapter 18; see also Comstock, 1989; The Lesbian and Gay Anti-Violence Task Force of Washington, DC, 1988; Governor's Task Force, 1988).

Most of the incidents occurred in the Mission district (53 or 24%) or the Castro/Upper Market district (27 or 12%). The highest concentrations of the survey respondents also lived in these two neighborhoods, which are strongly identified as gay or lesbian (61 or 15% in the Mission; 63 or 16% in the Castro/Upper Market).

Experience with anti-lesbian violence differed according to race and ethnicity. Of the 400 survey respondents, 69 (18%) were women of color, and many of them commented on the connections among their triple minority status and their experiences with violence. White lesbians were more likely to have experienced a verbal assault than were lesbians of color: 86% (235) of the White lesbians reported a verbal assault, compared with 65% (34) of the lesbians of color. The picture shifts, however, when physical violence, threats, vandalism, and rape are involved. Lesbians of color consistently experienced a higher level of all these types of anti-lesbian violence. Any generalizations from these data must be very tentative, however, because of the small number of cases.[3]

The Interviews

Although qualitative analysis of the in-depth interviews is not yet complete, three recurring themes have emerged. First, lesbians experience a continuous stream of harassment on the streets because of their gender. As women, they have been conditioned to cope with harassment as an inevitable part of life. Consequently, they often suffer silently with feelings of vulnerability and fear. Victims of anti-lesbian violence often minimize the impact of an incident, especially when it is "just" verbal. One woman said, "You realize that San Francisco is just like any other place and you're going to be harassed either for being a woman or for being a lesbian."

A second, closely related theme is that attacks often began as antiwoman and then added an anti-lesbian dimension. In several cases, the woman believed that her assailant did not know she was a lesbian (based, for example, on her clothing or appearance, her behavior, the location of the assault, or the assailant's initial remarks). Instead, the incident began when the man remarked upon her sex or made some unwanted reference about her being a woman. Only when the woman did not respond in a certain way did it escalate into an anti-lesbian incident. One woman commented, "My first incident was a lot of anti-woman thing and then when I confronted him it turned into an anti-gay thing because that's the worst thing that he can think of to say to me."

Men expect women to act in certain ways in response to their "come on." Carol Brooks Gardner (1980, p. 346), who has done research on street remarks, suggests that "retaliation is not considered feminine behavior." A woman who answers back or does something that is construed as retaliation is seen by her assailant as nonfeminine and therefore as engaging in behavior that is inappropriate for her gender. If the assailant is unhappy with the victim's response, one way of escalating the attack is to shift the harassment from antiwoman to anti-lesbian commentary.

One respondent illustrated this pattern in her analysis of an incident that began with a man asking to see her breast as she walked by him on the street. She ignored the comment and walked on. He continued the harassment by saying, "Dyke." She concluded, "So the worst kind of woman that he can imagine, a woman that won't respond to him at all, must be a lesbian. Otherwise I would've been flattered that he wanted to see my breast."

Based on these and other examples, I no longer frame the issue of violence against lesbians only in terms of sexual orientation. Instead, I conceptualize lesbianism as an extension of gender and conceptualize anti-lesbian violence as an extension of misogynistic violence. I have begun to view the types of remarks that the women experienced along a continuum ranging from exclusively antiwoman at one end to exclusively anti-lesbian at the other.

Of course, some incidents were clearly focused on the woman's lesbianism from the start. For example, one woman was standing at a bus stop with her lover and recounted, ". . . and we were talking about whatever and all of a sudden I hear goddamn bulldyke, goddamn fucking bulldyke." We should not assume, however, that this is always the pattern in anti-lesbian attacks.

A third theme that emerged from the interviews is that respondents necessarily developed habits of continually monitoring and analyzing their immediate social situations. Many of the women displayed considerable awareness of their own dress and behavior, the physical space between themselves and their assailant, and a host of other factors. They each constructed what I call a "safety map" through which they then analyzed their situation. The safety map includes such factors as their clothing and appearance, their interpersonal behavior, where they were going, who they were with, time of day, and location in the city. For example, one woman said,

> You're going to be harassed . . . and because of that you have to take precautions and that means letting go of the hand of the person you're with in certain areas or if certain groups of people are standing around looking menacing, and not going certain places late at night by yourself.

Another woman said,

> It's the outlying areas, like what I would call the suburbia of San
> Francisco, like the Richmond, Sunset. Out in those areas I won't say
> [I become] a little less obvious, I don't change the way I dress or
> anything but I may not be as out or open or whatever, subtle
> changes in body language or whatever.

A third woman's comments illustrate the level of sophistica-
tion that is involved in constructing the safety map:

> I put space between me, if I hear somebody walking behind me at
> night on the sidewalk I turn to see who it is . . . and if it's a man
> and it's late and dark and I'm alone I perhaps cross the street, de-
> pending on what he looks like he's doing. You know if he's carry-
> ing two bags of groceries and walking his dog just like I am and
> he's not just following me, I probably stay on the same sidewalk.
> But if he was sort of, whatever, then I'll walk faster or cross to the
> other side of the street or I'll stop and go in a store or pretend I'm go-
> ing in the store. I often try to make the person pass me; that clears up
> the whole mystery of whether or not they're following me.

Although use of the safety map may have helped women to
avoid some potentially threatening situations, it clearly does not
eliminate the threat of attack. Many of the factors considered by
the women were not under their personal control. For example, a
woman's income affects the part of the city in which she lives, how
she gets to and from work, and her free-time activities. Most of the
respondents (281 or 71%) made less than $29,000 in 1989; 101 (25%)
had an income under $10,000, which put them below the poverty
line. Also, few women have control over the location or hours of
their work. One of the respondents, for example, worked nights
and frequently had to walk home after midnight. In addition, each
woman's physical attributes (such as height, weight, age, ethnicity,
and race) affect her experiences on the street. Lesbians of color, for
example, must cope with racist violence in addition to violence
against them as women and as lesbians.

CONCLUSION

Because of the use of a nonrandom sample of volunteers, generalizations from the data presented here should be made only

with great caution. Nevertheless, three major conclusions can be drawn from this study. First, violence against lesbians appears to be widespread in San Francisco. Only a small percentage of the violence, however, is reported to any type of agency. Such reporting is crucial if we as a community and as a society are to prevent further violence and to respond to its victims.

Second, anti-lesbian violence is closely connected to violence against women in general. The study described here points to the importance of distinguishing between the two while at the same time seeing their interconnections.

Finally, lesbians not only react to specific attacks with specific responses but also alter their way of being because of the violence that surrounds them. All women have limited access to the streets in our society. What is clear from this study is that lesbians have even more limited rights to be themselves and to go about their daily lives free from violence.

APPENDIX
Questionnaire Items

1. During the last 12 months, have you experienced any of the following: Verbal threats; Threatened with physical harm; Objects thrown at you; Chased or followed; Punched, hit, kicked, or beat; Assaulted/wounded with a weapon; Property vandalized or set fire to; Sexually assaulted/raped; Robbed (person or property). [*Response alternatives: Yes, No*]

2. Have you ever been called "dyke," "faggot," "manhater," "queer," or any other anti-lesbian/gay names? [*No, Yes*] IF YES: How many times within the last 12 months?

3. Have people ever done any of the following to you *because* of their perception of your sexual orientation? (check *all* that apply): Threatened you with physical violence; Thrown objects at you; Chased or followed you; Punched, hit, kicked, or beat you; Assaulted/wounded you with a weapon; Set fire or vandalized your property; Sexually assaulted you; Robbed you? [*No; Yes, within last 12 months; Yes, previously*]

4. For the following section [Questions 4-10] if you have experienced more than one incident, please focus on and describe the *most recent physical assault*. If you have not experienced any incidents please skip to question 11. In what part of San

Francisco did this incident occur? [*Haight, Western Addition; Richmond; Sunset; Bernal Heights; Castro/Upper Market; Mission; Noe Valley; South of Market; Marina; Downtown/Tenderloin; Other*]

5. Where did the incident take place? [*Inside your home; In park, field, playground, etc.; Inside public building; On street, sidewalk, etc.; In a car; MUNI/BART/public transportation; Other (specify)*]

6. What were the injuries you suffered, if any? (Mark all that apply) [*Bruises, black eye, cuts, scrapes, swelling; Broken bones, teeth knocked out; Knife/gun shot wounds; Sexually assaulted, raped; Internal injuries, knocked unconscious; No physical injuries*]

7. Did you report the incident to the police? [*No, Yes*]

8. Did you receive any medical treatment? [*No, Yes*]

8A. IF YES: [*Emergency room outpatient; Stayed in hospital overnight or longer; Personal physician or clinic; Self treated or by friends*]

9. Did you contact any community service agencies after the incident? [*No, Yes*]

9A. IF YES: Who did you contact?

10. Was there any assistance you needed as a result of the incident that was not available to you? [*No, Yes*]

10A. IF YES: What kind? (Mark all that apply) [*Emotional support/counseling; Information/assistance with criminal justice system; Legal services; Medical services; Language/signing services; Financial assistance; Other*]

11. Are you familiar with Community United Against Violence (CUAV)? [*No, Yes*]

11A. IF YES: Have you ever contacted CUAV after an incident? [*No, Yes*]

11A-1. IF NO TO 11A: Why not?

11A-2. IF YES TO 11A: Were you satisfied with the services?

12. Where did you hear about CUAV? [*Advertising/news media; Police; Friend; Referral; Other (please specify)*]

13. Any additional comments?

NOTES

1. Four respondents did not report their sexual identity; four did not report their race; and five did not report their age.

2. Two surveys were unreadable and were dropped from the analysis.

3. These patterns are difficult to separate from overall crime statistics, which establish that people of color are more often the victims of violent crimes than Whites (see Koppel, 1987).

REFERENCES

Aurand, S. K., Addessa, R., & Bush, C. (1985). *Violence and discrimination against Philadelphia lesbian and gay people.* Philadelphia: Philadelphia Lesbian and Gay Task Force. (Available from Philadelphia Lesbian and Gay Task Force, 1501 Cherry St. Philadelphia, PA 19102)

Berrill, K. T. (1986). *Anti-gay violence: Causes, consequences, responses.* Washington, DC: National Gay & Lesbian Task Force. (Available from the National Gay & Lesbian Task Force, 1734 14th Street N.W., Washington, DC 20009)

Comstock, G. D. (1989). Victims of anti-gay/lesbian violence. *Journal of Interpersonal Violence, 4,* 101-106.

Conkin, D. (1990, December 6). Felony charges filed in Club Q incident. *Bay Area Reporter,* p. 1.

Gardner, C. D. (1900). Passing by: Street remarks, address rights, and the urban female. *Sociological Inquiry, 3-4,* 328-356.

Governor's Task Force on Bias-Related Violence. (1988). *Final report.* (Available from Division on Human Rights, 55 W. 125th Street, New York, NY 10027)

Gross, L., Aurand, S., & Addessa, R. (1988). *Violence and discrimination against lesbian and gay people in Philadelphia and the Commonwealth of Pennsylvania.* Philadelphia: Philadelphia Lesbian and Gay Task Force. (Available from Philadelphia Lesbian and Gay Task Force, 1501 Cherry St., Philadelphia, PA 19102)

Koppel, H. (1987). *Lifetime likelihood of victimization* (Reference No. NCJ-104274). Washington, DC: U.S. Department of Justice, Bureau of Justice Statistics.

The Lesbian and Gay Anti-Violence Task Force of Washington, DC. (1988). *Violence against lesbians and gay men in the Washington metropolitan area.* Washington, DC: Author. (Available from the DC Lesbian and Gay Anti-Violence Task Force, 1517 U St. N.W., Washington, DC 20009)

National Gay & Lesbian Task Force. (1984). *Anti-gay/lesbian victimization: A study by the National Gay Task Force in cooperation with gay and lesbian organizations in eight cities.* Washington, DC: National Gay & Lesbian Task Force. (Available from the National Gay & Lesbian Task Force, 1734 14th Street N.W., Washington, DC 20009)

4

Violence Against Lesbian and
Gay Male Youths

JOYCE HUNTER

Compared with adults, adolescents are disproportionately the victims of violent crime (Select Committee on Children, Youth, and Families, 1989). This violence is often targeted at subgroups of youths. Minority youths, for example, are at greater risk of violent and discriminatory behavior than are White youths. Mont-Reynaud, Ritter, and Chen (1990) found that 69% of Black youths and 54% of Latino youths enrolled in high schools have experienced discrimination, compared with 30% of White youths. Differences between minorities and Whites were even greater when frequent discrimination was examined: Only 6% of Whites, but 28% of Blacks and 25% of Latinos, experienced frequent discrimination.

Gay male and lesbian youths are another group believed to experience frequent violence, especially as a result of increasing societal homophobia in response to the AIDS epidemic (Chapter 1 of this volume; also Finn & McNeil, 1987; Gutis, 1989; Martin, 1988). In a survey of 2,823 junior and senior high school students, for example, the New York State Governor's Task Force on Bias-Related Violence found respondents to be not only negatively biased toward gay persons but "sometimes viciously and with threats of violence" (DeStefano, 1988, p. 7). These biases frequently are expressed in harassment and assault of gay- and lesbian-identified students (see Chapter 1). Such victimization has many consequences, including truancy and dropping out of school (Hunter & Schaecher, 1990). Violence toward youths also is believed to be associated with violence toward oneself, manifested in the form of suicidal behavior (Gibson, 1989; Hunter & Schaecher, 1990).

Although accounts of "gay-bashing" have increased in the popular press (Rotheram-Borus, Rosario, & Koopman, 1991), few data are available to document the incidence of such attacks among minority youths. Documentation of suicidal ideation and suicide attempts among minority youths also is needed. The goal of this chapter therefore is to document the frequency of violent attacks and suicidal behaviors reported by a sample of self-identifying lesbian and gay male youths who are also predominantly Black or Latino.

METHOD

Site

The Hetrick-Martin Institute is a community-based agency in New York City that provides a range of services targeting lesbian and gay male teenagers and their families. Youths who seek services at the agency are predominantly minority (35% Black, 46% Latino, with the remaining 19% White, Asian, or mixed), ranging in age from 14 to 21 years (mean = 16.8 years). Typically, they are referred by peers, media, schools, or emergency shelters. Approximately 80% of those seeking services are male, and 20% are female. Most self-identify as homosexual (67%), with the remainder reporting themselves to be bisexual (26%) or unsure about their sexual orientation (7%). The institute has six major service components, serving more than 1,000 youths per year: clinical counseling services, a street outreach program, the Harvey Milk High School, an after-school drop-in center program, educational services, and an HIV/health care program. This study is based on reports from all youths being seen at the institute except those in the street outreach program.[1]

Procedure

Data for this chapter were obtained from the charts of the first 500 youths seeking services at the agency beginning January 1, 1988 (which included charts through approximately November 1988). Each chart contained information collected during an initial intake interview that lasted from 90 minutes to two hours and was conducted with every youth presenting at the agency. This interview included assessment of demographic information (age, sex, race, sexual orientation, living situation, sources of financial support, religion), status of current psychosocial adjustment (including relations to family, peers, school, and the legal system), sexual abuse, problem behaviors, sexual and drug risk behaviors, health status, and knowledge of HIV and HIV risk.

Of particular relevance to this chapter, information was gathered on violence experienced by the youth (physical assaults), its source (family, peers, strangers), and whether or not it was gay related. Additionally, suicidal behavior was documented in terms of both suicidal ideation (thinking about suicide for more than three days in one week) and actual suicide attempts.

The six members of the clinical staff at the agency were trained to code each chart for the presence or absence of violent physical assaults and the type (anti-gay or not) and source of the violence as well as the presence or absence of suicidal ideation and attempts. To provide qualitative descriptions of the reports contained in the intake interviews, each counselor wrote a short case report and presented it in group supervision. Two typical cases have been selected for presentation here.

RESULTS

Of the 500 youths, 201 (40%) reported that they had experienced violent physical attacks. The youths reporting violence did not differ significantly from the general sample of youths seeking services at the Hetrick-Martin Institute. Their mean age was 17.1; 21% of them were female; 42% were Black, 40% Latino, 16% White, and 2% other. Of those reporting violent physical assaults, 46% reported that the assault was gay related; 61% of the gay-related violence occurred in the family. Suicidal ideation was found among 44% of those experiencing violent assaults; 41% of the girls and 34% of the boys reporting violent assaults had tried to kill themselves.

A description of two typical cases illustrates the psychological pain associated with violent attacks. Brian, a 16-year old Black youth, always knew that he was gay. He reported to his intake counselor that he also knew not to talk about his sexual orientation with family or peers. Because he did not pursue girls, a friend asked Brian about his sexual preferences. Brian responded honestly that he preferred males. Fearing that his friendship with Brian would lead to his own ostracism by peers, the friend informed others at school that Brian was gay, telling them in a manner that elicited harassment and ridicule toward Brian. Brian was shoved into lockers, ridiculed, and threatened on a daily basis. Over time, this emotional abuse evolved into physical abuse until, one day after school, Brian was attacked by his schoolmates. His home situation was similar. Brian's parents were unable to tolerate or accept his sexual orientation. His father taunted Brian and their arguments intensified until their relationship was characterized solely by abuse and ridicule. Brian attempted suicide several times before hearing about the Hetrick-Martin Institute and transferring to Harvey Milk High School.

Anna, an 18-year-old Latina, was living in a group home when coming to Hetrick-Martin. Her parents had filed a PINS (Persons in Need of Supervision) petition, requesting Anna's placement due to her sexual orientation. When Anna first told her parents that she was lesbian, they felt angry and guilty; they almost filed for divorce, each blaming the other for their daughter's homosexuality. With counseling, they chose not to divorce but to place Anna. She was angry and frequently became involved in arguments and fights, first at school and then in her several foster care and group home placements. Her anger was linked to insults and harassment for being lesbian. This harassment was invisible to the group home counselor, who saw only Anna's angry response and perceived her as victimizing the other youth. Only when Anna attempted suicide did the counselor begin to see Anna's victimization by the other residents. Referring Anna to the Hetrick-Martin Institute was a difficult and long-deliberated decision for the counselor and a relief for Anna.

DISCUSSION

The chart review revealed that 40% of youths had been violently assaulted; 46% of those assaults were gay related. Many of the violent incidents occurred at home. Suicide attempts were frequent among members of the group. Due to the limitations in the data, it remains unclear whether suicidal behavior was as common among youths who had not been victims of violence as among those who had been assaulted. Furthermore, it is unclear how often strangers perpetrated violence on gay-identified youths; such violence, however, is common among family members. These questions should be addressed in future research.

Our documentation was limited to physical attacks. Emotional and verbal abuse are probably even more common than physical violence. As revealed by the case vignettes and interviews conducted with clinicians at the agency, physical attacks typically were preceded by an escalating sequence of emotional abuse, name-calling, verbal attacks, and threats of violence.

The case vignettes demonstrate that at the root of violence toward lesbians and gay males are societal attitudes and discriminatory practices. The youths in this study were minority, working class, and homosexual. Many of them belonged to at least three risk groups. Therefore these youths are typically recipients of societal racism, sexism, and homophobia and have unusually stressful lives (Hunter & Schaecher, 1987; Rotheram-Borus et al., 1991). In addition, because adolescent suicide has increased threefold in the last 10 years (Fisher & Shaffer, in press), simply being young constitutes another risk factor for suicide. These youths thus constitute one of the highest-risk groups for adolescent suicide, with risk higher even than that for runaway and pregnant teens (Rotheram-Borus et al., 1991). Future research should attempt to replicate the finding of high rates of suicide attempts among gay youths. Researchers also must expand their focus to include additional risk behaviors that may reflect youths' reaction to their victimization by society. Black gay youths, for example, may be more inclined to provoke others to kill them rather than to commit suicide; such victim-precipitated homicide may mask the frequency of suicide in this group (Myers, 1989).

Lesbian and gay male youths are an invisible population. Many do not share their sexual orientation with family, friends, or peers because they fear rejection and violence. Consequently, documenting violence toward and suicide among them is difficult. Yet the data reported here indicate the need to develop responses to their victimization.

Bias-related violence against students in school, for example, needs to be documented and eliminated. School administrators, teachers, social workers, and counselors need to be trained to confront homophobia, counsel victims of bias-related violence, and demystify homosexuality (see Chapter 18). In New York City, the Harvey Milk High School was created as a haven for youths who self-identify as lesbian and gay. Ultimately, all schools must provide a safe environment in which children learn tolerance and acceptance of differences. Only when all youths can freely pursue their academic goals in traditional schools can we as a culture claim to be fostering true humanity toward other people.

NOTE

1. The street outreach program consists of homeless youths who are more likely than others to suffer violence due to conditions of life on the street and involvement with prostitution and drugs. These homeless youths are so different than the general lesbian and gay male teenage population in the New York metropolitan area that data concerning them will be reported elsewhere. Most of those youths not in the street outreach program (80%) live at home.

REFERENCES

DeStefano, A. M. (1988, May 10). NY teens anti-gay, poll finds. *Newsday*, pp. 7, 21.

Finn, P., & McNeil, T. (1987, October 7). *The response of the criminal justice system to bias crime: An exploratory review* (Contract report submitted to the National Institute of Justice, U.S. Department of Justice).

Fisher, P., & Shaffer, D. (in press). Facts about suicide: A review of national mortality statistics and records. In M. Rotheram-Borus, J. Bradley, & N. Oblensky (Eds.), *Planning to live: Suicidal youths in community settings*. Tulsa: University of Oklahoma Press.

Gibson, P. (1989). Gay male and lesbian youth suicide. In *Report to the Secretary's Task Force on Youth Suicide: Vol. 3. Prevention and intervention in youth suicide* (pp. 110-142). Washington, DC: U.S. Department of Health and Human Services.

Gutis, P. (1989, June 8). Attacks on U.S. homosexuals held alarmingly widespread. *New York Times*.

Hunter, J., & Schaecher, R. (1987). Stressors on lesbian and gay adolescents in schools. *Social Work in Education, 9*(3), 180-190.

Hunter, J., & Schaecher, R. (1990). Gay and lesbian youths. In M. Rotheram-Borus, J. Bradley, & N. Oblensky (Eds.), *Planning to live: Suicidal youths in community settings* (pp. 297-317). Tulsa: University of Oklahoma Press.

Martin, D. (1988, September 1). Young, gay—and afraid. *New York Times*, p. A-33.

Mont-Reynaud, R., Ritter, P., & Chen, Z. (1990, March). *Correlates of perceived discrimination among minority and majority youth in the Dornbush-Steinberg data set.* Paper presented at the biannual meeting of the Society for Research on Adolescence, Atlanta, GA.

Myers, H. F. (1989). Urban stress and mental health in Black youths: An epidemiological and conceptual update. In R. Jones (Ed.), *Black adolescents* (pp. 123-152). Berkeley, CA: Cobb & Henry.

Rotheram-Borus, M. J., Rosario, M., & Koopman, C. (1991). Minority youths at high risk: Gay males and runaways. In M. E. Colton & J. S. Gore (Eds.), *Adolescent stress: Causes and Consequences* (pp. 181-200). New York: Aldine de Gruyter.

Select Committee on Children, Youth, and Families, U.S. House of Representatives. (1989). *Down these mean streets: Violence by and against America's children.* Washington, DC: Government Printing Office.

SURVIVOR'S STORY

Bob Gravel

My name is Bob Gravel and my family has lived in Lewiston, Maine's second largest city, for 75 years. Until last year I had lived there all my life, working for the last 14 years as a shipping clerk for a shoe manufacturer.

In April, 1985, three young men whom I'd seen around the neighborhood began to call me names. At first they called me "Faggot," and "Queer." By summer the harassment had escalated. One night they threw a bottle at me; on another, they chased me in their van. One night in July I noticed this van on the street and left a note on the windshield: "We all live in the same neighborhood. You live your life. I'll live mine." I even called the mothers of two of the men and asked them to tell their sons to stop bothering me.

It did no good. On August 14, the same guys stopped me while I was taking groceries out of my car. They chased me, knocked me down, and kicked me. One said, "I'm going to kill you, faggot. I don't care how long it takes." He said it with such hatred that I knew he meant it.

On November 1, 1985, after eight months of harassment and threats, these people waited for me to come home. I spotted them in the alley near my home and stayed in my car. They pelted my car with rocks and bottles but I was able to escape. I saw a police car and informed them of the attack.

SOURCE: Reprinted from *Anti-Gay Violence* (Hearing before the Subcommittee on Criminal Justice of the Committee on the Judiciary, House of Representatives, 99th Congress, Second Session on Anti-Gay Violence; October 9, 1986). Washington, DC: Government Printing Office, Serial No. 132.

The police were getting impatient with me because this was my fifteenth complaint against this group. I was getting no positive response from the police. They seemed upset at me. One officer told me to stay home. Another told me I should move, but I didn't feel I should have to leave my home. I went to a lawyer and had a harassment notice served on the leader of the group and I continued to plead with the police to stop these people from harassing me.

I then borrowed a gun. I'd never had a gun and I don't like them. I was scared that these guys were going to come to my house. At 9:00 p.m. on November 3, 1985, they did come to my home. I looked out the window and saw one of them in the driveway. I called the police. One of them knocked at the front door and yelled obscenities at me. I was frightened. Suddenly another one began kicking the back door. They kicked and kicked at my door until the door began to break apart. I went to the bedroom and got the gun and called the police again. I could see them all outside. I felt cornered. I lost it. I ran downstairs and when one of them came at me, I fired one shot into the air. He kept coming. I shot again and killed him.

I became a different man. I became very ill, was unable to function, and lost my self-esteem. It's a terrible thing to have killed a man. I have spoken with his family and visited his grave, but this feeling continues. I cannot enjoy life again.

The same guys came to my home again in March of 1986, just four months after the shooting. Again they hollered and threw objects in my apartment windows. I called the police. The cop told me, "Gravel, you'll have to understand that these guys will go out and get drunk and start thinking about what you did to their friend."

My landlord asked me to move because he was scared of this group. Where was I to go? If I moved to another street, these people would just track me down again. I couldn't go out. I couldn't even go to the market. So the best solution was to move far away. I had to leave most of my furnishings. I lost my job. I lost the comfort of being with my family and friends. I was forced from my home.

My life is now hell. I had to begin at the bottom and take a janitor job. I am earning $100 less a week than at my former job. I have $4,000 in attorney's fees. I paid for damages around my former home, damages to my car, hospital and psychiatrist bills. The most severe damage to me was emotional; I cannot believe I had to kill to live free.

The leader of this group finally went to court. He received a $35 fine. The court told me they plea-bargained because the court didn't have time for a trial.

One man lost his life, another man lost the will to live; the court assessed $35.

PART II

THE CONTEXT

5

The Social Context of Hate Crimes: Notes on Cultural Heterosexism

GREGORY M. HEREK

Hate crimes against lesbians and gay men in the United States must be understood in context: Anti-gay violence is a logical, albeit extreme, extension of the heterosexism that pervades American society. *Heterosexism* is defined here as an ideological system that denies, denigrates, and stigmatizes any nonheterosexual form of behavior, identity, relationship, or community.[1] Like racism, sexism, and other ideologies of oppression, heterosexism is manifested both in societal customs and institutions, such as religion and the legal system (referred to here as *cultural heterosexism*), and in individual attitudes and behaviors (referred to here as *psychological heterosexism* and discussed in Chapter 9).

This chapter has three principal goals. First, it describes cultural heterosexism in the contemporary United States as the backdrop against which anti-gay violence occurs. Second, it explores how key components of the cultural ideologies of sexuality and gender foster heterosexism and, ultimately, anti-gay violence. These components of ideology create conditions whereby gay people remain

AUTHOR'S NOTE: Portions of this chapter originally appeared in the article, "The Context of Anti-Gay Violence: Notes on Cultural and Psychological Heterosexism," *Journal of Interpersonal Violence, 5*, 316-333 (1990).

largely invisible while the concept of homosexuality is imbued with various symbolic statuses (e.g., deviance, sickness, evil). Finally, the chapter considers how societal transformations now in progress might affect cultural heterosexism and its underlying ideologies. The overall question to be addressed is not so much why homosexuality is stigmatized in American society but how heterosexism is transmitted through cultural institutions.

INSTITUTIONAL MANIFESTATIONS OF CULTURAL HETEROSEXISM

Through cultural heterosexism, homosexuality is largely hidden in American society and, when publicly recognized, is usually condemned or stigmatized. This alternation between invisibility and hostility is readily apparent in four major societal institutions: religion, the law, psychiatry and psychology, and mass media.

In prescribing guidelines for moral living, modern Christian and Jewish religious institutions stress the inherent virtue of committed marital relationships through which children are conceived and raised in the faith. Marriages are heterosexual by definition; homosexual behavior is widely condemned; same-sex relationships and families are not recognized (see Boswell, 1980, for historical background). Some denominations and congregations recently have adopted more accepting positions concerning homosexuality. They have opposed discrimination, allowed gay people to join the clergy, and, in rare cases, blessed gay relationships (Diamond, 1989; Fernandez, 1990; Goldman, 1989; Lattin, 1988). Others, however, have reaffirmed and even intensified their rejection. The Catholic church, for example, officially opposed extending civil rights protection to gay people in a Vatican statement that also was widely interpreted as condoning anti-gay violence. After deploring "violent malice in speech or in action" against homosexual persons, the document nevertheless seemed to blame such malice on the movement for gay civil rights: "When civil legislation is introduced to protect behavior to which no one has any conceivable right, neither the Church nor society at large should be surprised when other distorted notions and practices gain ground, and irrational and violent

Figure 5.1. Sodomy Laws in the United States
NOTE: As this book goes to press, sodomy laws in Kentucky, Michigan, and Texas have been overturned by state courts. In each case, the sodomy law was found to violate the state's constitutionally protected right to privacy. Each decision is under appeal, however.

reactions increase" (Congregation for the Doctrine of the Faith, 1986, paragraph 10; reprinted in Gramick & Furey, 1988, pp. 5-6). In the third paragraph of that document, homosexual feelings are described "as ordered toward an intrinsic moral evil," which leads to the conclusion that homosexuality "itself must be seen as an objective disorder" (Gramick & Furey, 1988, p. 2).

Gay men and lesbians also remain largely outside the law (Melton, 1989). Except in four states (Wisconsin, Massachusetts, Hawaii, and Connecticut) and several dozen municipalities (including San Francisco, New York City, and Chicago), discrimination on the basis of sexual orientation is not prohibited in employment, housing, or services. Gay relationships generally have no legal status, and lesbian and gay male parents often lose legal custody of their children when their homosexuality becomes known (Falk, 1989). Nearly one half of the states outlaw private consenting homosexual acts (Figure 5.1), and their right to do so was upheld by the U.S. Supreme Court in 1986 (*Bowers v. Hardwick*, 1986). In a clear illustration of the linkage between legal philosophies and religious teachings, Justice White and Chief Justice Burger refused to find a constitutional right for adults to engage privately in consenting homosexual behavior, based on the fact that legal proscriptions against sodomy have ancient origins and that condemnation of homosexuality is firmly rooted in Judeo-Christian moral and ethical standards (*Bowers v. Hardwick*, 1986).

In contrast to other institutions, the mental health field has made homosexuality highly visible; this visibility, however, historically has been within a discourse of pathology. Despite Freud's refusal to label homosexuality a sickness, mainstream American psychiatry and psychoanalysis spent much of the twentieth century seeking its cure (Bayer, 1987; for a personal account, see Duberman, 1991). When finally subjected to rigorous scientific testing, however, the theory that homosexuality is linked with psychopathology proved to be without basis (Gonsiorek, 1982, 1991; Hooker, 1957). Consequently, the American Psychiatric Association finally dropped homosexuality as a diagnosis from its *Diagnostic and Statistical Manual* in 1974 (Bayer, 1987). Since then, the American Psychological Association (APA) has led other scientific and professional organizations in removing the stigma so long associated with homosexuality (APA, 1975). Nevertheless, the *International Classification of Diseases* (*ICD*) continues to label homosexuality as a mental illness, and the language of pathology still infuses public perceptions and popular debate.

A fourth institution that reflects and perpetuates cultural heterosexism is the electronic mass media. Mirroring the larger society, media portrayals of homosexuality are relatively infrequent and, when they occur, typically are negative. Russo's (1981) study of Hollywood films, for example, demonstrated that most homosexual characters in the past have died before the end of the movie, usually from suicide or murder. In children's cartoons, characters whose homosexuality is implied through their violation of gender roles long have been targeted for ridicule, contempt, and violence (Russo, 1989). Even when gay characters have been portrayed positively in more recent films and television programs, they almost always appear in a story because they are gay, that is, because their homosexuality is important to the plot (Gross, 1984). Thus all characters are heterosexual unless explicitly identified as homosexual, in which case the story focuses on their sexuality rather than their day-to-day nonsexual lives.

As these examples show, homosexuality is normally kept invisible and, when it becomes visible, is condemned and attacked by cultural institutions. In the next section, the ideological systems that underlie this dual negation are explored.

CULTURAL IDEOLOGIES OF SEXUALITY AND GENDER

A cultural *ideology* is defined here as a system of beliefs, values, and customs that form the basis for group members' shared perceptions of social reality. It reflects a worldview that is shared by the members of society and a set of institutions based on that notion of reality; both the worldview and the institutions evolve continuously as people interact.[2] Heterosexism is one component of two broader and overlapping ideologies: the ideology of sexuality and the ideology of gender.[3] Although these ideologies vary among different groups within American society, the themes of denial and stigmatization, and invisibility and hostility concerning homosexuality recur repeatedly. In this section, the roots of those themes are considered for each ideology.

Heterosexism and the Ideology of Sexuality

Since the nineteenth century, Western societies have come to define who people *are* in terms of what they *do* sexually, giving rise to social categories based on sexual behavior, preference, and relationships. I refer to the social roles and psychosocial identities deriving from these categories as *socioerotic identities*. Historically, socioerotic identities became incorporated into the Western worldview as various economic and social changes permitted individuals to leave traditional kin-based lives to seek out others with sexual proclivities like their own (D'Emilio, 1983; Weeks, 1977). This trend coincided with shifts in social consensus about the primary goal and cultural focus of sexuality: from reproduction to intimacy and personal happiness, and from family and community to the individual (D'Emilio & Freedman, 1988).

Social categories developed to describe those who transgressed the boundaries of existing marital and reproductive roles, namely, homosexuals and bisexuals. These categories describe "master statuses" to which all other characteristics of an individual are subordinated in others' perceptions (Becker, 1963). From the first, the modern concept of the homosexual developed more in opposition to normalcy than to heterosexuality per se and was stigmatized as sinful, illegal, and sick (D'Emilio & Freedman, 1988; Duberman, Vicinus, & Chauncey, 1989; Foucault, 1976/1978; Plummer, 1981; Weeks, 1977).

In theory, all members of society can be categorized according to their socioerotic identity. However, just as White Americans typically do not think of themselves as White (e.g., Wellman, 1971), and men usually can think of themselves as human beings rather than as males (e.g., De Beauvoir, 1953), so most adults think of themselves not as heterosexuals but as husbands or wives, fathers or mothers. Those identities, however, largely negate the experiences of gay and bisexual people. Like members of other minorities, they must define themselves in terms of the characteristic (sexual orientation) that relegates them to unequal status and sets them in opposition to the dominant group.

Socioerotic identity, based as it is entirely on sexuality, is inherently problematic for at least two reasons. First, although it is a public identity, it is based on something that society prescribes should be private—namely, sexuality. Second, because homosexual behavior is regarded negatively by society, an identity based on such behavior is inevitably stigmatized.

Privatization and invisibility: The personal-public dichotomy. In a questionnaire study of heterosexuals' attitudes toward lesbians and gay men (reported in Herek, 1987), one college student wrote: "Homosexuals would be more acceptable if they wouldn't flaunt their homosexuality." Another student wrote: "Gay people have a right to live their own lives as long as they keep it to themselves and don't display the fact in public." Expressing a sentiment widespread in American society, these comments reflect an important component of sexual ideology: the belief that sexuality belongs only in the personal or private sphere of life. This aspect of sexual ideology perpetuates homosexuality's invisibility and creates a basis for stigmatizing it when it becomes visible.

The cultural dichotomy between public and private spheres of life, with sexual intimacy and pleasure relegated to the latter, is a fairly recent historical development (D'Emilio & Freedman, 1988). Ostensibly, all sexuality is privatized. Private heterosexuality, however, has public counterparts through which it is implicitly acknowledged and affirmed. The institution of marriage publicly legitimizes heterosexual partnerships through such mechanisms as wedding rituals, tax and inheritance laws, employee benefits programs, and immigration and naturalization policies. The institutions of parenthood and the family are heterosexually identified: The birth of children (which implicitly is interpreted as affirming the parents' heterosexuality) is recognized by the larger community through birth announcements, gift giving, religious rituals, tax deductions, and other customs.

Homosexuality, however, has no corresponding public institutions. Because same-gender marriage is illegal, gay relationships remain invisible. Because gay men and lesbians have often been accused of being unfit parents (Herek, 1991a), those who have children often have kept their sexual orientation hidden. When gay people engage in behaviors allowed for heterosexuals (such as holding hands or kissing), they make public what society has prescribed should be private. They are accused of flaunting their sexuality and thereby are perceived as deserving or even asking for retribution, harassment, or assault.

Consider, for example, an employee who keeps a photograph on her desk in which she and her husband smile for the camera and embrace affectionately. While explicitly conveying information to others about the woman's relationship status, the photograph implicitly conveys information about her private sexual behavior. Yet the fact that she is heterosexual is mundane, taken for granted. Because he has a public identity as a husband, most onlookers (if they even notice the photo) do not think of her partner primarily in sexual terms. Rather, their interest probably centers upon his physical appearance, social status, occupation, and personality. They do not perceive the displaying of the photograph to constitute an inappropriate intrusion of the private sphere into public life.

If the photograph instead shows the woman in the same pose with a same-sex partner, everyone is likely to notice. As with the first example, the photograph conveys the information that she is in a relationship. But the fact that the partner is a woman overwhelms all other information about her. The sexual component of the relationship is not mundane and implicit as with a heterosexual spouse; the private-public barrier is perceived to have been violated. Thus this seemingly innocent act of displaying a photograph fundamentally changes the employee's social status and work relationships.

Sexualization and stigmatization. In addition to violating the public-private dichotomy, a socioerotic identity is problematic for gay men and lesbians because the type of sexuality that is made public (homosexuality) is devalued by the culture. As Rubin (1984, pp. 280-281) summarized, "normal" sexuality "should ideally be heterosexual, marital, monogamous, reproductive, and non-commercial. It should be coupled, relational, within the same generation, and occur at home. It should not involve pornography, fetish objects, sex toys of any sort, or roles other than male and female."

Gay sexuality violates many of these rules. It is not reproductive by definition and not marital by statute. In many gay relationships, the partners have agreed not to be sexually exclusive (Bell & Weinberg, 1978; Herek, 1991a). Some homosexual men have staked out cruising areas for sexual behavior that are semipublic (Altman, 1982; Humphreys, 1970). Because of the culture's abiding suspicion of and hostility toward such merely pleasurable sexuality,[4] gay sexuality is " 'bad,' 'abnormal,' or 'unnatural' " (Rubin, 1984, p. 281).

Thus not only are gay people defined solely in sexual terms, but that sexuality is equated with deviance and abnormality. Further, it is stereotyped as pathological, predatory, and compulsively promiscuous (Adam, 1978; Herek, 1991b). At best, gay people are perceived as basing their identity and life-style upon a trivial pursuit, namely, sexual pleasure. At the worst, homosexuality is stigmatized as inherently sick or dangerous and worthy of punishment through legal (the criminal justice system) or extralegal (in the form of anti-gay hate crimes) means.

Heterosexism and the Ideology of Gender

Whereas biological sex is about physiology, gender is about behavior. The ideology of gender is a set of shared beliefs, values, and customs concerning "masculinity" and "femininity." Children internalize the rules for behavior prescribed by this cultural ideology in the course of defining their gender identity, that is, their core sense of self as male or female (Money, 1987; Money & Ehrhardt, 1972). Because the meanings attached to masculinity and femininity are learned at such an early age, they seem "natural" to adults, something that always has been a part of oneself rather than something that was socially constructed and learned.

Although gender identity is distinct from socioerotic identity, the two are closely related.[5] Heterosexuality is equated ideologically with "normal" masculinity and "normal" femininity, whereas homosexuality is equated with violating norms of gender. Although no inherent connection exists between sexual behavior and gender conformity, gay men are widely stereotyped as highly effeminate and lesbians as hypermasculine (Herek, 1984, 1986, 1991b). This ideological linkage between sexuality and gender has at least three consequences.

First, gay people are stigmatized not only for their erotic behaviors but also for their perceived violation of gender norms. Second, because homosexuality is associated with deviation from something so "natural" as masculinity or femininity, its labeling as abnormal receives further justification. Heterosexuals with deep-seated insecurities concerning their own ability to conform to cultural standards for masculinity or femininity may even perceive homosexuality as threatening their own sense of self as a man or woman. Third, a dual pattern of invisibility and hostility, denial and condemnation, is associated with gender that parallels that previously described for cultural heterosexism. People who do not conform to gender roles—regardless of their actual sexual orientation—often are labeled as homosexual and stigmatized or attacked. Fear of such labeling leads heterosexuals and homosexuals alike to monitor their own behavior carefully to avoid any appearance of gender nonconformity (Lehne, 1976).

TRANSFORMATIONS IN HETEROSEXIST IDEOLOGY: IMPORTANT RECENT TRENDS

The feminist and gay movements, coupled with the struggles for civil rights for racial minorities, have had a profound impact on socioerotic self-definitions, perceptions of the public and the private, and gender roles during the past 25 years (Adam, 1987; Altman, 1982). Additionally, lesbians and gay men have achieved increasing visibility through community action and by individually coming out. Since the early 1980s, the AIDS epidemic has influenced this process in ways that perhaps will not be recognized for years to come. In the final section of this chapter, some of these changes and their possible implications for cultural heterosexism are briefly considered.

Heterosexism and Sexuality

From private to public. Through intense political struggle, lesbians and gay men have begun to make what previously was the private world of homosexuality a focus for public discourse. This discourse has itself evolved. The liberationist approach of the early 1970s, which celebrated a polymorphously perverse sexuality, has yielded to a paradigm that defines homosexuals as members of a minority community similar to those of ethnic groups (Altman, 1982; Levine, 1979; Murray, 1979). Lesbians and gay men now are often perceived as a quasi-ethnic minority group struggling for civil rights (Herek, 1991a, 1991b). Consequently, they are beginning to attain the rudiments of a public identity that is based on community membership as well as individual sexual behavior.

This public identity also has begun to include parental and relational roles. Growing numbers of openly gay people are raising children, thereby defining parenthood as a component of their gay identity (Kolata, 1989). Lesbian and gay male relationships, long hidden from heterosexual society, are becoming increasingly visible and are receiving some degree of official recognition. New York's highest court, for example, ruled that a gay lover constitutes family for purposes of rent control laws (Gutis, 1989). Former New York Mayor Koch expanded benefits such as funeral leave to include gay city employees ("Koch Signs Domestic Partners Law," 1989). The California Secretary of State now allows gay families to register as unincorporated nonprofit associations (Hull, 1990). On February 14, 1991, a domestic partners law took effect in San Francisco. It creates a legal mechanism for members of an unmarried couple (gay or heterosexual) to register their relationship (Bishop, 1991; Figueroa, 1991).

Opposition to societal recognition of gay families has been vigorous. A 1989 version of the San Francisco domestic partners bill, which closely resembled an ordinance vetoed seven years earlier by then-Mayor Diane Feinstein, was defeated by voters in a citywide referendum. Both the mayoral veto and the referendum campaign were heavily influenced by religious groups (Keane, 1989; Lattin, 1989; Rannells, 1982).

The AIDS epidemic has given further visibility to gay relationships and communities. Media coverage has included reporting on the devoted care that gay men with AIDS have received from their lovers and gay families, often while their biological relatives rejected them because of their homosexuality. Such portrayals, along with increasingly frequent personal interactions as more gay people come out in response to the epidemic, no doubt have changed public perceptions of gay relationships—showing both that they exist and that they can include such socially valued attributes as self-sacrifice and commitment.

Thus recognition and legitimation of gay communities, relationships, and families have begun to infiltrate American society. Gay men and women have increasing access to public identities that allow them to affirm their sexual orientation on the basis of community membership and relational commitment but without violating privacy barriers or being "merely" sexual. Public debate is expanding to include a discourse on community and family as well as sexual self-expression.

The legitimizing of socioerotic identities. Because it is a public manifestation of what society prescribes should be private, socioerotic identity heretofore has been inherently stigmatized. Because it is concerned with "mere" sexuality, it also has been perceived as inconsequential by many heterosexuals. This may change, however, as heterosexuals themselves increasingly feel compelled to make explicit their own socioerotic identities. Individual Whites often become aware of their own racial identity for the first time when they are surrounded by highly visible racial minority cultures (Walsh, 1990). Similarly, as gay relationships and families become increasingly visible, individual heterosexuals may experience greater pressure to assert and prove their socioerotic identity rather than simply defining themselves in terms of marital and familial status. As a result, socioerotic identity may become less trivialized and accorded greater importance by heterosexual society. Ironically, it may simultaneously become less salient to lesbians and gay men who will have relational, familial, and community-based identities newly available to them. To the extent that homosexuality remains stigmatized, this process may have a negative consequence, at least in the short term: Pressures to affirm one's heterosexuality may become even more intense for adolescents and young adults, especially males. In the absence of effective violence-prevention programs, this pressure may foster an increase in anti-gay attacks by young males strongly concerned about their own sexuality and social acceptance.

Heterosexism and Gender

An early goal of the gay movement was to foster sexual liberation, which required, in part, the breaking down of rigid gender roles (Altman, 1971). Although the range of experiences available to each gender has expanded somewhat, the importance of gender conformity remains relatively unchanged: People who seriously transgress gender roles (e.g., "drag queens" and "bar dykes") remain at the low end of the hierarchy of acceptability among gay people as well as among heterosexuals. But a change has occurred, albeit not the one originally foreseen by gay liberationists: The traditional equating of homosexuality with gender norm violation appears to be weakening.

As heterosexual Americans have begun to have more contact with openly gay people, the inaccuracy of stereotypes equating a homosexual orientation with the adoption of cross-gender mannerisms and behavior has become more evident. As conceptualizations of gay people become more complex and differentiated, global stereotypes (such as the "sissy" and the "bull dyke") are being replaced by multiple subcategories of various types common in gay communities (e.g., "lipstick lesbian," "homo politico," "clone"). Heterosexuals may well continue to dislike effeminate men and masculine women (as do some gay people) but may not equate this with dislike of all homosexuals. As a result, gay people whose outward behavior conforms to cultural conceptions of masculinity and femininity may achieve greater acceptance (Rubin, 1984).

CONCLUSION

Anti-gay violence and victimization in the United States today cannot adequately be understood apart from cultural heterosexism. By alternately denying and stigmatizing homosexuality, this ideology creates the conditions under which lesbians and gay men can be routinely victimized. The analysis presented here highlights the importance of a comprehensive approach to eliminating anti-gay violence. Although interventions clearly are needed that focus specifically on violence and victimization, they will not be sufficient to eliminate the ultimate causes of anti-gay violence. Making lesbians and gay men visible and removing the stigma that has so long been attached to a homosexual orientation will require institutional changes (see Chapter 18) as well as personal interventions (Herek, 1991b). These issues are considered further in Chapter 9.

NOTES

1. This definition may itself appear to be heterosexist, because it is framed entirely in terms of heterosexuality. Obviously, the principal referents here are homosexual behavior; same-gender relationships; and lesbian, gay male, and bisexual identities and communities. The definition, however, is framed in such a way that it could be expanded to include other requirements of "normal" heterosexuality (e.g., that it be monogamous, marital, and reproductive; Rubin, 1984). Further, the definition corresponds to the way in which heterosexism actually works. As explained in this chapter, it simultaneously defines human experience in terms of heterosexuality and renders alternatives such as same-gender relationships invisible.

2. The term *ideology* has been used differently by philosophers, sociologists, political scientists, psychologists, and others (see Drucker, 1974; Lane, 1962). The usage here derives primarily from a social psychological approach to cultural systems of values and beliefs.

3. Some confusion arises in discussing these two ideologies because the word *sex* in the English language refers both to gender (the female sex, the male sex) and to erotic activity and desire (to have sex). As Rubin (1984, p. 307) noted, this dual definition reflects a cultural assumption that sexuality is reducible to sexual intercourse and that it is a function of the relations between women and men. Although teasing apart the two ideologies clearly would be a valuable endeavor, such a task is beyond the scope of this chapter. For purposes of clarity, reference will be made to the ideologies of sex and gender when discussing components that seem common to both.

4. As Rubin (1984) notes, a telling illustration of this discomfort with merely pleasurable sexuality is the perseverance of obscenity statutes, which outlaw

production and commercial distribution of materials whose sole purpose is sexual arousal (without artistic, scientific, or other purposes).

5. Whether or not the cultural organization of sexuality can be understood apart from that of gender is a topic for debate. Some authors have asserted that heterosexism can be analyzed only as part of the cultural ideology of gender (e.g., Rich, 1980), whereas others have argued for the necessity of analytically separating sexuality from gender to understand the distinct (though related) social organization of each (Rubin, 1984).

REFERENCES

Adam, B. D. (1978). *The survival of domination.* New York: Elsevier North-Holland.
Adam, B. D. (1987). *The rise of a gay and lesbian movement.* Boston: Twayne.
Altman, D. (1971). *Homosexual: Oppression and liberation.* New York: Outerbridge & Dienstfrey.
Altman, D. (1982). *The homosexualization of America, the Americanization of the homosexual.* New York: St. Martin's.
American Psychological Association (APA). (1975). Minutes of the Council of Representatives. *American Psychologist, 30,* 633.
Bayer, R. (1987). *Homosexuality and American psychiatry: The politics of diagnosis* (2nd ed.). Princeton, NJ: Princeton University Press.
Becker, H. S. (1963). *Outsiders: Studies in the sociology of deviance.* New York: Free Press.
Bell, A. P., & Weinberg, M. S. (1978). *Homosexualities: A study of diversity among men and women.* New York: Simon & Schuster.
Bishop, K. (1991, February 15). Not quite a wedding, but quite a day for couples by the Bay. *New York Times,* p. A12.
Boswell, J. (1980). *Christianity, social tolerance, and homosexuality: Gay people in western Europe from the beginning of the Christian era to the fourteenth century.* Chicago: University of Chicago Press.
Bowers v. Hardwick, 478 U.S. 186 (1986).
Congregation for the Doctrine of the Faith. (1986). *Letter to the bishops of the Catholic church on the pastoral care of homosexual persons.* Vatican City: Author.
De Beauvoir, S. (1953). *The second sex.* New York: Knopf.
D'Emilio, J. (1983). *Sexual politics, sexual communities: The making of a homosexual minority in the United States, 1940-1970.* Chicago: University of Chicago Press.
D'Emilio, J., & Freedman, E. B. (1988). *Intimate matters: A history of sexuality in America.* New York: Harper & Row.
Diamond, R. (1989, December 17). First gay Episcopal priest is ordained. *San Francisco Examiner,* p. A-6.
Drucker, H. M. (1974). *The political uses of ideology.* London: Macmillan.
Duberman, M. (1991). *Cures: A gay man's odyssey.* New York: Dutton.
Duberman, M. B., Vicinus, M., & Chauncey, G., Jr. (1989). *Hidden from history: Reclaiming the gay and lesbian past.* New York: New American Library.
Falk, P. (1989). Lesbian mothers: Psychosocial assumptions in family law. *American Psychologist, 44*(6), 941-947.

Fernandez, E. (1990, January 21). Gays ordained as ministers in affront to ban. *San Francisco Examiner*, p. B-1.

Figueroa, A. (1991, February 15). City's domestic partners debut. *San Francisco Examiner*, p. A2.

Foucault, M. (1978). *The history of sexuality: Vol. 1. An introduction* (R. Hurley, Trans.) New York: Pantheon. (Original work published 1976)

Goldman, A. L. (1989, June 27). Reform conference debates allowing homosexuals to become rabbis. *New York Times*, p. A8.

Gonsiorek, J. C. (1982). Results of psychological testing on homosexual populations. *American Behavioral Scientist, 25*, 385-396.

Gonsiorek, J. C. (1991). The empirical basis for the demise of the illness model of homosexuality. In J. C. Gonsiorek & J. D. Weinrich (Eds.), *Homosexuality: Research implications for public policy* (pp. 115-136). Newbury Park, CA: Sage.

Gramick, J., & Furey, P. (Eds.). (1988). *The Vatican and homosexuality*. New York: Crossroad.

Gross, L. (1984). The cultivation of intolerance: Television, Blacks, and gays. In G. Melischek, K. E. Rosengren, & J. Stappers (Eds.), *Cultural indicators: An international symposium* (pp. 345-363). Wien: Verlag der Österreichischen Akademie der Wissenschaften.

Gutis, P. S. (1989, July 7). Court widens family definition to gay couples living together. *New York Times*, pp. A1, A13.

Herek, G. M. (1984). Beyond "homophobia:" A social psychological perspective on attitudes toward lesbians and gay men. *Journal of Homosexuality, 10*(1/2), 1-21.

Herek, G. M. (1986). On heterosexual masculinity: Some psychical consequences of the social construction of gender and sexuality. *American Behavioral Scientist, 29*, 563-577.

Herek, G. M. (1987). Can functions be measured? A new perspective on the functional approach to attitudes. *Social Psychology Quarterly, 50*, 285-303.

Herek, G. M. (1991a). Stigma, prejudice, and violence against lesbians and gay men. In J. C. Gonsiorek & J. D. Weinrich (Eds.), *Homosexuality: Research implications for public policy* (pp. 60-80). Newbury Park, CA: Sage.

Herek, G. M. (1991b). Myths about sexual orientation: A lawyer's guide to social science research. *Law and Sexuality, 1*(1).

Herek, G. M., & Glunt, E. K. (1988). An epidemic of stigma: Public reactions to AIDS. *American Psychologist, 43*, 886-891.

Hooker, E. (1957). The adjustment of the male overt homosexual. *Journal of Projective Techniques, 21*, 18-31.

Hull, T. (1990, December 14). State lets gay couples register. *San Francisco Examiner*, pp. A1, A28.

Humphreys, L. (1970). *Tearoom trade: Impersonal sex in public places*. New York: Aldine.

Keane, T. G. (1989, May 24). SF Archbishop assails "domestic-partners" law. *San Francisco Chronicle*, p. A4.

Koch signs domestic partners law. (1989, August 8). *San Francisco Chronicle*, p. A4.

Kolata, G. (1989, January 30). Lesbian partners find the means to be parents. *New York Times*, p. A13.

Lane, R. E. (1962). *Political ideology*. New York: Free Press.

Lattin, D. (1988, October 26). Episcopalians endorse gay marriages. *San Francisco Chronicle*, p. A8.

Lattin, D. (1989, July 10). How religious groups stopped partners law. *San Francisco Chronicle*, pp. A1, A20.

Lehne, G. (1976). Homophobia among men. In D. David & R. Brannon (Eds.), *The forty-nine percent majority: The male sex role* (pp. 68-88). Reading, MA: Addison-Wesley.

Levine, M. P. (1979). Gay ghetto. In M. P. Levine (Ed.), *Gay men: The sociology of male homosexuality* (pp. 182-204). New York: Harper & Row.

Melton, G. B. (1989). Public policy and private prejudice: Psychology and law on gay rights. *American Psychologist, 44*(6), 933-940.

Money, J. (1987). Sin, sickness, or status? Gender identity and psychoneuroendocrinology. *American Psychologist, 42*, 384-399.

Money, J., & Ehrhardt, A. E. (1972). *Man & woman, boy & girl: Differentiation and dimorphism of gender identity from conception to maturity*. Baltimore: Johns Hopkins Press.

Murray, S. O. (1979). The institutional elaboration of a quasi-ethnic community. *International Review of Modern Sociology, 9*, 165-177.

Plummer, K. (Ed.). (1981). *The making of the modern homosexual*. London: Hutchinson.

Rannells, J. (1982, December 10). Live-in lover plan vetoed. *San Francisco Chronicle*, p. A1.

Rich, A. (1980). Compulsory heterosexuality and lesbian existence. *Signs, 5*(4), 631-660.

Rubin, G. G. (1984). Thinking sex: Notes for a radical theory of the politics of sexuality. In C. S. Vance (Ed.), *Pleasure and danger: Exploring female sexuality* (pp. 267-319). Boston: Routledge & Kegan Paul.

Russo, V. (1981). *The celluloid closet: Homosexuality in the movies*. New York: Harper & Row.

Russo, V. (1989, June). *Nelly toons: A look at animated sissies*. Introduction to a program at the 13th Lesbian and Gay Film Festival, Castro Theater, San Francisco.

Walsh, J. (1990, February 4). School colors. *San Francisco Examiner* (This World sec.), pp. 9-11.

Weeks, J. (1977). *Coming out: Homosexual politics in Britain, from the nineteenth century to the present*. London: Quartet.

Weissman, E. (1978, August). Kids who attack gays. *Christopher Street*, pp. 9-13.

Wellman, B. (1971). Social identities in black and white. *Sociological Inquiry, 41*, 57-66.

The Ecology of Anti-Gay Violence

HOWARD J. EHRLICH

The purpose of this chapter is to consider that which is general and that which is unique to anti-gay prejudice and violence. I start my inquiry from a theory of prejudice that I first presented in *The Social Psychology of Prejudice* (Ehrlich, 1973).

SOME SOCIAL PSYCHOLOGICAL CONSIDERATIONS

Herek (see Chapters 5, 9) has addressed the social heritage of anti-gay prejudice in an original and thoughtful manner. This social heritage refers to the body of cultural practices, social norms, values, attitudes, and beliefs that is "there" for every child and young adult to learn. How they learn it, when they learn it, and whether or not they accept or reject this heritage are significant questions to ask. A successful program of attitude change cannot be instituted without an understanding of the origins of the attitude.

Habits of prejudice are communicated within the parental family. People develop attitudes similar to those of their primary

AUTHOR'S NOTE: This chapter is reprinted with minor revisions from the *Journal of Interpersonal Violence*, 5, 359-365 (1990).

agents of socialization. Parents communicate attitudes often as explicitly as they teach the child other modes of behavior. They also control the child's opportunities and experiences and, not least, provide models of behavior for the growing child.

As Kevin Berrill (1989) has pointed out, the language of anti-gay prejudice is essentially sexist. More research is needed on this point, but observation suggests that some anti-gay prejudice is based in traditional sex role attitudes transmitted by parents. For people who believe in male superiority, gays and lesbians are ideological renegades. They have rejected the appropriate hierarchy of beliefs, attitudes, and behavior.

Prejudice originates in less explicit parental teaching as well. Again, more research is needed to establish firmly that some prejudice toward lesbians and gay men originates in the patterns of development of self-attitudes and sex role attitudes. Certainly one of the most well-confirmed principles of prejudice is that, the more negative one's self-attitudes, the greater the number of unacceptable others one will find and the more negative one's attitudes toward them will be. I expect self-rejection is directly related to the acceptance or rejection of one's gender identity. Those who negatively regard their own ability to meet (their idealized) sex role expectations may find models of homosexual behavior anxiety provoking (for a good, first test of this hypothesis, see Herek, 1987). The response to such anxiety we know to be an increased closed-mindedness and greater rejection of the dissimilar other (Ehrlich, 1978).

It may be that both factors—closed belief systems and self-image deficits—may combine to form virulent prejudice. We know that people who are prejudiced toward one group tend also to be prejudiced toward other groups (Ehrlich, 1973). There appear to be relatively few people whose prejudice is directed solely at a single group of people. Further, the perpetrators of violence against a religious, ethnic, or racial group are also the perpetrators of homophobic violence. I think this is as important to understand for policy reasons as it is for its scientific implications. "An injury to one is an injury to all" was an old organizing slogan of the Industrial Workers of the World; it ought to be a slogan of human relations workers and gay activists as well.

If the family of orientation facilitates the development and transmission of prejudice, larger social forces point to and legitimate

certain groups as appropriate targets for the expression of prejudice. How early attitudes develop toward any "out-group" depends upon the group's visibility, the distinctiveness and
salience of stereotypes about the group, and whether or not the
community is polarized over intergroup relations. So, for example, in a community where Black-White relations are conflictual,
where Blacks are highly visible, and where the stereotypes of
them are well defined, children (both Black and White) learn
these group attitudes much earlier than in communities where
these conditions do not prevail (Ehrlich, 1973).

It is an important fact that anti-gay violence persists not solely
because of individual psychology but also because of the structure
of the society in which we live. Patterns of prejudice are normative,
the result of social and historical processes. The maintenance and
expression of anti-gay prejudice is possible primarily because it is
in keeping with the current social norms. These norms are main-
tained, formally, through the routine operation of the major social
institutions—school, church, mass media, and family.

THOUGHTS ABOUT VIOLENCE

Although it may seem to be one of those simple-minded veri-
ties of social science, it needs assertion: To understand violence
against gay men and lesbians, one needs to understand violence.
We really do not know why some people act in a violent manner. Clearly, not all prejudiced persons act out their prejudices
in ethnoviolence. (*Ethnoviolence* is a term I introduced to refer to
an act or attempted act in which the actor is motivated to do
psychological or physical harm to another, where the "other" is
perceived as a group representative or is identified with a
group, and where the motivation for the act is group prejudice.)

To begin with, we need to recognize that violence, like prejudice, is woven into the social fabric. This is a violent society. The
majority of Americans have lived through at least one war; their
adult recollections of important events are dominated by World
War II, Vietnam, or other group conflicts or national acts of violence (Schumann & Scott, 1989). *Family violence* may be a new
term in our lexicon, but it points to long-standing and long-hidden
forms of violence: spouse battering, marital rape, child abuse, and

abuse of the elderly. A majority of American children are physically punished, and, in perhaps as many as half of all families, the use of physical punishment does not stop until the child leaves the parental home (Straus, 1983). Children's cartoon television currently features 23 acts of violence an hour, and all prime-time television averages 14 violent acts per hour (NCTV News, 1989-1990). The adolescent male gang that goes out gay-bashing one night may already have collectively witnessed over 50,000 violent acts on television.

Most Americans regard some forms of violence as socially acceptable in some situations. We do not yet know under what conditions specific forms of violence are evoked. Nor do we know why, under ostensibly the same conditions, one person will act violently and another will not. These ought to be questions high on our research agenda.

Harry's analysis (in Chapter 7) suggests that, for some adolescent males, violence is an expressive act, that is, an end in itself. This notion of "recreational violence" requires closer examination and empirical research. I believe, however, that most violence is instrumental, that is, a habitual pattern of behavior adopted to achieve a set of personal needs or ends. One of the reasons I choose not to use the popular term *hate violence* is that I think it presupposes the motivation of the actor. The violent actor may lose control after initiating the act, but I think that the violence is usually perpetrated to meet an end.

If violence is instrumental, then what are the ends in view? Some ethnoviolence is motivated by attempts to gain power and control. In those cases, my guiding hypothesis is that three basic threats evoke a violent response: violations of territory or property, violations of the sacred, and violations of status. Here is a single example of all three themes in a homophobic diatribe printed in the October 1989 issue of a campus magazine.

> Homosexuals are . . . committed to destroying the traditional Christian values [*the sacred*] on which this nation is founded. . . . If these deviates chose to keep their sins to themselves [*territory*], perhaps it could be tolerated. But as it is, they are seeking rights that are reserved for normal citizens [*status*] . . . such as marriage and adoption. These people are unfit to live, let alone to raise children. (Bartolomeo, 1989)

This excerpt introduces another theme in ethnoviolence motivated by attempts at power and control, that is, the theme of "dehumanization." In war as in the propaganda of bigots, the enemy comes to be defined as something less than human. A related theme is the rationalization of violence by "blaming the victim"; that is, the victim's behavior or potential behavior is defined by the actor as leaving no choice but to respond with violence. In other words, the actor's own behavioral repertory does not include a nonviolent response.

Although power and control may often be at issue, I suspect that some magnitude of ethnoviolence is motivated less by a person's need for power and more by a need for affiliation and social conformity. The violent spectacles of history, after all, were primarily populated by people acting in compliance or conformity with the demands of the state or religion. Of course, to assert that one of the ends of violent behavior is conformity to the dominant norms of a group is not to deny that motivations are complex. In any given act for any given actor, there may be elements of power, affiliation, and conformity as well as a "recreational" or expressive component.

NOTES ON PERPETRATORS

Who are the perpetrators of ethnoviolent acts? Most people respond to that query by pointing to adolescent males, usually in a small gang. I believe that they are wrong. From some campus case studies, we know that as many as 70% of all anti-gay or anti-lesbian incidents were never reported (Chapter 18). If an incident is never reported, we cannot know who perpetrated it. Our research at the National Institute Against Prejudice and Violence indicates that what gets reported varies by the site of the incident. There are different reporting rates for street incidents, for incidents occurring in residential neighborhoods, and for those on campus or at the workplace. Statements about the characteristics of perpetrators based only on victims' making reports inevitably are based on biased samples, and we don't even know what the character of the bias may be. Furthermore, from our research, I would estimate that, in at least half of all ethnoviolent acts, the victim did not see the perpetrator. When victims have seen them, the assailants were often perceived to be over 30 years or older and frequently alone. Perpetrator characteristics also seem to vary by the site of the incident. Younger people seem more involved in neighborhood and street settings; older people are the actors in workplace settings (Ehrlich, Larcom, & Weiss, 1990).

NOTES ON VICTIMIZATION

We want two kinds of information about people who have been victimized: How did they cope and, given their pattern of coping behavior, what more can be done to provide assistance? We know from past research that a substantial proportion do not report what happened to them. Even more significant, as indicated by the preliminary findings of the national group violence project (Ehrlich, Larcom, & Weiss, 1990), almost two of every five people who are victimized either did not talk about the incident with friends, neighbors, or relatives or, when they did, received no support. This is a striking level of isolation. I suspect that those not reporting the incident to anyone are also isolated. (These data are not specific to gay victims. In the final analyses, we will be able to examine victim groups separately.)

One of the guiding hypotheses of the study is that ethnoviolence has a greater impact on its victim than do other forms of victimization. The substantive character of ethnoviolence victims' responses is quite serious, ranging across the standard psychophysiological indicators of increased stress. These include higher levels of depression and withdrawal, increased sleep difficulties, anxiety, and loss of confidence. Further, an extraordinary percentage of victims report serious interpersonal difficulties with friends and significant others.

In the preliminary analysis, using only the Black population sample ($N = 1,013$), we divided the respondents into those who had not been victimized in the past 12 months ($n = 287$), those who were victims of crimes or attempted crimes ($n = 656$), and those who were victims of ethnoviolent acts ($n = 70$). For all but 2 of 25 behavioral and psychological symptoms,[1] victims of ethnoviolence displayed greater trauma than did other victims. In turn, the other victims displayed greater trauma than did the control sample of Black nonvictims. In all, victims of ethnoviolence report an average of almost two and one-half times more symptoms than do victims of other kinds of violence.

We do not yet know how long these dysfunctional symptoms last nor whether they recur after a period of absence. These are also critical questions for our research agenda.

FINAL THOUGHTS ON RESEARCH

To summarize, we need empirical research on the social and familial determinants of anti-gay violence, the motivations for individual acts of anti-gay violence, the characteristics of perpetrators, and the problems experienced by victims. We need also to ask about the witnesses to violence, especially those who stand by without intervening. What is the mental health cost of such behavior? Is the witness also a victim? Finally, we need to look at ourselves—researchers and service providers. What about ourselves? What is the effect upon us of continually performing a role that makes us participant-observers to the perpetrators of violence and to the miseries of their victims?

Sociologist Johann Galtung once described violence as anything that prevents an individual from fully developing her or his full potential (Galtung, 1980). That definition comes closer than any to identifying the essence of violence. Whatever we do in building our research agenda, we should not let legal norms or custom define our problem. To do so would be not just to ignore but to delegitimize the pain of thousands of survivors of violence in this society.

NOTE

1. The behavioral and psychological symptoms included the following: felt more nervous than usual; felt depressed or sad; had sleep problems (bad dreams, trouble falling asleep); had physical problems (headaches, stomachaches, shortness of breath); had trouble concentrating; used more alcohol, prescriptions, and other drugs; was afraid to answer the phone or leave the house; felt very angry; felt ashamed; perseverated on incident; felt exhausted for no reason; lost people one thought were friends; tried to be less visible.

REFERENCES

Bartolomeo, N. (1989, October 20). George Washington student in an uproar over anti-gay article. *Washington Blade*, p. 4 (District of Columbia).

Berrill, K. T. (1989, June). *Incidence and prevalence: Overview of extent and scope of anti-gay violence.* Paper presented at a research workshop, "Mental Health Aspects of Violence Towards Lesbians and Gay Men: Research Issues and Directions," sponsored by the National Institute of Mental Health, Bethesda, MD.

Ehrlich, H. J. (1973). *The social psychology of prejudice.* New York: John Wiley.

Ehrlich, H. J. (1978). Dogmatism. In H. London & J. Exner (Eds.), *Dimensions of personality* (pp. 129-164). New York: John Wiley.

Ehrlich, H. J., Larcom, B., & Weiss, J. C. (1990). *The national group violence project.* Unpublished manuscript.

Galtung, J. (1980). *The true worlds: A transnational perspective.* New York: Free Press.

Herek, G. M. (1987). Can functions be measured? A new perspective on the functional approach to attitudes. *Social Psychology Quarterly, 50,* 285-303.

NCTV News. (1989, November-1990, January). Prime time violence edges downward. *Newsletter of the National Coalition on Television Violence,* pp. 1, 8.

Schumann, H., & Scott, J. (1989). Generations and collective memories. *American Sociological Review, 54,* 359-381.

Straus, M. A. (1983). Ordinary violence, child abuse, and wife-beating: What do they have in common? In D. Finkelhor, R. J. Gelles, G. T. Hotaling, & M. A. Straus (Eds.), *The dark side of families: Current family violence research.* Beverly Hills, CA: Sage.

7

Conceptualizing Anti-Gay Violence

JOSEPH HARRY

This chapter attempts a conceptualization of the motivations and situations surrounding the hate crime of violence against gay males and lesbians. (The term *gay* will henceforth be used to refer both to gay males and to lesbians. *Gay males* and *lesbians* will be used to discriminate between the groups.) Violence is anti-gay when its victims are chosen because they are believed to be homosexual. This definition excludes common crimes committed against gay males or lesbians when the homosexuality of the victim is unknown or irrelevant to the choice of victim. Although some research has been done on the victims of anti-gay violence (Committee on the Judiciary, 1986; Harry, 1982; Miller & Humphreys, 1980), there is little knowledge about the perpetrators. In this chapter, I attempt to enlarge on this scarce data.

MOTIVATIONS FOR ANTI-GAY VIOLENCE

As Berk and his colleagues suggest in Chapter 8, the perpetrators of anti-gay violence are very largely male, in their late teens or early twenties, strangers to the victim(s), in groups, and not engaged in victimization for profit. Anti-gay violence seems to be committed during the peak years of delinquency/ criminality (Hindelang, Gottfredson, & Garofalo, 1978). Anti-gay violence may thus be but one element of the general delinquency complex in which correlations are found among most kinds of illegal behaviors. If so, it may require little special explanation beyond those usually offered for delinquency and crime; that is, no special psychological propensities on the part of the offender need be assumed.

Even if, however, the typical anti-gay offender is a generic criminal disengaged from the conventional moral order, some closer examination is required to explain why or when he may engage in a particular type of offense (male pronouns are used throughout to highlight the likelihood that perpetrators are male). Whereas disengaged delinquents are free to commit a variety of illegal activities, such freedom does not mean they will engage in any one particular activity. Motivations and situational circumstances are needed to focus their attention on a particular illegal possibility. Why commit anti-gay violence versus rape or armed robbery or burglary? What is there about beating homosexuals that appeals to offenders?

I suggest that most anti-gay violence arises out of the interactions of male groups in their late adolescence or early twenties. For many persons, the period of adolescence constitutes an extended "moral holiday" during which bonds to the adult moral order are attenuated by involvement in an adolescent subculture, the principal emphases of which are hedonism and autonomy from adult control. Such adolescents find themselves most at home not in school or in the family but in the company of same-age peers. Such company is unstructured, informal, and largely devoted to recreational pursuits, both legal (e.g., sports) and illegal (e.g., drugs). Although the social groups of the adolescent and immediately postadolescent worlds consist of both same-sex and mixed-sex groups, groups of gay-bashers seem to be almost exclusively male. In a few accounts of gay-bashing incidents, a female consort of the offenders served as appreciative audience. This acknowledged, it remains that the offenders are overwhelmingly male and usually act in groups.

One depiction of such male adolescent groups has been provided by Matza (1964, pp. 49-64) in what he calls the "situation of company." In this situation, adolescents are constantly mutually pressured to prove their commitment to the male gender role. Engaging in a variety of illegal or deviant acts is one way to prove their daring, their maleness, their adulthood. In the rather primitive eyes of the adolescent male, sexual and violent acts are the two main means through which they can prove their male commitment. For example, adolescent males have been found much more likely than females (68% versus 44%) to tell their friends about their first experience with sexual intercourse (Carns, 1973), apparently because reporting such intercourse has status value in the eyes of peers.

Although violence can also validate one's commitment to being a male, it has risks. In the legitimate forms of sports, one can lose. Also, many forms of available sports are supervised by adults and hence do not fit well with the emphases of the adolescent subculture. Most illegal forms of violence, such as fighting, offer the possibilities of losing, being injured, possibly being arrested, and having one's status considerably deflated. Hence, although it is important for the adolescent male to be able to talk a good fight, actually engaging in one is risky business.

The option of gay-bashing offers a nearly ideal solution to the status needs of the immature male. When done in groups, it offers little risk of injury. It provides immediate status rewards in the eyes of one's peers because, unlike verbal reports of sexual conquest, it provides direct and corroborated evidence of one's virility. It offers only minimal likelihood of arrest both because the offenders are rarely known to the victim and because the victim is unlikely to report the incident to the police. Gay-bashing serves to validate one's maleness in the areas of both violence and sexuality. It is a sexual, but not homosexual, act because it reaffirms one's commitment to sexuality exclusively in its heterosexual form. Occasionally, gay-bashing incidents include forcible rape, either oral or anal. Given the context of coercion, however, such technically homosexual acts seem to imply no homosexuality on the part of the offenders. The victim serves, both physically and symbolically, as a vehicle for the sexual status needs of the offenders in the course of recreational violence.

The offenders' choice of victim is made appropriate by the institution of gender. Although young males living in the situation of company and morally adrift may find anti-gay violence appealing, such behavior requires that the laws and norms of civil society be morally neutralized. In cases of gay-bashing, the offender is not simply on a moral holiday, as he may be when committing common property offenses, nor is he simply grabbing excuses out of thin air to justify seriously criminal behavior. He is resorting to an alternative set of norms based upon the institution of gender: that set of norms, imbibed mostly unconsciously from birth, that prescribes our sense of what is "masculine" and what is "feminine" in thought, affect, and behavior.

The gender institution often operates as a set of subterranean values justifying illegal conduct when more acceptable justifications (e.g., self-defense) cannot be found within the law. Our dominant institution of gender contributes to the view that male-female rape is justified if the victim behaved in a "provocative" or "unladylike" manner. It also allows the perpetuation of wife-beating. Gay-bashing seems similarly to be based on a popularly accepted belief, in this case that the only justifiable forms of sex are those between males and females. In the case of gay-bashing at least, moral neutralization is based upon "denial of the victim" (Sykes & Matza, 1957) and of her or his moral worth as a human being. By viewing the victim as worthy of punishment for having violated gender norms, the offender not only excuses himself from opprobrium but sees himself as rendering gender justice and reaffirming the natural order of gender-appropriate behavior.

The above arguments may seem to predict too much gay-bashing, just as Matza (1964, pp. 25-26) argued that cultural theories of delinquency predict too much delinquency because they imply a continuing commitment by the juvenile to delinquent behaviors. Matza's point was that, if juveniles are so committed to delinquency, they would engage in it almost on a full-time basis. Similarly, if anti-gay violence is an ideal means for the attainment of sexual status by young males and is based on such a basic institution as gender, it would seem that gay-bashing should be a daily occurrence involving significant percentages of both the homosexual and the heterosexual populations. To deal with this issue, we need some idea of the extent of anti-gay violence. Because relevant statistics are few, we divide gay-bashing incidents into three types based on the age of the victim.

First are *serious physical assaults and homicides committed against adult lesbians and gay males* such as those reported in the House Criminal Justice Subcommittee hearings on Anti-Gay Violence

(Committee on the Judiciary, 1986). These *reported* assaults are clearly the most serious ones and do not include the common, random beatings of homosexuals that occur in the streets, parks, and parking lots of America. Most assaults go unreported either because the victim fears being discredited by family, the law, or employers or because the assault was less serious, although still criminal.

Second are *assaults and related harassments of lesbian and gay male adolescents by their peers,* such as those that gave rise to the Harvey Milk School in New York City for homosexual adolescents. The existence of such a school implies that mistreatment of homosexual adolescents is pervasive in the adolescent world.

Finally, probably far more common than either of the other forms of assault and harassment are the *beatings of effeminate boys, both future homosexuals and heterosexuals* (Saghir & Robins, 1973, pp. 18-23) that occur during childhood. These beatings occur because the boys do not conform to the extremely rigid rules of the male gender role. They also reaffirm the offender's commitment to that role before his peers. Psychologically, they serve the same function as the more serious gay-bashing of adulthood. They differ from the latter in two ways, however. First, they are more accepted in conventional adult norms. Second, they do not suggest as much criminality and probable moral disengagement from the norms of civil society on the offenders' part as does adult gay-bashing. Culturally, however, the childhood and adult incidents are the same. Whether persons who engage in adult gay-bashing have also engaged in childhood "sissy-bashing" is unknown.

If we view the above three age-based types of incidents as gay-bashings that differ only in the ages of the participants involved, the ideas offered to explain anti-gay violence may not predict too much. Gay-bashing may be endemic during childhood and decline in frequency with age while at the same time it increases in seriousness and lethality. As males approach adulthood, most become more secure in their gender roles, so that proving their gender adequacy becomes less obsessive and gender deviance in others becomes less salient. Hence the motivations for gay-bashing may decline with the advent of an adulthood that is not defined in the stark imagery of the immature male.

THE SITUATIONS OF ANTI-GAY VIOLENCE

The views of gay-bashers are clearly in agreement with those of the large majority of the population who disapprove of homosexuality (see Chapter 5). Reporting data from the General Social Survey (National Opinion Research Center, 1988) in 1987, 82% of the population found homosexuality "always wrong" or "almost always wrong." This percentage has changed little since 1973 and may have increased slightly since the 1970s. For purposes of analysis, we divide this 82% into three categories. Most strongly opposing homosexuality are a small number of *activists* who go out of their way to find homosexuals to assault. Such strongly motivated persons would typically go to a place where homosexuals are known to gather such as a gay ghetto (Levine, 1980) or to the environs of a gay bar. Somewhat less opposed to homosexuality would be the larger number of *opportunists* who are not sufficiently motivated to seek out homosexuals to victimize but will assault them as occasions arise. Such situations would typically arise in non-gay-defined settings when persons who are visibly homosexual appear. The remainder of the 82% are those who disapprove of homosexuality but not strongly enough to engage in gay-bashing. This group is theoretically important because it is by far the largest of the three and it consists of those who might normally be expected to serve as guardian citizens in cases of assault (Cohen & Felson, 1979). In the case of common crimes among heterosexual participants, such guardians serve the function of being interveners or of calling the police. In cases of anti-gay violence, however, it is doubtful that many of this large group who disapprove of homosexuality would be willing to actively assist the victim. Hence gay males and lesbians may be largely lacking in guardians due to the widespread disapproval of homosexuality in the general population.

Gay men who reside in a gay-defined neighborhood are more likely to have experienced gay-bashing than those living in other areas of a large city (Harry, 1982). Because outsiders are the perpetrators of anti-gay violence in gay areas, the ratio of victimizations of gays resident in a gay area to victimizations of gays resident in other areas may be taken as an approximate indicator of the ratio of victimizations by activists to those by opportunists. It is true that a gay area may have a high rate of victimizations not because of many visiting activists but because of the great concentration of available targets for the opportunists resident in the area. But, as an area becomes more densely populated by gays, one would assume that activists and opportunists would be the first to be displaced from that area.

The ratio of activist to opportunistic gay-bashing probably varies directly with city size. Larger cities have more gay-defined places to which activist bashers may resort, whereas potential bashers in smaller places may have to wait for an occasion to present itself. This implies that anti-gay violence in smaller places is probably more geographically diffuse and opportunistic in nature. The overall rates of anti-gay violence in smaller places may actually be lower than those in large cities for two reasons. First, there are no or few gay-defined places for activists to find victims reliably. Second, the more conservative cultures typical of most smaller communities may induce homosexuals to go to greater lengths to conceal their sexual identity. Better data on these ideas may become available after the U.S. Department of Justice has implemented its new mandate to gather data on hate crimes, including those based on sexual orientation.

Simply being in a gay-defined area is not sufficient to be identified as a target, however, because such areas normally contain nonhomosexuals at most times of the day or night. The potential victim must also conform to the offender's image of a gay male or lesbian. Klassen, Williams, and Levitt (1989, p. 430) found that 70% of both males and females in the general population "strongly agree" or "somewhat agree" that "homosexuals act like the opposite sex." There is little reason to believe that gay-bashers differ in their views from the general population. In the case of gay men, this means that the potential victim should appear and act effeminate, and in the case of lesbians, that the potential victim should appear and act in a masculine manner. Supporting this interpretation, Harry (1982) found that those gay men who described themselves as "a little feminine" or "very feminine" were twice as likely as other gays to have experienced gay-bashing. Those gay men who affect hypermasculine styles of personal deportment, however, which were quite common during the late 1970s, may also have a heightened rate of victimization. The association between hypermasculine styles and homosexuality in males appears to have become known among the broader public and that association could serve as an alternative cue for identifying potential targets.

Although the visibility of potential victims partially resides in their dress, their style of personal deportment, and their associates, it is also the result of conscious decisions to allow their homosexuality to be known to others—to be "out." Coming out, especially coming out to heterosexuals, often requires not only emotional, psychological, and political bravery but physical bravery as well (Dank, 1971; Harry, 1990; Troiden, 1979). In one survey, 31% of gay males who agreed or strongly agreed that "it is important to me to 'be out' to straight people I know" had experienced gay-bashing versus 21% of other respondents (Harry, 1990). In addition, it has been reported that those gays most of whose friends were also gay had a higher rate of gay-bashing (Harry, 1982). These phenomena no doubt persuade many gays to stay closeted in the hope of avoiding victimization and also contribute to Weinberg and Williams's finding (1974, p. 107) that 29% of their male homosexual sample "strongly agreed" or "agreed" that "I do not like to associate with a person who has a reputation (among heterosexuals) of being homosexual."

OTHER ISSUES

I have attempted to describe the victimization of both gay men and lesbians. Differences between these groups' victimization experiences, however, are likely. Gay men may be more likely than lesbians to have experienced physical assault (Committee on the Judiciary, 1986, p. 45). Part of this difference may arise because lesbians are less visible than gay males. Gender nonconformist deportment has generally been less disapproved in women than in men. In a national sample of 1,500 fathers, for example, it was found: "It was more important to these fathers that a boy act like a boy should than that a girl act like a girl should" (Duncan & Duncan, 1978, p. 272). Similarly, affectionate behavior in public between women has been more accepted than it has been between men. Because of the less stringent criteria that our culture imposes on the behavior of women, any nonconforming behavior is less visible and less likely to be taken as an indicator of homosexuality. Lesbians also seem to be more circumspect in revealing their homosexuality to others such as fellow workers and neighbors (Bell & Weinberg, 1978, pp. 296-297), thereby providing less opportunity for bashers (see Chapter 1 for further discussion of gender differences in victimization).

The type of anti-gay victimization discussed above is street crime between strangers. There are, however, other kinds. Gay-bashing can occur within the family. Harry (1989) recently reported, in comparing samples of gay and heterosexual male students, that the gay males had experienced more physical abuse from their parents than the others. Considerable anti-gay violence by the police has also been reported (Committee on the Judiciary, 1986). This underscores the earlier point that homosexuals may be largely lacking in guardians, both official (police) and unofficial (citizens; see also Chapter 1).

Although not technically anti-gay violence, property damage is another variety of hate crime directed against gays. The circumstances of this form of crime differ from those of violence against the persons of gays. In property crimes, the offender relies on such cues as neighborhood gossip or (if a car is damaged) proximity to a gay establishment to identify his victim rather than on cues provided directly by the victim. I personally never have seen a gay bumper sticker, a fact that may reflect the belief of many gay people that such a sticker would very likely result in vandalism to the car.

CONCLUSIONS

The ideas outlined in this chapter suggest that the following elements are required for gay-bashing to occur: (a) the *institution of gender*, which defines departure from a gender role, and especially sexual departure, as an abomination; (b) *groups of immature males* who feel the need to validate their status as males; (c) *disengagement* by those males from the conventional moral order; and (d) *opportunities for gay-bashing—gay neighborhoods for activists, visibly homosexual persons for opportunists*.

REFERENCES

Bell, A., & Weinberg, M. (1978). *Homosexualities: A study of diversity among men and women.* New York: Simon & Schuster.

Carns, D. (1973). Talking about sex: Notes on first coitus and the double sexual standard. *Journal of Marriage and the Family, 35,* 677-688.

Cohen, L., & Felson, M. (1979). Social change and crime rate trends. *American Sociological Review, 44,* 588-608.

Committee on the Judiciary. (1986). *Anti-gay violence: Hearing before the Subcommittee on Criminal Justice of the Committee on the Judiciary, House of Representatives* (Serial No. 132). Washington, DC: Government Printing Office.

Dank, B. (1971). Coming out in the gay world. *Psychiatry, 34,* 180-197.

Duncan, B., & Duncan, O. (1978). *Sex typing.* New York: Academic Press.

Harry, J. (1982). Derivative deviance: The cases of extortion, fag-bashing, and shakedown of gay men. *Criminology, 19,* 546-564.

Harry, J. (1989). Parental physical abuse and sexual orientation in males. *Archives of Sexual Behavior, 18,* 251-261.

Harry, J. (1990). *Fag-bashing and lifestyle theory.* Unpublished manuscript.

Harry, J., & DeVall, W. (1978). *The social organization of gay males.* New York: Praeger.

Hindelang, M., Gottfredson, M., & Garofalo, J. (1978). *Victims of personal crime.* Cambridge, MA: Ballinger.

Klassen, A., Williams, C., & Levitt, E. (1989). *Sex and morality in the U.S.* Middletown, CT: Wesleyan University Press.

Levine, M. (1980). Gay ghetto. In M. Levine (Ed.), *Gay men: The sociology of male homosexuality* (pp. 182-204). New York: Harper & Row.

Matza, D. (1964). *Delinquency and drift.* New York: John Wiley.

Miller, B., & Humphreys, L. (1980). Lifestyles and violence: Homosexual victims of assault and murder. *Qualitative Sociology, 3,* 169-185.

National Opinion Research Center. (1988). *General social surveys, 1972-1988: Cumulative codebook.* Chicago: Author.

Saghir, M., & Robins, E. (1973). *Male and female homosexuality.* Baltimore, MD: Williams & Wilkins.

Sykes, G., & Matza, D. (1957). Techniques of neutralization. *American Sociological Review, 22,* 664-670.

Troiden, R. (1979). Becoming homosexual: A model of gay identity acquisition. *Psychiatry, 42,* 362-373.

Weinberg, M., & Williams, C. (1974). *Male homosexuals.* New York: Oxford University Press.

8

Thinking More Clearly
About Hate-Motivated Crimes

RICHARD A. BERK
ELIZABETH A. BOYD
KARL M. HAMNER

California Senate Bill 39, which was introduced in 1989, required that the State's Department of Justice "acquire data to be used for statistical analysis concerning any crime or attempted crime which causes physical injury, or property damage, which is, or appears to be, motivated by the race, religion, sexual orientation, or ethnicity of the victim (Peri & Freshour, 1986, p. 4).[1] The legislation reflects growing concern in California about "hate-motivated" crimes, first officially articulated by the Governor's Task Force on Civil Rights (1982) and repeated by the California Fair Employment and Housing Commission (1982). Both bodies believed that "crimes motivated all or in part by race, ethnicity, and religion occur throughout California . . . [have] intensified in some parts of California and [have] permeated society to a

AUTHORS' NOTE: This chapter is a revised version of Dr. Berk's article, "Thinking About Hate-Motivated Crimes," in the *Journal of Interpersonal Violence*, 5(3), 334-349 (1990). Research for this chapter was completed under grant No. 1 RO1 MH44704-01 from the Violence and Antisocial Behavior branch of the National Institute of Mental Health.

greater degree than is commonly believed" (Peri & Freshour, 1986, p. 1). Some local police departments in the state have apparently reached similar conclusions or have been pressured to act. For example, in fall 1987, the Los Angeles Police Department began requiring investigation of all incidents motivated by "hatred or prejudice against a person based on sexual orientation, whether or not the incident is a crime" (Los Angeles Police Department, 1987, p. 3). Outside of California, racially motivated assaults reported to the police in New York apparently have increased sharply, stimulated in part by the Howard Beach Incident (a homicide in Brooklyn, New York, in which several White young men attacked and killed a Black teenager in what was later claimed to be a case of mistaken identity). In addition, congressional hearings on "hate crimes" have been held, and the "Hate Crime Statistics Act" was passed in 1990 (May, 1988; see also the Introduction to this volume).

The California bill built on an earlier mandated study (S.B. 2080) designed to make recommendations about which state agencies should collect data on hate-motivated crimes, what procedures should be used, and what definitions should be applied. Eight police agencies, serving about 10% of California's population, participated. After extensive training of local law enforcement personnel, data were collected during a 4-month interval. Each reported incident was reviewed by California Department of Justice researchers with the result that some cases were rejected and some reporting errors were uncovered and corrected. In the end, 66 cases were found that were motivated by race, 5 cases by ethnicity, 3 cases by religion, and 5 by sexual orientation. Figures for a 12-month period are probably about three times larger (approximately 250 incidents), whereas figures for the state as a whole are perhaps ten times larger. Because San Francisco, Los Angeles, and San Diego were virtually unrepresented in the study, however (and because most of California's gay men and lesbians probably live in Los Angeles or San Francisco), these numbers probably substantially underestimate the number of reported assaults on gay men and lesbians and reported damage to their property. In short, there are in a given year perhaps 3,000 reported hate-motivated crimes in California, with perhaps several hundred directed against gay men and lesbians.[2]

The problem with interpreting "official" estimates is that the term *hate motivated* is not clearly defined. Consider the following examples (based in part on actual events reported to the Los Angeles Police Department). (a) A drug sale between a Black and a White goes sour, and racial insults are used in the ensuing fight. (b) A Lebanese couple is assaulted by a group of "Skinheads," who incorrectly assume that the couple is Jewish. (c) Two Jewish neighbors have a falling out and one of them, in an effort to frighten the other, spray-paints a swastika and anti-Semitic slogans in the first neighbor's driveway. (d) A city bus is spray-painted with racial insults as it sits in a particular neighborhood; no one seems to care until the bus later passes through another neighborhood, where the spray-painting is taken to be offensive. (e) A group of Latino gang members kill a Black gang member in a drive-by shooting. Should the police classify any of these incidents as hate motivated?[3]

In practice, much more would be known about each of these illustrative incidents, but the additional information might actually confuse things further. The point is that much of the available data on hate-motivated crimes rests on unclear definitions; it is difficult to know what is being counted as hate motivated and what is not.

The common practice of reporting crime *rates* adds to the confusion. For example, using the total population of a jurisdiction for calculating the proportion of people who are victimized can be misleading because it assumes that all individuals are equally at risk. In reality, some groups are at much greater risk than others in part because of visible attributes that potential perpetrators use to identify their targets. Further, the base of people "at risk" might not be defined (let alone accurately estimated). For instance, who qualifies as being at risk for a hate-motivated assault against gay people? And how many such people are there? This is important because, for crime rates to be interpretable, the standardizing base must be sensible. For example, if there are more hate-motivated assaults against gay men and lesbians in Los Angeles than in Chicago, is that because Los Angeles has more people "at risk" (i.e., more gay people)?

Finally, little is known about (a) the attributes of hate-motivated crimes; (b) trends over time; (c) what role AIDS has in any aggregate trends for gay men and lesbians, Blacks, and Latinos;

and (d) the import of particular "risk factors." These and other empirical concerns (e.g., Herek, 1989) motivate this chapter. The goal is to inject a bit more clarity into current claims about the nature of hate-motivated crimes and their prevalence, time trends, and causes. (There also are a host of operational issues such as the fit between how victims interpret their experience and how police report it, but there is not space to discuss these concerns here.) Conceptions of hate-motivated crime will be considered first.

SOME CONCEPTIONS OF HATE-MOTIVATED CRIMES

As concerned as one might be about the empirical validity of claims made about hate-motivated crimes, it is important to appreciate that an absence of sound data is only a part of the problem. Indeed, without better conceptual foundations, it is not clear what any data set could contribute. Perhaps the following "data" will help illustrate the conceptual swamp in which we find ourselves.

One afternoon, as the senior author of this chapter (Berk) drove up to his home, he had to stop to allow the garage door opener to work. Berk lives on a narrow street where there is only room for a single car to pass. Immediately after he stopped, another car pulled up behind him and the driver began honking his horn. The other driver could clearly see why Berk had stopped and that there was no way for him to pull to one side to let a vehicle pass. But the other driver sat on his horn. Berk got annoyed, turned back to the driver and yelled, "What the . . . do you expect me to do?" The driver, who was Black and about 18, yelled back something about Berk's relations with his mother, his lineage, and his skin color (all in one phrase). Several seconds later the garage door opened, and Berk entered. The other car drove on. Berk got out of his car, closed the garage door, and began walking toward the front door of his house when the other car, after apparently circling the block, pulled past the garage; a second (Black) person in the car threw an empty whiskey bottle at the garage door. There were also some new racially linked insults, although Berk could not easily be seen from the street. The bottle struck as intended and shattered.

Was Berk a victim of a hate-motivated crime? A neighbor, who is Black, did not think so. He saw the whole thing and offered: "That's just a few teenagers acting up." Yet many of the pieces fit. Indeed, Berk's experience probably would have been counted as a hate crime by the Los Angeles County Commission on Human Relations. By their definition, Berk is victimized several times a year by similar kinds of hate crimes (as are a very large number of ordinary people). Of course, a lot depends on difficult judgments about the motives and intentions of the "assailants." For example, would the events described here have unfolded differently had Berk been Black?

The criminology literature is almost totally silent on the topic of hate-motivated crimes (e.g., Glaser, 1974; Sykes, 1978; Weis, 1987; Wilson & Herrnstein, 1985). Somewhat in contrast, writings on collective behavior (Berk, 1974a, 1974b; Smelser, 1962; Turner & Killian, 1957), particularly when focused on racial violence (Berk, 1972; Graham & Gurr, 1970, Pt. IV; Grimshaw, 1969a; Short & Wolfgang, 1972), touch on many instructive issues but typically are concerned with very serious violence committed infrequently by large groups of people. Lynchings (Phillips, 1987) and riots (e.g., Masotti & Bowen, 1968) are common instances. In short, it is difficult to find much direct guidance in existing scholarship.

Symbolic crimes. In this light, perhaps the best place to begin is with the broad observation by Grimshaw (1969b), Sterba (1969), and Nieburg (1972) that one key ingredient in hate-motivated violence is the "symbolic status" of the victim. Thus Grimshaw (1969b, p. 254) speaks of violence as "social" when "it is directed against an individual or his property solely or primarily because of his membership in a social category." A social category is defined by one or more attributes that a set of individuals share, which have implications for how the individuals are perceived or treated. There is no logical necessity to the kinds of social categories or social interactions that are important for a particular collection.[4] The symbolic content may derive from a wide variety of processes: competition between groups over scarce resources (Grimshaw, 1969b), long-standing social rituals (Nieburg, 1972), unresolved childhood traumas (Sterba, 1969), conceptual efforts to simplify the social environment, and other processes.

Unfortunately, there do not seem to be any credible scientific efforts to sort out these explanations (such as they are).

Actuarial crimes. In addition to the symbolic status of the victim, the victim's "actuarial status" (Messinger & Berk, 1987) may be important. People routinely make lay estimates of central tendencies associated with particular social categories. For example, an emergency room nurse might be more concerned about drawing blood from a male homosexual than a male heterosexual not because of homophobia but because the homosexual man is judged more likely to be infected with human immunodeficiency virus (HIV). Likewise, a group of street thugs may mug a gay man not because of what his sexual orientation represents to them but because they apply a stereotype to him implying an upper-middle-class income and a disinclination to fight back.[5] In this example, the victim's symbolic status is used as a marker to retrieve relevant "factual" information about him. It is the factual information that motivates the crime, not the marker itself.

The distinction between symbolic and actuarial crimes suggests a potentially useful boundary between hate-motivated crimes and other offenses. Whereas symbolic crimes would be classified as hate motivated under almost any reasonable definition, actuarial crimes might more usefully be placed in some other category. If the definition of hate-motivated crimes depends fundamentally on the motivation of the offender, and if actuarial crimes reflect the use of social categories as a means to some nonsymbolic end (such as robbery), then actuarial crimes are not really hate *motivated*. This is not to deny that such crimes are traumatic for victims or that victims may experience them as hate motivated whatever the offender's real motivation. Nor it is to say that making clear empirical distinctions between symbolic crimes and actuarial crimes would be easy in practice. To establish in general the role of an offender's motives is difficult; to disentangle different but related motives may be nearly impossible.

The role of uncertainty. The symbolic categories that form the basis for hate-motivated crimes are presumably linked to one or more invidious distinctions. For example, the hate-crime perpetrator may perceive gays as immoral, Jews as avaricious, Blacks as surly, and so on. Sometimes, however, more important than the specific content of particular social categories is the *absence of information*; it is substantial *uncertainty* that really matters.

To begin, an individual may have an assessment of what is "typical" for a given group but also be aware of significant variation around that central tendency. For example, whereas gay men may be perceived as responsible citizens on the average, they may also be perceived as having among their numbers a relatively large population whose lives revolve around parties, drugs, and "promiscuous" sex. The central tendency does not fully capture potential concerns; variation *around* the central tendency counts as well.

Then, because of large variation around the central tendency or because of very limited experience (i.e., lack of information), the lay estimate of what is typical may be somewhat unstable. There is substantial uncertainty in the central tendency estimate itself. (The concern here is with uncertainty in the estimated central tendency, whatever its accuracy. Whether the central tendency is reasonably accurate or not is a different issue.) Thus some Whites may be uneasy with Blacks in social situations primarily because they have had little firsthand social experience with Blacks; in effect, they do not know what to expect. Likewise, a lot of what looks like homophobia may have as much to do with a felt ignorance about gays and fears stemming from that felt ignorance. A young heterosexual male's lack of information about what to expect from a gay teammate in the locker room, for example, may be aversive. When the content of social categories is evaluated, this absence of information may be as important as the presence of particular kinds of other information.

Expressive and instrumental motives. Given the importance of a victim's symbolic status, it should be clear that any derivative violence can be expressive, instrumental, or both. "Gay-bashing," for instance, may be a purely homophobic reaction or may be seen by the assailant as a way to keep a particular individual from moving into a certain neighborhood. Equally important, the violence itself may take on a symbolic character with messages for the victim, members of the victim's social or actuarial category, other prospective assailants, public officials, and the public at large (Berk, 1972; Nieburg, 1972). For example, gay-bashing may, in part, be a way to teach "those people" a lesson.

The role of premeditation. The degree of premeditation may be an issue in at least two related aspects of a hate-motivated crime: the motive and the choice of target/victim. At one extreme, a small group of teenagers might plan for weeks to vandalize a particular synagogue or to mail death threats to a particular person thought to be of Jewish descent. At the other extreme, while cruising around town on a Saturday night looking for some excitement, those teenagers might get involved in a fight with teenagers from another neighborhood, or the robbery of a 7-Eleven market, or the harassment of a homeless person camped out in a local park, or an assault on a male homosexual waiting at a bus stop. In the first example, a particular hate-motivated crime was planned well in advance. In the second case, the hate-motivated crime was but one of several options selected from among opportunities that may have presented themselves in an unpredictable fashion. And there are variations in between. For example, the group might have set out to harass customers leaving a local bar frequented by gays but have no specific victims in mind.

Initial causes, proximate causes, and mixtures of causes. At the least, the category of hate-motivated crimes includes (a) those based on the victim's symbolic status, (b) those stemming from the perpetrator's instrumental or expressive motives, (c) those generated by the perpetrator's uncertainty about members of the victim's group, and (d) those with and without substantial premeditation. This complex picture becomes even less clear when "hate motives" are mixed with other crime motives. For example, the apparent sexual orientation of a victim may provide the impetus for a series of events that ultimately culminate in a robbery; although the victimization initially was hate motivated, the ensuing robbery was motivated solely by economic need. Or a crime may involve a simultaneous mix of hate and other motives. Violence associated with a drug deal gone bad, for instance, may involve economic and racial motives.

We know of no consensus on how the mix or sequence of motives should affect the definition of hate-motivated crimes. Our experience with law enforcement officials, however, suggests that, for a crime to be categorized as hate motivated, a "but for" criterion is commonly applied: But for the hate motivation, the crime would not have occurred. The hate motivation is at least a necessary condition. Under this conception, where the hate motives enter a sequence of events is unimportant. Some law enforcement officials, however, require that the hate motive also be the proximate cause. For example, harassment of a gay man that turns into a robbery would not be a hate-motivated crime if the proximate cause were economic gain.

To summarize, perhaps the essential feature of hate-motivated crimes is their symbolic content. Crimes motivated solely by the victim's actuarial status would seem best included in another category. In addition, the hate motivation should probably be a necessary condition for the crime, whether the motivation stems from firmly held beliefs or substantial uncertainty about the victim's group. Finally, the degree of premeditation or instrumentality should not matter.[6]

ATTRIBUTES OF HATE-MOTIVATED CRIMES

It is useful to distinguish between definitions of hate-motivated crimes and the statistically common attributes of those crimes. To take one example, whereas hate-motivated crimes may often be committed by individuals who are unknown to the victim, the feature of "unknown assailants" is not included in most hate-crime definitions. Yet, insofar as these assaults are initiated by individuals who are unknown to the victim, they present the theoretical challenge to find out why such crimes are perhaps very likely to be "stranger" crimes. Part of the explanation may be that existing stereotypes are especially likely to dominate the assailant's perceptions in interactions between strangers. That is, the perpetrator has very little countervailing, particularized information about the victim. Assailants also may be more readily able to "distance" themselves from the victim in those interactions so that they may act upon hostile feelings. In any case, from fragmentary evidence that exists, a list of empirical attributes of certain kinds of hate-motivated crime might include (a) the number of perpetrators (more than one); (b) ages of perpetrators (late teens to early twenties); (c) ratio of perpetrators to victims in person crimes (2 to 1); (d) relationship to victim (a stranger or distant acquaintance); (e) location (outside of residences for person crimes); (f) when it occurs (in the evenings and over weekends); (g) gender of perpetrator(s) (male); and (h) other associated crimes (none).

We can make no strong claims about the associations between these attributes and hate-motivated crimes. Because current data are scanty, the attributes of hate-motivated crimes remain an empirical question. Moreover, hate-motivated crimes are heterogeneous. Thus the attributes listed above may be important for person crimes but not for property crimes or they may be more relevant for crimes based on race than those based on sexual orientation (e.g., the offenders in assaults on gays often may be family members). Any associations, insofar as they exist, begin to raise rather concrete substantive questions.

The majority of non-hate-motivated assaults, for example, typically involve two individuals (one victim and one perpetrator or two "mutual combatants") who know each other well. Why might hate-motivated crimes be different? Or, in a very large fraction of property crimes, something of value is taken. In hate-motivated crimes, it is apparently more likely that something of value is damaged or destroyed.

We are very uneasy with any explanations of hate-motivated crime in the absence of well-documented empirical regularities. And any explanations must effectively account for those regularities. For example, although it is hard to deny that in principle "racism" has something to do with racially motivated hate crimes, little in the concept can account for the eight attributes listed above. In fact, "racism" is closer to a defining aspect of racially motivated crimes than to an explanation of them. The same argument would seem to hold for homophobia (Herek, 1988; Larsen, Reed, & Hoffman, 1980; Stevenson, 1988). Accounting for empirical regularities in anti-gay hate crimes would require a number of auxiliary theories that may have little to do with homophobia.

REPORTING HATE-MOTIVATED CRIMES

Current data on the number, kinds, and distribution of hate-motivated crimes must be viewed very skeptically. Hate-motivated crimes may be a more or less serious problem than currently suspected or the problem may be rather different than the way it is currently perceived. Part of the confusion is caused by data that are generated by advocacy or service organizations, which reach out only to particular segments of a population at risk. Perhaps the best example is "hot lines" provided by minority or gay advocacy groups. Because many victims of hate-motivated crimes will not use such hot lines, serious underreporting results. Equally important, the received calls constitute a convenience sample; it is typically impossible to know to what extent the data from such samples can be generalized to a larger population. For example, gay men and lesbians whose sexual orientation is publicly acknowledged may be overrepresented in hot line calls, in part because they are more likely to be involved with gay advocacy groups. Because of possible life-style differences, they also may be vulnerable to hate crimes that differ somewhat from those experienced by gay people whose sexual orientation remains a secret.

Data from law enforcement agencies have serious problems as well. Like advocacy and service organizations, law enforcement organizations face serious underreporting problems. Gay victims, for instance, may choose not to report an incident to police for fear of an unsympathetic or even hostile response (i.e., a secondary victimization; see Chapter 18 by Berrill & Herek). Whether or not the secondary victimization is "real," however, the widespread perception that it has occurred may fuel still more underreporting.[7] An additional problem is that many law enforcement agencies have no systematic way to designate hate-motivated crimes and no systematic means to record them. Some even lack an articulated agency definition. When definitions and recording mechanisms are provided, a range of crimes may be designated as "hate motivated" with little effort made to determine whether the designation is appropriate. That is, after an initial report from a patrol officer, there may be no follow-up by detectives (as might occur in burglary cases, for example). In short, there is insufficient concern with data quality control (which is not to say that there are no departments whose handling of hate-motivated crime is exemplary).

Even agencies that have seriously tried to develop clear reporting procedures for hate-motivated crimes often face significant implementation obstacles. For example, some police officers, perhaps

with the best of intentions, may place the burden of proof so that
the number of hate crimes is minimized. That is, given the real
world of difficult judgment calls, a crime will not be defined as
hate motivated unless the evidence is overwhelming. This is especially likely if the police jurisdiction is very busy with crimes ordinarily thought to be far more serious, such as homicide or rape,
and if the labeling of a crime as hate motivated requires a different
and demanding police response.[8] For example, a symbolic hate
crime may be interpreted as an actuarial hate crime, which then is
categorized as a regular robbery, burglary, or battery. Alternatively, if there are serious sanctions for officers who fail to properly
report hate-motivated crimes, the burden of proof may be placed
in the opposite direction. Actuarial hate crimes, for instance, might
routinely be "upgraded" to symbolic hate crimes.

TIME TRENDS AND THE ROLE OF AIDS

Assuming that good data are available, it might seem a simple
matter to determine whether the number of hate-motivated crimes
is increasing, decreasing, or remaining about the same. One can
collect data over several years on the number of incidents and calculate summary statistics and significance tests to determine what
trends may exist (e.g., Gottman, 1981). It is not at all clear, however, what conclusions properly follow. In particular, any patterns
that materialize may reflect trends in crime more generally or in,
say, all crimes of violence. Thus an increase in hate-motivated
crimes may reflect a general increase in crime. (The increase also
may be totally a reporting phenomenon. Increasing activity by gay
and minority advocacy groups may reduce the level of underreporting.) The inferential problems become still more vexing if one
is trying to estimate the impact of some exogenous factor. Suppose
that, in particular, one hoped to provide information on whether
there is any evidence that AIDS has affected violence against male
homosexuals. An increasing time trend in such violence could result from a variety of factors: the age mix of the population, the
availability of handguns, the growth of gangs, and so on.
      Consequently, there is an important role for one or more com-
parison groups of about the same size as the groups of initial interest (Rosenbaum, 1987). Comparable data on *non*-hate-motivated

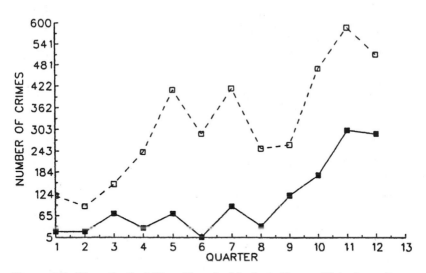

Figure 8.1. Hypothetical Time Trends: Nonhate Versus Hate Assaults

crimes is essential. For example, if assaults on gay males are increasing but assaults on other males are not, some important competing explanations can be ruled out, and the argument for the impact of AIDS becomes more plausible. The case can be made still stronger by making such comparisons within racial groups, geographic areas, and age groups. In effect, this is a matching strategy for picking comparison groups (Cochran, 1983).

What might such data look like? Suppose that in Figure 8.1 the higher line represents non-hate-motivated assaults and the lower line represents hate-motivated assaults. Also assume that the hypothetical data in the two series only include assaults against White males between 18 and 30 years of age that were committed by Whites unknown to the victim. Both series are plotted over 3 years by quarter.

The time trend for the hate-motivated assaults is gently upward from about 20 crimes per quarter at the beginning of the series to about 300 at the end of the series; most of the increase occurred during the last four quarters. These hypothetical data could be interpreted as clearly indicating that a particular kind of hate-motivated crime is on the rise. Moreover, insofar as the prevalence of infection with human immunodeficiency virus

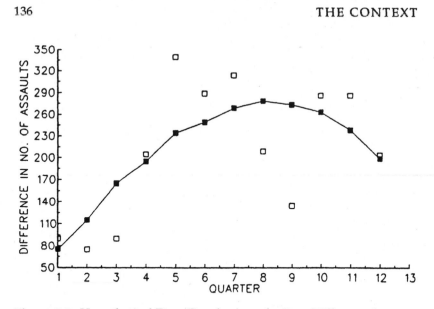

Figure 8.2. Hypothetical Time Trends: Assaults Data Differenced

(HIV) and publicity about AIDS have grown of late at an increasing rate, there is a prima facie case that AIDS is driving up the assault rate. (Recall that the two series include only White-on-White assaults against male strangers.) But the data also reveal that the non-hate-motivated crimes are increasing and show a similar acceleration during the last four quarters. Relative to non-hate-motivated crimes, it is not apparent that hate-motivated crimes are becoming relatively more common. Indeed, both may be driven by similar social processes.

It is possible to be far more precise. Figure 8.2 shows with open squares a plot of the difference between the two series in Figure 8.1. "Differencing" (i.e., subtracting one series from the other) is a means of removing from both trends, period by period, the impact of forces affecting both series in a similar manner. One assumes, in effect, that, for each time period, each series is shifted up or down some constant amount or, more realistically, that each is shifted a constant amount plus a random "shock." If either assumption holds, differencing produces a trend line that can be properly treated as primary data in further analyses (D. Rubin, personal communication, 1988).

The solid squares and solid line in Figure 8.2 show one reasonable "smoothing" of the data.[9] The story from these hypothetical data is straightforward. For the first eight quarters of the time series, the frequency of non-hate-motivated assaults grew faster than hate-motivated assaults, but this relative rate of growth was decreasing. For the last four quarters, hate-motivated assaults grew faster than non-hate-motivated assaults. One interpretation is that public anxiety about AIDS began to cause an increase in hate-motivated assaults early in the time series so that, by the last third of the time series, the number of hate-motivated assaults was gaining on non-hate-motivated assaults. Note that these effects are felt over and above whatever else may be affecting both time series in a similar fashion (e.g., levels of gang violence). Fortunately, real data on hate-motivated crimes and non-hate-motivated crimes are increasingly available (e.g., for Los Angeles). Moreover, statistical analyses of these data may be enriched with the inclusion of explanatory variables and by undertaking the analyses for different kinds of hate-motivated crimes.

RISK FACTORS

By *risk factors*, one usually means characteristics of the victim or the environment that are causes of victimization or *proxies* for causes. An association exists that may or may not be causal. For example, living in the Castro district of San Francisco may be a cause if prospective assailants assume that males living there are gay. In contrast, a Castro district zip code is a proxy for residence that might be used for statistical analysis; it is not a cause because prospective assailants are very unlikely to know it or use it.

Very little is known about risk factors for hate-motivated crimes. Even in the case of race, where skin color and other physical features are relevant, no quantitative estimates exist that separate the impact of race from other related risk factors. For example, given residential patterns in the United States, race is associated with the kind of place in which one lives, and violence of all kinds is more common in some locales than others. Thus young men in a Black neighborhood may be especially vulnerable in part because they live adjacent to a working-class White neighborhood.

Once one moves beyond a few very obvious risk factors, not even much speculation is relevant. For example, how do prospective assailants determine whether a pair of young men walking together are gay? Are interracial male/female couples more vulnerable than Black male/female couples? Are the risks higher in urban areas than in rural areas, other things being equal? How important are the activities of hate groups such as the KKK, especially in the immediate aftermath of a gathering (e.g., after a rally)? Ideally, answers to such questions should be found through prospective studies of risk factors (Fleiss, 1973). That is, data should be collected on a representative sample of prospective victims and their victimization measured at some later point. Alternatively, data should be collected on a representative sample of individuals some of whom had been victimized and some not. The critical methodological point is that the sample should be chosen as a simple random sample of some relevant population or through a stratified sample, with strata defined by explanatory (exogenous) variables rather than by the dependent variable of victimization. For example, one might survey equal proportions of gay and heterosexual men selected by probability procedures.[10]

CONCLUSIONS

There is no doubt that many crimes are committed consistent with most definitions of "hate motivated." There also is no doubt that such crimes have occurred throughout the history of this country (and all others) and that public concern about them has fluctuated considerably over time. In this context, it is difficult to know what to believe about current claims. We are in a situation much like one 15 years ago when controversial assertions were being made about "family violence." There are also interesting parallels to more recent pronouncements about child abuse and missing children. All of these crimes were associated, quite properly, with widespread moral outrage. Fuzzy definitions made informed discussion nearly impossible, however, and almost all of the key factual questions were either ignored or answered with seat-of-the-pants science. A few especially heinous crimes at the tail of a distribution were often taken to represent a central tendency. Or very different kinds of events were commonly aggregated under a particularly alarming title. Or huge extrapolations were routinely made from the very few facts that were known. The good news is that, after a lot of excellent research, we now are a lot wiser. The bad news is, in an atmosphere in which people of goodwill rapidly wanted to do something constructive, the requisite research base took years to develop.

NOTES

1. The bill passed, but without an appropriation. A comparable bill with appropriation was introduced in 1990, but a budget shortfall made sufficient funding unlikely.
2. These figures, of course, represent only those crimes coming to the attention of the police; many crimes are seriously underreported and the hate-motivated sort are no doubt among them (see Chapter 18 by Berrill & Herek). Still, the California figures seem roughly consistent with data from other sources. For example, using a somewhat broader definition of a *crime* (e.g., vandalism of a synagogue, even if there is no other information), the Los Angeles County Commission on Human Relations reported that, for Los Angeles County in 1987, there were 79 racially motivated hate crimes, 115 religiously motivated hate crimes, and 52 hate crimes in which the motivation was sexual orientation. For racially motivated hate crimes, about half were directed at Blacks and about 20% each at Asians and Latinos. For religiously motivated hate crimes, the vast majority were directed against Jews.
3. If gang incidents such as that described in the fifth example were counted as "hate crimes" in Los Angeles, the number of reported hate-motivated crimes in Los Angeles might well double. In the opinion of the Los Angeles Police Department, however, it is gang status itself that puts a person at risk. Even if gang definitions and histories depend heavily on racial and ethnic characteristics, these characteristics are no longer the key motives for the attack; they have been superseded by gang membership.
4. It is perplexing to us that rape is not considered a hate-motivated crime despite the common observation that rape is closely linked to misogyny.
5. Similar processes operate routinely in daily life. A mathematics teacher may pay less attention to female students not because of misogynist feelings but because of an assumption that female students are less interested in mathematics than male students. This does not excuse the behavior or make it any less damaging to female students.
6. They should not matter for the definition but might well matter when convicted hate-crime offenders are sentenced (as is the case with other crimes). For example, premeditated hate crimes may be more aggravated than others and so would receive harsher sentences. Likewise, the extent of victim provocation in a particular incident might well affect the kind of sentence given, even though it should not affect the definition of the incident as a hate-motivated crime.

7. Whereas police often fail to respond properly and professionally to the victimization of gays, it also is true that relatively neutral police behavior is sometimes incorrectly interpreted as anti-gay. For example, on Friday and Saturday nights in a busy jurisdiction, police may be slow to respond to most calls, not just those involving assaults on gays. Likewise, detectives may fail to follow up aggressively on many kinds of less serious property crimes (e.g., smashing the windows of a new car), not only those involving vandalism of property owned by gays. And sometimes state law effectively ties the hands of police officers responding to a wide variety of calls, despite strong public pressure that the police "do something." For example, it is very difficult for police to intervene *before* a battery has been committed, even if there are credible threats.

8. If the hate-motivated crime is a homicide or rape, it would have been given top priority in any case. Another point worth mentioning is that certain precincts in large city police departments receive hundreds of calls on Friday and Saturday nights involving very serious person crimes. If the crime leads to an arrest, the arresting officers may be tied up for several hours transporting the offender to jail and then doing the necessary paperwork.

9. More specifically, the solid squares and solid line in Figure 8.2 show the conditional expectations (predicted values) for a descriptive (not causal) regression analysis of the differenced data, using a quadratic function of time (i.e., in units 1, 2, . . . 12). The quadratic function fits reasonably well (R^2 = .66), and including higher-order polynomials in the equation did not appreciably improve matters.

10. Samples chosen by probability procedures, whether unstratified or stratified by explanatory variables, can be analyzed in conventional ways. For example, one might regress the number of victimizations that individuals experience on some set of risk factors (perhaps using some form of Poisson regression; see Cameron & Trivedi, 1986) and interpret the regression coefficients as measures of the impact of each factor on the likelihood of victimization. Alternatively, sampling may be done on the dependent (endogenous) variable. Consider a study of risk factors associated with cancer (smoking, stress, diet, and so forth). A common approach is to select a sample of patients with cancer and a sample of patients without; patients are chosen depending on their status on the outcome being examined. Then an effort is made to determine on what possible risk factors the two groups differ. Such studies are retrospective in design (Fleiss, 1973). It is widely known that "endogenous sampling" makes conventional statistical analysis inappropriate (Amemiya, 1985, pp. 319-348). In brief, the problem is that the ways in which the data are collected are confounded with the causal effects to be estimated. The Poisson regression analysis mentioned above, for example, would produce biased and inconsistent estimates of the regression coefficients.

Basically, there are two options. First, if one knows the true proportions for the dependent variable, some conventional procedures may be altered to remove the bias (Amemiya, 1985, pp. 319-348; Bye, Gallicchio, & Levy, 1987). Second, if one is prepared to use the odds ratio (or odds multiplier) as one's measure of relative risk (Fleiss, 1973, pp. 56-59), then garden-variety logistic regression will, in principle, produce unbiased estimates (Fleiss, 1973, pp. 46-49; Holland & Rubin, 1990; Rosenbaum, 1987). This follows because the odds ratio is symmetrical; its value is the same whether X is regressed on Y or Y is regressed on X. And this property holds when there is more than one explanatory variable.

REFERENCES

Amemiya, T. (1985). *Advanced econometrics*. Cambridge, MA: Harvard University Press.

Athens, L. H. (1980). *Violent criminal acts and actors: A symbolic interactionist study*. Boston: Routledge & Kegan Paul.

Berk, R. A. (1972). The emergence of muted violence in crowd behavior: A case study of an almost race riot. In J. F. Short & M. E. Wolfgang (Eds.), *Collective violence* (pp. 309-328). Chicago: Aldine Atherton.

Berk, R. A. (1974a). *Collective behavior*. Dubuque, IA: William C Brown.

Berk, R. A. (1974b). A gaming approach to crowd behavior. *American Sociological Review, 39*, 355-373.

Berk, R. A. (1989). Police responses to family violence incidents: An analysis of an experimental design with incomplete randomization. *Journal of the American Statistical Association, 83*, 70-76.

Berk, R. A., & Newton, P. J. (1985). Does arrest really deter wife battery? An effort to replicate the findings of the Minneapolis spouse abuse experiment. *American Sociological Review, 50*, 253-262.

Berk, R. A., & Sherman, L. (1985). Data collection strategies in the Minneapolis domestic assault experiment. In L. Burstein, H. E. Freeman, & P. H. Rossi (Eds.), *Collecting evaluation data* (pp. 35-48). Beverly Hills, CA: Sage.

Berkowitz, L. (1980). Is criminal violence normative behavior? Hostile and instrumental aggression in violent incidents. In E. Bittner & S. L. Messinger (Eds.), *Criminology review yearbook* (Vol. 2, pp. 387-400). Beverly Hills, CA: Sage.

Brandt, A. M. (1987). *No magic bullet: A social history of venereal disease in the United States since 1880*. New York: Oxford University Press.

Bye, B. V., Gallicchio, S. J., & Levy, J. M. (1987). Estimation of discrete choice models in retrospective samples: Application of the Manski and McFadden conditional maximum likelihood estimator. *Sociological Methods and Research, 15*, 467-492.

California Fair Employment and Housing Commission. (1982). *Public hearing on racial and ethnic discrimination and violence in north San Diego County*. San Francisco: Author.

Cameron, A. C., & Trivedi, P. K. (1986). Econometric models based on count data: Comparisons and applications of some estimators and tests. *Journal of Applied Econometrics, 1*, 29-53.

Castro, K. G., Lieb, S., Jaffe, H. W., Narkunas, J. P., Calisher, C. H., Bush, T. J., Witte, J. J., & Belle Glade Field-Study Group. (1988). Transmission of HIV in Belle Glade, Florida: Lessons for other communities in the United States. *Science, 239*, 193-197.

Cochran, W. G. (1983). *Planning and analysis of observational studies*. New York: John Wiley.

Cohen, L. E., & Land, K. C. (1984). Discrepancies between crime reports and crime surveys: Urban and structural determinants. *Criminology, 22*, 499-530.

Efron, B. (1982). *The jackknife, the bootstrap and other resampling plans*. Philadelphia: Society for Industrial and Applied Mathematics.

Felber, B. K., & Pavlakis, G. N. (1988). A quantitative bioassay for HIV-1 based on trans-activation. *Science, 239,* 184-190.

Fishman, G., Rattner, A., & Weimann, G. (1987). The effect of ethnicity on crime attribution. *Criminology, 25,* 507-524.

Fleiss, J. L. (1973). *Statistical methods for rates and proportions.* New York: John Wiley.

Glaser, D. (Ed.). (1974). *Handbook of criminology.* Chicago: Rand McNally.

Glass, R. I. (1986). New prospects for epidemiologic investigations. *Science, 234,* 951-963.

Gottman, J. M. (1981). *Time-series analysis.* New York: Cambridge University Press.

Gove, W. R., Hughes, M., & Geerken, M. (1985). Are Uniform Crime Reports a valid indicator of the index crimes? An affirmative answer with minor qualifications. *Criminology, 23,* 451-501.

Governor's Task Force on Civil Rights. (1982). *Report on racial, ethnic, and religious violence in California.* Sacramento: California Department of General Services, Office of State Printing.

Graham, H. D., & Gurr, T. R. (1970). *Violence in America: Historical and comparative perspectives.* New York: Bantam.

Granger, C. W. J., & Newbold, P. (1986). *Forecasting economic time series* (2nd ed.). Orlando, FL: Academic Press.

Grimshaw, A. D. (1969a). Factors contributing to color violence in the United States and Britain. In A. D. Grimshaw (Ed.), *Racial violence in the United States* (pp. 254-287). Chicago: Aldine.

Grimshaw, A. D. (1969b). Three views of urban violence: Civil disturbance, racial revolt, class assault. In A. D. Grimshaw (Ed.), *Racial violence in the United States* (pp. 385-396). Chicago: Aldine.

Herek, G. M. (1988). Heterosexuals' attitudes toward lesbians and gay men: Correlates and gender differences. *Journal of Sex Research, 25*(4), 451-477.

Herek, G. M. (1989). Hate crimes against lesbians and gay men: Issues for research and policy. *American Psychologist, 44,* 948-955.

Holland, P. W., & Rubin, D. B. (1990). Causal inference in retrospective studies. *Evaluation Review, 12*(3), 203-231.

Hsiao, C. (1986). *Analysis of panel data.* New York: Cambridge University Press.

Hsieh, D. A., Manski, C. F., & McFadden, D. (1985). Estimation of response probabilities from augmented retrospective observations. *Journal of the American Statistical Association, 80,* 651-662.

Larsen, K. S., Reed, M., & Hoffman, S. (1980). Attitudes of heterosexuals toward homosexuality: A Likert-type scale and construct validity. *Journal of Sex Research, 16*(3), 245-257.

Little, R. J. A., & Rubin, D. B. (1987). *Statistical analysis with missing data.* New York: John Wiley.

Los Angeles County Commission on Human Relations. (1987). *Hate crime in Los Angeles County, 1987.* Los Angeles, CA: Los Angeles County Commission on Human Relations.

Los Angeles Police Department. (1987, August 10). *Special order no. 11* (Internal document). Los Angeles: Author.

Lubin, J. H., & Gail, M. H. (1984). Biased selection of controls for case-control analyses of cohort studies. *Biometrics, 40*, 63-75.

Maddala, G. S. (1983). *Limited-dependent and qualitative variables in econometrics.* New York: Cambridge University Press.

Masotti, L. H., & Bowen, D. R. (Eds.). (1968). *Riots and rebellion: Civil violence in the urban community.* Beverly Hills, CA: Sage.

May, C. D. (1988, January 18). Hearings by a house panel to examine "hate crime." *New York Times,* p. 13.

McNemar, Q. (1962). *Psychological statistics.* New York: John Wiley.

Messinger, S. L., & Berk, R. A. (1987). Review essay: Dangerous people. *Criminology, 25*, 767-781.

Nieburg, H. L. (1972). Agonistics-rituals of conflict. In J. F. Short, Jr., & M. E. Wolfgang (Eds.), *Collective violence* (pp. 82-99). Chicago: Aldine Atherton.

Peri, D., & Freshour, D. (1986). *Racial, ethnic, and religious crimes project: Preliminary steps to establish statewide collection of data* (Report prepared by the California Department of Justice pursuant to Senate Bill 2080). Sacramento, CA: Bureau of Criminal Statistics, Division of Law Enforcement.

Phillips, C. D. (1987). Exploring relations among forms of social control: The lynching and execution of Blacks in North Carolina, 1889-1918. *Law and Society Review, 21*, 361-374.

Rosenbaum, P. R. (1987). The role of a second control group in an observational study. *Statistical Science, 2*, 293-316.

Sherman, L. W., & Berk, R. A. (1984). The specific deterrent effects of arrest for domestic assault. *American Sociological Review, 49*, 261-272.

Short, J. F., Jr., & Wolfgang, M. E. (Eds.). (1972). *Collective violence.* Chicago: Aldine Atherton.

Smelser, N. J. (1962). *Theory of collective behavior.* New York: Free Press.

Stephan, W. G., & Rosenfield, D. (1982). Racial and ethnic stereotypes. In A. G. Miller (Ed.), *The eye of the beholder: Contemporary issues in stereotyping* (pp. 112-148). New York: Praeger.

Sterba, R. (1969). Some psychological factors in Negro race hatred in anti-Negro riots. In A. D. Grimshaw (Ed.), *Racial violence in the United States* (pp. 408-413). Chicago: Aldine.

Stevenson, M. R. (1988). Promoting tolerance for homosexuality: An evaluation of intervention strategies. *Journal of Sex Research, 25*(4), 500-511.

Sykes, G. M. (1978). *Criminology.* New York: Harcourt Brace Jovanovich.

Sudman, S. (1976). *Applied sampling.* New York: Academic Press.

Toch, H. (1980). Normatively hostile, purposefully hostile, or disinhibitedly bloody angry? In E. Bittner & S. L. Messinger (Eds.), *Criminology review yearbook* (Vol. 2, pp. 401-410). Beverly Hills, CA: Sage.

Turner, R. H., & Killian, L. M. (1957). *Collective behavior.* Englewood Cliffs, NJ: Prentice-Hall.

Weis, J. G. (1987). [Special issue]. *Criminology, 25*(4).

Wilson, J. Q., & Herrnstein, R. J. (1985). *Crime and human nature.* New York: Simon & Schuster.

SURVIVOR'S STORY

William Edward Hassel

[The incident] occurred just a few years ago. I had gone to a bar on Wisconsin Avenue [in Washington, DC]. . . . I noticed two people who entered a few minutes afterward because one of them was an unfamiliar face. The other one I had seen there before, but I didn't know him. Other than telling the two how to sign up to play pool on the pool table, I did not speak to them at all. . . . When I left the bar, they followed me outside. . . .

Out on the street, they were very friendly. One of them was sexually aggressive toward me. They said they were American University students. They asked me if I wanted to go over to a party at American University that was going on that night. Well, I had also been a student at American University. I knew the gay group on American University's campus.

I perceived these two to be lovers. I didn't suspect that there would be a problem. And, like a fool, I agreed to go with them to a party on American University's campus.

Instead, they took me to Battery Kimball Park, which is over behind Georgetown University off Chain Bridge Road in the District. They forced me at knife-point to strip. They beat me. One of them stood on my wrists leaning over my face holding a knife point at my throat so that any way I moved would dislodge him and he would fall into me, forcing the knife through my throat, while the other one systematically kicked me in the groin, in the side.

They made me address them as "Sir." They made me beg to be made into a real woman. They threatened to castrate me. They

SOURCE: Excerpted from *Anti-Gay Violence* (Hearing before the Subcommittee on Criminal Justice of the Committee on the Judiciary, House of Representatives, 99th Congress, Second Session on Anti-Gay Violence; October 9, 1986). Washington, DC: Government Printing Office, Serial No. 132.

threatened to emasculate me. They called me "Queer," "Faggot."
One of them urinated on me. They threatened me with sodomy.

They kept me this way for about an hour. And there is an old
Southern expression called "playing possum." I kept trying, but
they were hurting me so badly that I couldn't help but cry out in
pain.

Finally, I think I probably was close to passing out—I don't
know—but finally I fooled them. They thought I had passed out.
They relaxed a little bit. They stopped kicking me around for a
few moments while they talked.

One of them said to the other one, "Let's finish him off and get
out of here." The one holding the knife raised the knife over his
head and swung it at my throat. I reached up and grabbed the
blade of the knife to avoid it going through my throat and managed to roll my body into his legs. He fell across me. I managed
to get out from under him, and I ran for my life.

One of them chased me on foot. The other one went back and
got into the truck they had been driving and went out to the
road waiting to run me down when I came across the road.
Luckily, the path I chose out of the park didn't cross the road
where he thought I would be, or I probably would have not lived.

Also luckily, even completely nude, bleeding and badly hurt—I
guess adrenalin or whatever—it managed to enable me to out-
run the one pursuing me on foot. He followed me about 400
yards through the park, across Chain Bridge Road and into a
woman's yard. He only quit following me when the woman awak-
ened at 2:00 in the morning—this whole thing had started at
12:30—turned on the lights in the house, and let me in. . . . She
called the police and an ambulance.

The police arrested the one who had been following me on foot
within minutes. The two young men were seniors at St. John's
College High School here in Washington. It is a prestigious
Catholic military prep school. . . .

I spent five days in the hospital. My condition was bad enough
those five days that they chose not to operate to repair the damage in my hand until I had recovered physically. A month later, I
went back to the hospital again for five days to repair damage to
my hand. I went in again a month and a half later for one day to
repair further damage to my hand. I remained under medical
observation for about five months for damage to my groin. . . .

The boys were at school the next day. That is how long they stayed in police custody. They were charged by a grand jury with 11 felonies. There was a plea bargaining session that reduced the charge to assault with a deadly weapon, a knife. The charges originally included intent to commit murder, mayhem, assault with intent to kill, and armed robbery. . . .

Judge Nunzio put off sentencing at the convenience of the boys' high school graduation. After they graduated, he held a sentencing hearing. He had the prosecuting attorney make a statement. He asked me if I wanted to make a statement, and I said a little bit about what had happened.

Then he asked the defense attorney to make a closing statement, and in that statement the defense attorney invented two new witnesses as to my sexual behavior. . . . I had never seen either of them before in my life. The defense attorney described explicitly the kinds of things I liked to do with these people in the most gross and debased terms imaginable.

There was a reporter sitting next to me who turned to me and asked what this was, if I had ever heard of this before, and I turned to him and shook my head and said no.

The judge stood up and said, "Young man, you have had your chance to speak in this court. If you say another word, I will hold you in contempt." Then he proceeded to give the two boys unsupervised probation for a period of three years, and 400 hours of community service in a soup kitchen, on the grounds they were intoxicated when it occurred—not to my knowledge, they weren't—and it was a homosexual provocation on my part and an overreaction on their part.

Subsequently, I pursued the thing through civil court. I spent two days being cross-examined during which they accused my doctors of being gay, they accused me again of situations that I was not involved in, they accused me of going to the bar specifically to pick up young men.

The outcome was I got a settlement of $28,400, of which $8,000 was punitive damages. That doesn't cover my medical expenses, much less the legal expenses involved in pursuing it. And it is highly unlikely that I will ever be able to collect that. . . .

[One of the boy's parent's] comment on leaving the room was that he certainly wasn't going to pay some faggot for getting his son in trouble.

PART III

PERPETRATORS

9

Psychological Heterosexism and Anti-Gay Violence: The Social Psychology of Bigotry and Bashing

GREGORY M. HEREK

Roughly two thirds of Americans[1] condemn homosexuality or homosexual behavior as morally wrong or a sin; this pattern has not changed significantly since the late 1970s.[2] According to Gallup polls (Colasanto, 1989), only a plurality of Americans felt in 1989 that homosexual relations between consenting adults should be legal (47% versus 36% who say they should not be legal). Many heterosexual Americans also reject gay people at the personal level. In 1987 a Roper poll found that 25% of the respondents to a national survey would strongly object to working around people who are homosexual, and another 27% would prefer not to do so; only 45% "wouldn't mind." In a 1985 *Los Angeles Times* poll, 35% of the respondents reported that they felt discomfort around either gay men (6%) or lesbians (11%) or both (18%); 50% reported that they did *not* feel *un*comfortable around gay people.

Despite this evidence for widespread condemnation and avoidance of lesbians and gay men, other data indicate that heterosexual Americans are increasingly reluctant to condone discrimination on the basis of sexual orientation (e.g., Colasanto, 1989; Schneider & Lewis, 1984; see Rayside & Bowler, 1988, for evidence of a similar trend in Canada). Roper surveys found that the proportion of Americans agreeing that "homosexuals should be guaranteed equal treatment under the law in jobs and housing" rose from 60% in 1977 to 66% in 1985, while the proportion supporting legalized discrimination declined from 28% to 22%. Similarly, the proportion of American adults surveyed by the Gallup organization who say that homosexual men and women should have equal rights in terms of job opportunities increased from 56% in 1977 to 59% in 1982 and to 71% in 1989; the proportion opposing such rights declined from 33% to 28% to 18%, respectively (Colasanto, 1989).

Respondents sometimes show more willingness to discriminate when asked about specific occupations, but a steady trend toward supporting gay rights still is evident. In Gallup polls (Colasanto, 1989), the proportion stating that gay people should be hired as doctors increased from 44% in 1977 to 56% in 1989; similar increases were observed for hiring them as salespersons (from 68% to 79%), members of the armed forces (51% to 60%), clergy (36% to 44%), and elementary school teachers (27% to 42%). For all of these occupations, the long-term trend appears to be toward increased public opposition to discrimination on the basis of sexual orientation.

CULTURAL AND PSYCHOLOGICAL HETEROSEXISM

In Chapter 5, I defined *heterosexism* as an ideological system that denies, denigrates, and stigmatizes any nonheterosexual form of behavior, identity, relationship, or community. I described how cultural heterosexism, like institutional racism and sexism, is manifested in societal customs and institutions. Through cultural heterosexism, homosexuality is rendered invisible and, when it becomes visible, is condemned by society. The poll data cited above make it clear that, although cultural heterosexism is pervasive in society, Americans display considerable variability in their individual attitudes toward lesbians and gay men. This observation reveals the inadequacy of an analysis of heterosexism that is restricted to its cultural manifestations.

In this chapter, I discuss *psychological heterosexism*—the manifestation of heterosexism in individuals' attitudes[3] and actions—and its role in violence against lesbians and gay men. In particular, I consider how psychological and situational factors affect the attitudes and behaviors of heterosexual individuals. The chapter is based on the assumptions that (a) psychological heterosexism and anti-gay violence are often functional for the person who manifests them; (b) the principal function served by these attitudes and actions differs for each person, depending upon her or his psychological needs; and (c) the translation of individual needs into anti-gay attitudes and behaviors involves a complex interaction of deep-seated personality characteristics, salient aspects of the immediate situation, and cultural definitions of sexuality and gender. In short, no single explanation of psychological heterosexism applies to all people.[4]

In the next section of the chapter, I discuss heterosexism as an attitude or prejudice and consider how it can serve different psychological functions for different people. Following that, I apply a similar analysis to overt acts of anti-gay behavior.

The Psychological Functions of Heterosexism

Why do some heterosexuals feel strongly hostile toward gay people while others are tolerant or accepting in their attitudes? In my own empirical research (Herek, 1984, 1987), I have tried to answer this question by using a perspective that earlier researchers applied to Whites' attitudes toward Blacks and Americans' attitudes toward Russians (e.g., McClintock, 1958; Smith, Bruner, & White, 1956). This perspective is called the *functional approach* to attitudes. Its central assumption is that people hold and express particular attitudes because they get some sort of psychological benefit from doing so. In other words, attitudes and opinions serve psychological functions for the person who holds them. According to the functional approach, two people can have very different motivations for expressing what appears to be the same attitude. Or they can express opposing opinions for essentially the same reason. Further, an individual's attitudes are more likely to change when they stop being functional or actually become dysfunctional.

Using this perspective, I analyzed essays about homosexuality written by 205 heterosexual college students (Herek, 1987) and found three principal psychological functions underlying the students' attitudes. I labeled the first of these the *experiential* function.[5] Attitudes serving an experiential function assisted the students in making sense of their previous interactions with gay people. Those who had experienced pleasant interactions with a gay man or lesbian generalized from that experience and accepted gay people in general. For example, one woman wrote:

> [I have generally positive attitudes because] I have come to know some of these people and find them no different from any other people. This has not always been the case. In junior high and high school I didn't condemn so to speak but I held strong opinions against them. This was an attitude formed without any knowledge of homosexuality or homosexuals. When I first came to [college] I still had some of the same attitudes. Little did I know that the guy in the next room was gay. We became good friends and did things together all the time. Eventually he told me and it was then that I realized that homosexuals only differ in sexual preference.

Others reported negative attitudes resulting from their unpleasant experiences with gay men or lesbians. Another woman wrote:

> Personally, I don't like most male homosexuals. I once worked under one and worked with some and they were everything homosexuals are stereotyped to be—someone once said "male homosexuals have all the bad qualities of women" (shrewishness, pettiness, etc.)—and unfortunately, for the men I worked with this statement applied.

Whether favorable or unfavorable, experiential attitudes help an individual to make sense of past experiences and fit them into a larger worldview, one that is organized primarily in terms of her or his own self-interest.

Because only about 30% of American adults know an openly gay person,[6] most heterosexuals' attitudes are not based on actual experiences with gay people. The attitudes of some of the remaining 70% probably serve an *anticipatory* function. Like the experiential function, the anticipatory function helps an individual to understand the world and to develop strategies for maximizing rewards and minimizing negative experiences. Unlike the experiential function, however, the anticipatory function is not based on past experiences with lesbians and gay men.

Rather, it is based on the anticipation of future interactions with them.

For most of the 70% of Americans who do not personally know lesbians or gay men, however, homosexuality and gay people are primarily symbols. Whereas attitudes toward people with whom one has direct experience function primarily to organize and make sense of those experiences, attitudes toward symbols serve a different kind of function. Such attitudes help people to increase their self-esteem by expressing important aspects of themselves—by declaring (to themselves and to others) what sort of people they are. Affirming who one *is* often is accomplished by distancing oneself from or even attacking people who represent the sort of person one *is not* (or does not want to be).

Many respondents in my study wrote essays that appeared to serve this type of function. Some essays, for example, manifested what I call a *social identity* function:[7]

> I have generally positive attitudes toward homosexuals because I don't think sexual preferences are a basis of judgment of someone's character or personality. Sexual preferences are a personal matter, and as long as a homosexual doesn't offend anyone or force his temptations on someone who is unwilling, there is no reason to condemn him/her. Homosexual tendencies aren't a deficit in someone's upbringing. I have these attitudes because of my own upbringing to be open-minded and non-stereotypical or non-judgmental.

An example of negative social identity attitudes:

> [I have generally negative attitudes because] in the Bible it clearly states that homosexuality is a *sin*. I believe that no one can be a Christian if he/she is a homosexual. I believe the Bible is correct, and I follow its beliefs word for word. I am a Christian.

The opinions expressed in these essays appeared to help the authors to increase their feelings of self-esteem in two ways. Consequently, I divided the social identity function into two interrelated components. The first of these is the *value-expressive* function. Attitudes serving a value-expressive function enable people to affirm their belief in and adherence to important values that are closely related to their self-concepts. In one of the latter essays printed above, for example, the author expressed her personal philosophy of "live and let live." For her, being gay represented a personal issue; her values dictated that people should not be condemned for what they do in their personal lives so long as they do not force themselves on unwilling others. Expressing her views about gay people allowed her to express her personal values about individual liberties, which were fundamental to her perception of herself as an open-minded person.

Although the last essay above conveyed a considerably different message, it also manifested a value-expressive function. Through it, the writer expressed her need to perceive herself in terms of her religious faith. In her view, opposing homosexuality was an integral part of being a good Christian, which was of central importance to feeling good about herself. It was not homosexuality per se that was important; homosexuality was a symbol for all that is immoral and contrary to her religious views. If her religion were to define left-handedness as it now defines homosexuality, she would probably express comparable hostility toward left-handed people.

The second component of the social identity function is *social expression*. With this function, expressing an attitude strengthens one's sense of belonging to a particular group and helps an individual to gain acceptance, approval, or love from other people whom she or he considers important (e.g., peers, family, neighbors). When social-expressive attitudes are hostile, gay people are perceived as the epitome of outsiders; denigrating them solidifies one's own status as an insider, one who belongs to the group. When social-expressive attitudes are positive, lesbians and gay men are regarded favorably by one's group or are members of that group. In either case, the approval that is won through expressing these attitudes increases the individual's own self-esteem, which is of central importance to her or him. Sometimes social support for attitudes is experienced directly, as when others tell us that they agree with our opinions or approve of our actions, that they accept us and like us. At other times, the support is indirect or imagined, as when we experience satisfaction because we feel that others would approve of us if they knew what we were saying or doing. The writers in these two essays most likely experienced both kinds of reinforcement for their attitudes. Their friends and family probably directly supported one's open-mindedness and the other's religiosity. At the same time, expressing their views probably helped them to feel kinship with larger social groupings (namely, open-minded people and good Christians).

I observed one other attitude function that also treats lesbians and gay men as symbols: the *ego-defensive* function. Defensive attitudes lower a person's anxiety resulting from her or his unconscious psychological conflicts, such as those surrounding sexuality or gender. This function is summarized in the notion that heterosexuals who express anti-gay prejudice do so out of fear that they themselves are latent homosexuals. This explanation for anti-gay prejudice has become widespread in recent years. Although it is used more often than is appropriate, it does fit some people for whom lesbians or gay men symbolize unacceptable parts of themselves (e.g., "effeminacy" for some men, "masculinity" for some women). Expressing anti-gay hostility represents an unconscious strategy through which they can avoid an internal conflict by externalizing it—projecting it onto a suitable symbol apart from themselves. By rejecting (or even attacking) gay people, the defensive individual can deny that unacceptable aspect of him- or herself while also symbolically attacking it. Defensive attitudes are often expressed in strong feelings of disgust toward homosexuality or in perceptions of danger from gay people of one's own gender. For example, one woman wrote:

[I have generally negative attitudes] because I feel homosexuality is not a normal lifestyle. I do, however, feel more comfortable with a male homosexual than with a lesbian. Male homosexuals may have a different lifestyle but they are not physically dangerous to me as a woman, and I feel casual friendships between myself and male homosexuals are less tense. Lesbianism, however, is disgusting to me.

Another essay with defensive themes hinted strongly at some of the author's struggles with his own sexuality. Denying that anyone is truly homosexual, he expressed the unrealistic belief that society encourages young people to become gay:

I don't believe such tendencies come about because of a person's true feelings. Our society keeps telling everyone that it's okay to be a les or fag, and that there's nothing wrong with it. Many guys and girls who have never had sexual relations with the opposite sex think they're "different" right away and they turn gay because everyone says it's okay anyway. I don't think anyone should hold the passive view that "if they don't bother me, let them be" because they are ruining this country's morals in a very disguised fashion. I feel people with these tendencies aren't that abnormal—they've just been taken in by society's view that it's okay. Let's give these people help so they can enjoy life to its fullest like everyone else.

The value-expressive, social-expressive, and ego-defensive functions share a common characteristic: With all of them, anti-gay prejudice helps people to define who they are by directing hostility toward gay people as a symbol of what they are not. With the value-expressive function, a heterosexual's attitudes help to define the world according to principles of good and evil, right and wrong; by opposing the embodiment of evil (gay people), the individual affirms her or his own morality and virtue. With the social-expressive function, one's attitudes help to designate who is in the in-group and who is in the out-group; by denigrating outsiders (lesbians and gay men), the individual affirms her or his own status as an insider. With the defensive function, attitudes toward gay people help to affirm and "own" the good or acceptable parts of the self while denying the bad or unacceptable parts. Unacceptable feelings (such as homoerotic desires, "feminine" tendencies for men, or "masculine" tendencies for women) are projected onto gay people, who are then disliked. In this way, individuals can symbolically (and often unconsciously) prove to themselves that those unacceptable feelings are not their own.

Here then is a nexus between psychological and cultural heterosexism: *Psychological heterosexism can serve these functions only when an individual's psychological needs converge with the culture's ideology.* Anti-gay prejudice can be value expressive only when an individual's self-concept is closely tied to values that also have become socially defined as antithetical to homosexuality. It can be social expressive only insofar as an individual strongly needs to be accepted by members of a social group that rejects gay people or homosexuality. It can be defensive only when lesbians and gay men are culturally defined in a way that links them to an individual's own psychological conflicts.

The functions discussed here are summarized in Table 9.1, from which it can be seen that the benefits received from attitudes toward lesbians and gay men are contingent upon either of two principal sources. One source is gay people themselves. With attitudes

TABLE 9.1 The Psychological Functions of Heterosexism

Name of Function	Description	Benefit to Individual
Evaluative functions:		
Experiential	Generalizes from past experiences with specific lesbians or gay men to create a coherent image of gay people in relation to one's own interests.	Makes sense of past experiences and uses them to guide behavior.
Anticipatory	Anticipates benefits or punishments expected to be received directly from lesbians or gay men.	In absence of direct experience with gay men or lesbians, plans future behavior so as to maximize rewards and minimize punishments.
Expressive functions:		
Social identity:		
Value-expressive	Lesbians or gay men symbolize an important value conflict.	Increases self-esteem by affirming individual's view of self as a person who adheres to particular values.
Social-expressive	Lesbians or gay men symbolize the in-group or out-group.	Increases self-esteem by winning approval of others whose opinion is valued; increases sense of group solidarity.
Defensive:	Lesbians or gay men symbolize unacceptable part of the self.	Reduces anxiety associated with a psychological conflict by denying and externalizing the unacceptable aspect of self and then attacking it.

NOTE: With the evaluative functions, benefit is contingent upon direct experiences with lesbians and gay men. With the expressive functions, benefit is contingent upon the consequences of expressing the attitude.

serving an experiential function, lesbians and gay men have been the source of pleasant or unpleasant experiences in the past. Holding and expressing attitudes consistent with that earlier experience allows an individual to exert some control over future experiences, either by avoiding what has been unpleasant or by seeking out what has been pleasant. With the anticipatory function, the individual has not had direct interactions with lesbians or gay men in the past but expects to have them in the future and expects gay people to be the source of either benefit or detriment; the attitude helps the individual to prepare for those anticipated interactions. Because these attitudes involve an evaluation or appraisal of gay men and lesbians as a group in terms of whether they have been or will be a source of reward or punishment, I refer to them as the *evaluative* attitude functions (Herek, 1986b).[8]

With the social identity (value-expressive and social-expressive) and defensive functions, in contrast, the source of benefit is not contingent upon the actions or characteristics of lesbians and gay men but upon what happens when the individual expresses her or his attitudes. Lesbians and gay men serve as symbols of personal values, group membership, or unconscious conflicts. They are a means to an end: Expressing a particular attitude toward them helps the individual to affirm her or his self-concept in terms of important values, to feel accepted by significant others, or to reduce anxieties. Consequently, I refer to them as the *expressive* functions.

Distinguishing between the evaluative and expressive functions is useful because it suggests different strategies for reducing prejudice. Prejudice that serves one of the evaluative functions can best be reduced through direct experiences with lesbians and gay men. Prejudice that serves an expressive function can be reduced through addressing the individual's identity needs, affiliation needs, or unconscious conflicts. Some implications of this distinction for reducing psychological heterosexism are discussed more fully in the final section of this chapter.

THE PSYCHOLOGICAL FUNCTIONS OF ANTI-GAY VIOLENCE

In the discussion so far, psychological heterosexism has been examined as an attitude—that is, something "in the heads" of individuals. But what about behaviors such as actively discriminating against gay people or physically attacking them? When a teenage boy participates in a gang attack against a gay man on the street, for example, do his actions serve psychological functions for him in the same way that heterosexist attitudes do? In this section, I consider how the functional approach can be applied to hate crimes against lesbians and gay men.

Violence Serving Evaluative Functions

Some anti-gay crimes may serve an experiential function by enabling the attacker to make sense of his or her past negative interactions with a particular lesbian or gay man. Although discussions of anti-gay violence usually focus on the victim's status as a representative of the lesbian or gay male community, it should be recognized that gay people are not immune from attacks based on personal dislike or vengeance. They can be targeted by an individual with whom they have previously had an argument or disagreement unrelated to their sexual orientation. Or a perpetrator may have had a negative experience with someone who is gay and then attacked another gay person (e.g., a friend of the first individual) as a proxy. From the viewpoint of the victim, the attack may well be experienced as a hate crime regardless of the assailant's actual motives. But from the perpetrator's perspective, the attack was directed at a specific individual rather than all gay women and men.

Other violent attacks against gay people may be based on an anticipatory function. For example, the perpetrator perceives gay people to be vulnerable and unlikely to resist and consequently targets them for robbery (Harry, 1982). The assailant's primary motivation in this case is the desire for personal gain with minimal risk. In Chapter 8, Berk and his colleagues use the term *actuarial* to describe such crimes. The victim and the larger community are likely to experience this as a hate crime, especially if anti-gay epithets are uttered by the assailant. But the perpetrator might well have been responding more to situational cues than to personal prejudice—for example, an unexpected opportunity to rob an easy target.

Violence Serving an Expressive Function

Value-expressive violence. Value-expressive violence provides a way for perpetrators to express important values that are the basis for their self-concepts. The value-expressive motivation was illustrated in an interview conducted by journalist Michael Collins (see Chapter 12) with members of a Los Angeles gang called the Blue Boys. At one point in Collins's interview, the gang's leader justified their actions in value-expressive terms. Characterizing homosexuality as a serious societal problem, he stated that the gang members would not "sit back and watch the poisoning of America" (see Chapter 12). He further portrayed the group members as upholding important values when he compared their violent assaults on gay men to "the work of Batman or some other masked avenger." His comments are consistent with the rhetoric of hate groups such as the Ku Klux Klan, which regularly appeal to moral authority (see Segrest & Zeskind, 1989). As Harry observed in Chapter 7, value-based justifications for anti-gay violence often derive from societal norms surrounding the institution of gender. Although disengaged from the conventional moral order, perpetrators may develop rationalizations that designate gay people as worthy of punishment and that allow attackers to see themselves as "rendering gender justice and reaffirming the natural order of gender-appropriate behavior."

Social-expressive violence. As Hamner explains in Chapter 11, membership in a social group often is a central component of one's identity. By clearly differentiating and then attacking an out-group, anti-gay violence can help in-group members to feel more positive about their group and, consequently, about themselves as well. For example, Weissman (see Chapter 10) interviewed several young men who had thrown eggs and oranges at gay men at a gay bar in Greenwich Village. They generally described the incident as a practical joke, but it appears also to have strengthened their sense of group solidarity. The informal leader explained, "Peer pressure has a lot to do with it. Sometimes you're forced into doing something to prove yourself to others." Another group member described his feelings after the incident: "Relief. A kind of high. There was also a strong, close feeling that we were all in something together."

Social-expressive motivations also were apparent among the Blue Boys (see Chapter 12). They had a clearly formed in-group, signified by their "uniform" of blue baseball jackets, their blue bats, and their framed "Statement of Principals," which they claimed to have signed in blood. Additionally, the Blue Boys' leader also seemed to seek recognition and acceptance from a larger audience; he fantasized that people who read about the group's exploits would cheer them on, much the way that baseball fans cheer a home run.

Perpetrators of anti-gay sexual assaults also may be motivated by needs to maintain status and affiliation with their peers. From a series of interviews with perpetrators of male-male rapes, for example, Groth and Burgess (1980, p. 808) concluded, "Some offenders feel pressured to participate in gang rape to maintain status and membership with their peers. . . . [A]cceptance and recognition by one's peers becomes a dynamic in group rape, and mutual participation in the assault serves to strengthen and confirm the social bond among the assailants."

Ego-defensive violence. Anti-gay assaults can provide a means for young males to affirm their heterosexuality or masculinity by attacking someone who symbolizes an unacceptable aspect of their own personalities (e.g., homoerotic feelings or tendencies toward effeminacy). This process may be partly conscious, as evidenced in comments by the Blue Boys (in Chapter 12). Their leader repeatedly affirmed that they were "*real* men" who were "out there fucking chicks every night" and explained that they "chose the blue baseball bats because it's the color of the boy. The man is one gender. He is not female. It is male. There is no confusion. Blue is the color of men, and that's the color that men use to defeat the anti-male, which is the queer."

The Blue Boys appeared to use their anti-gay beatings as a way of establishing their own manhood. Their brutal assaults on men whom they perceived as the antithesis of masculinity may have been an attempt to deny any trace of femininity in themselves.

The ego-defensive motivations of anti-gay attacks probably often are hidden from the perpetrators themselves. A dramatic example can be found in the brutal murder of Robert Hillsborough by a gang of young men in San Francisco in the summer of 1977 (Shilts, 1982). One of the men convicted of the murder, 19-year-old John Cordova, stabbed Hillsborough 15 times while shouting "Faggot, faggot." What makes this story a possible example of defensive attitudes is the interesting fact that Cordova was sexually attracted to men but he could not admit it to himself. He had an occasional sexual relationship with a male construction contractor, who said that Cordova often initiated sexual encounters but "never wanted to act like he knew what he was doin'" during them (Shilts, 1982, p. 168). Cordova would always wake up as if he were in a daze, insisting he had no idea what had happened the night before. When he stabbed Hillsborough over and over, Cordova may have been unconsciously attacking and striking out at his own homosexual desires.

Ego-defensive motives also can underlie sexual assaults in which the perpetrator apparently wished to punish the victim as a way of dealing with his own unresolved and conflictual sexual interests. Groth and Burgess (1980, p. 808) quoted an assailant who had assaulted a young hustler after having sex with him:

> After I came, I dragged him out of the car and punched him out and called him a punk. I told him I was going to kill him. Then I threw his clothes out of the car and took off. I was angry at him. I don't know why. At what I was doing, I guess, is what I was really angry at.

Groth and Burgess (1980) speculated that assailants in male-male rape who are conflicted about their own homosexual attraction may see the victim as a temptation and may subsequently use rape in an attempt to punish him for arousing them.

Violence with Multiple Motivations

In many anti-gay assaults, the perpetrators act from several motives simultaneously. Multiple motivations seem especially likely in street assaults by young male perpetrators. Such assailants are at an age when establishing their adult identity, including their manhood, is of considerable importance (Erikson, 1963). Many of them strongly embrace what the culture has defined as "masculine" characteristics, while rejecting "feminine" characteristics (Horwitz & White, 1987). Identity formation is both a personal and a social process; it must be done for oneself, for one's peers, and for the larger society. Consequently, gay men and lesbians may serve simultaneously as multiple symbols for young male gangs. They may represent (a) unacceptable feelings or tendencies experienced privately by each gang member (for example, deviations from heterosexuality or culturally pre-scribed gender roles), (b) the out-group, and (c) what society has defined as evil. At the same time, such attacks may be based in part on past experiences with gay people. The perpetrator, for example, may have had an unpleasant interaction with an indi-vidual who incidentally was gay and may seek vengeance by at-tacking a proxy for that individual. Consequently, gang attacks may simultaneously serve experiential, ego-defensive, social-expressive, and value-expressive functions for the perpetrators.

Other perpetrators also are likely to have multiple motives for their anti-gay attacks. Police officers, for example, work to uphold societal values in an institution where the sense of the in-group is strong and where masculinity traditionally has been revered (Niederhoffer, 1967). Some have interacted with gay people only when arresting them. Especially for young policemen, who may still be solidifying their adult identities, anti-gay violence may serve psychological functions quite similar to those previously dis-cussed for street gangs. Similarly, parents who assault their lesbian daughters or gay sons may have multiple motivations: They may be trying to banish unacceptable feelings from a child whom they consider to be an extension of their own identity (an ego-defensive function), while fulfilling their culturally defined parental role of imparting society's values to their children (a value-expressive function) and while seeking to protect the integrity of their family from what they perceive as outside, perhaps alien influences (a social-expressive function). The assault also may result in part from the parent's feelings of anger and frustration that have built up toward the child during a long series of unpleasant interactions (an experiential function).

Situational Influences on Anti-Gay Violence

From the examples in this section, it should be clear that the primary cause of anti-gay violence is not always the attacker's own personal prejudice against lesbians and gay men. Although anti-gay (or, for that matter, progay) actions may reflect an individual's deeply felt attitudes and beliefs, this is not always the case. A heterosexual person's behaviors toward lesbians and gay men may be more a product of immediate circumstances than of her or his strong dislikes (or likes) for lesbians and gay men. In this sense, I agree with Ehrlich's (Chapter 6) observation that the term *hate crime* can be misleading if it implies that the attacker's motivation always is intense personal hatred for the victim's group. Acts of anti-gay violence need not always be driven primarily by psychological heterosexism (although it is likely to be present to some extent in all anti-gay hate crimes). Instead, such crimes can serve a variety of social and psychological functions for those who commit them. Rather than acting from their own bigotry, for example, some perpetrators of violence against lesbians and gay men may be responding primarily to peer pressure or other situational factors. This was illustrated in the comments of a young man interviewed by Weissman (see Chapter 10): "We were trying to be tough to each other. It was like a game of chicken—someone dared you to do something and there was just no backing down."

This observation points to another reason for distinguishing between psychological and cultural heterosexism. Whereas psychological heterosexism may not always be the principal reason for an anti-gay attack (e.g., a gang might well have selected another type of "outsider" as a suitable victim), the importance of cultural heterosexism cannot be underestimated. For it is cultural heterosexism that defines gay people as suitable targets that can be "used" for meeting a variety of psychological needs. And anti-gay attacks, regardless of the perpetrator's motivation, reinforce cultural heterosexism. Thus, when a teenage gang member attacks a gay man on the street, it is a hate crime *not* because hate necessarily was the attacker's primary motive (it may or may not have been) but because the attack expresses cultural hostility, condemnation, and disgust toward gay people and because it has the effect of terrorizing the individual victim as well as the entire lesbian and gay community. The attack in effect punishes the gay person for daring to be visible.

In summary, although cultural heterosexism is the principal determinant of anti-gay hate crimes as a cultural phenomenon, additional factors must be considered to explain why a particular person commits a specific act of anti-gay violence. Among these are the individual's past experiences with the victim (if any), her or his psychological needs and personality characteristics, and the demands created by the immediate situation (e.g., peer pressures).

STRATEGIES FOR CHANGE

The functional approach is important not only because it explains the motivations for individuals' attitudes and actions but also because it suggests a strategy for combating anti-gay prejudice and violence, namely, by making them dysfunctional. This involves determining what psychological functions are served by a person's feelings or behaviors and then intervening in either of two ways: preventing the individual's anti-gay attitudes or actions from fulfilling that psychological need or helping her or him to meet the same need in another, less destructive way.

Consider, for example, someone whose anti-gay attitudes result from a value-expressive need to perceive herself as a religious person. Attempts to reduce her prejudice by eliminating the role played by religious values in her self-concept is not likely to succeed. It might be possible, however, to disentangle her condemnation of gay people from her moral beliefs so that she can continue to express her religious values but without attacking lesbians and gay men. This might be accomplished by presenting her with alternative, noncondemnatory theological perspectives on homosexuality by religious leaders whom she respects. She also might be influenced by juxtaposing her religious values against equally important but contradictory values. If she places a high value on patriotism, for example, she might be influenced by arguments that appeal to justice and liberty. A third source of change might be her realization that a person whom she loves (e.g., a close friend or relative) is gay. This might create a conflict between her moral condemnation of homosexuality as a symbol and her feelings for the flesh-and-blood individual whom she has always considered to be a good person and whom she now knows to be gay (see Herek, 1984, 1986b, 1987, 1991, for further discussion).

This approach requires that institutions and society, as well as individuals, be targeted for change. Individual anti-gay attitudes and actions will become dysfunctional when they are no longer supported by religious and political institutions, when they are not reinforced by social norms, and when they are not integral to society's images of sexuality and gender. Even more broadly, anti-gay prejudice and violence will become much less functional when the majority of heterosexual Americans stop perceiving homosexuality in symbolic terms and instead associate it with their close friends and loved ones who are lesbian or gay.

Coming out to heterosexuals is perhaps the most powerful strategy that lesbians and gay men have for overcoming psychological heterosexism and anti-gay violence. Empirical research with other minority groups has shown that intergroup contact often reduces prejudice in the majority group when the contact meets several conditions: When it makes shared goals salient, when intergroup cooperation is encouraged, when the contact is ongoing and intimate rather than brief and superficial, when representatives of the two groups are of equal status, and when they share important values (Allport, 1954; Amir, 1976). These conditions occur most often when lesbians and gay men disclose their sexual orientation to their relatives, friends, neighbors, and coworkers. When heterosexuals learn that someone about whom they care is gay, formerly functional prejudice can quickly become dysfunctional. The untruth in stereotypes becomes obvious, social norms are perceived to have changed, and traditional moral values concerning sexuality are juxtaposed against the values of caring for a loved one. Thus having a friend, coworker, or family member who is openly gay can eventually change a prejudiced person's perception of homosexuality from an emotionally charged, value-laden symbolic construct to a mere demographic characteristic, like hair color or political party affiliation.

Coming out, however, is difficult and possibly dangerous. It requires making public an aspect of oneself that society perceives as more appropriately kept private (see Chapter 5). It can mean being defined exclusively in terms of sexuality by strangers, friends, and family. It also can mean being newly perceived as possessing some sort of disability or handicap, an inability to be what one should be as man or woman. In the worst situations, it can mean being completely rejected or even physically attacked by those to whom one has come out. Many gay people remain in the closet because they fear these negative interpersonal consequences as well as discrimination and stigmatization. Additionally, continually having to overcome invisibility is itself a frustrating experience; allowing others to assume that one is heterosexual often is the path of least resistance.

The challenge, therefore, is for all people who abhor heterosexism to do whatever they can to remove these barriers, to create a social climate in which coming out is safer and easier. This requires a comprehensive approach in which we all confront heterosexism in both its cultural and its psychological manifestations. As a first step, we must confront hate crimes against lesbians and gay men and other minority groups; we must clearly establish that these crimes are unacceptable and punish the perpetrators. We also must work to change the individual attitudes that give rise to such attacks and that tolerate them. And we must change the institutions that perpetuate prejudice by keeping lesbians and gay men invisible and punishing them when they come out.

Our culture already has witnessed the beginnings of a transformation as more and more lesbians and gay men have come out to those around them and as they have challenged heterosexism in its many forms—both psychological and cultural. Prejudice and violence work to prevent this transformation; they threaten to set back the clock by making gay people invisible once again. It is up to each of us to confront prejudice, to challenge violence, and to fight invisibility.

NOTES

1. Following popular usage, the word *American* is used in this chapter to describe residents of the United States of America.

2. For example, see polls by ABC (August, 1987), the *Los Angeles Times* (August, 1987), Roper (September, 1985), Yankelovich (March, 1978), and Gallup (November, 1978). When not otherwise indicated, the national survey data described in this chapter were obtained through the Roper Center, University of Connecticut at Storrs. I am grateful to Professor Bliss Siman of Baruch College, City University of New York, for her assistance in securing these data.

3. In this chapter, the term *attitude* is used to refer to an individual's evaluative stance toward a particular group of persons or objects. Such an evaluation might be described with terms such as *good-bad, like-dislike,* or *favorable-unfavorable.* The term *opinion* is used interchangeably with *attitude.* An attitude or opinion can be expressed privately (to oneself) or publicly (through speaking, writing, or some other observable behavior).

4. In this chapter, I purposely avoid the term *homophobia,* which has often been used to describe such attitudes (Herek, 1984; Smith, 1971; Weinberg, 1972). Any single word is necessarily limited in its ability to characterize a phenomenon that encompasses issues of morality, legality, discrimination, civil liberties, violence, and personal discomfort. *Homophobia* is particularly ill-suited to this purpose, however, for three reasons. First, it is linguistically awkward; its literal meaning

168   PERPETRATORS

is something like "fear of sameness." Second, anti-gay prejudice is not truly a phobia; it is not necessarily based on fear; nor is it inevitably irrational or dysfunctional for individuals who manifest it (Fyfe, 1983; Herek, 1986a; Nungesser, 1983; Shields & Harriman, 1984). Third, using homophobia can easily mislead us into thinking of anti-gay prejudice in exclusively individual terms, as a form of mental illness rather than as a pattern of thought and behavior that can actually be adaptive in a prejudiced society.

5. In my earlier papers (Herek, 1986b, 1987), I used the term *experiential-schematic*. This somewhat cumbersome term has been shortened for the current chapter.

6. For example, 29% of the respondents to a 1986 *Newsweek*/Gallup poll indicated they knew a gay person. In a 1983 *Los Angeles Times* poll, the figure was 30%.

7. In my earlier papers (Herek, 1986b, 1987), I used the term *social expressive*. For greater clarity, I have substituted the term *social identity* in this chapter.

8. The term *instrumental* also might be used to describe these functions, in that they are based on the attitude object's instrumental value to the person holding the attitude. All attitudes can be considered instrumental, however, to the extent that they provide some sort of psychological benefit to the holder. I think that understanding this dual usage of *instrumental* helps to resolve Ehrlich's (Chapter 6) disagreement with Harry (Chapter 7) over whether violence is instrumental or symbolic. Harry uses the term in the more specific sense of benefits derived directly from the victim (e.g., valuables obtained through robbery); his usage matches the evaluative functions described here. Ehrlich's use of *instrumental* refers to the actor's need for some general benefit from the violence; this usage includes both evaluative and expressive violence and matches the more general concept of *function* as used in this chapter.

REFERENCES

Allport, G. (1954). *The nature of prejudice*. New York: Addison-Wesley.
Amir, Y. (1976). The role of intergroup contact in change of prejudice and inter-group relations. In P. Katz (Ed.), *Towards the elimination of racism* (pp. 245-308). New York: Pergamon.
Colasanto, D. (1989, October 25). Gay rights support has grown since 1982, Gallup poll finds. *San Francisco Chronicle*, p. A21.
Erikson, E. H. (1963). *Childhood and society* (2nd ed.). New York: Norton.
Fyfe, B. (1983). "Homophobia" or homosexual bias reconsidered. *Archives of Sexual Behavior, 12*, 549-554.
Groth, A. N., & Burgess, A. W. (1980). Male rape: Offenders and victims. *American Journal of Psychiatry, 137*(7), 806-810.
Harry, J. (1982). Derivative deviance: The cases of extortion, fag-bashing, and shakedown of gay men. *Criminology, 19*, 251-261.
Herek, G. M. (1984). "Beyond homophobia:" A social psychological perspective on attitudes toward lesbians and gay men. *Journal of Homosexuality, 10*(1/2), 1-21.
Herek, G. M. (1986a). The social psychology of homophobia: Toward a practical theory. *NYU Review of Law & Social Change, 14*(4), 923-934.

Herek, G. M. (1986b). The instrumentality of attitudes: Toward a neofunctional theory. *Journal of Social Issues, 42*(2), 99-114.

Herek, G. M. (1987). Can functions be measured? A new perspective on the functional approach to attitudes. *Social Psychology Quarterly, 50*, 285-303.

Herek, G. M. (1991). Stigma, prejudice, and violence against lesbians and gay men. In J. Gonsiorek & J. Weinrich (Eds.), *Homosexuality: Research implications for public policy* (pp. 60-80). Newbury Park, CA: Sage.

Horwitz, A. V., & White, H. R. (1987). Gender role orientations and styles of pathology among adolescents. *Journal of Health and Social Behavior, 28*, 158-170.

McClintock, C. (1958). Personality syndromes and attitude change. *Journal of Personality, 26*, 479-492.

Niederhoffer, A. (1967). *Behind the shield: The police in urban society.* Garden City, NY: Doubleday.

Nungesser, L. G. (1983). *Homosexual acts, actors, and identities.* New York: Praeger.

Rayside, D., & Bowler, S. (1988). Public opinion and gay rights. *Canadian Review of Sociology and Anthropology, 25*, 649-660.

Schneider, W., & Lewis, I. A. (1984, February). The straight story on homosexuality and gay rights. *Public Opinion*, pp. 16-20, 59-60.

Segrest, M., & Zeskind, L. (1989). *Quarantines and death: The Far Right's homophobic agenda.* (Available from the Center for Democratic Renewal, P.O. Box 50469, Atlanta, GA 30302)

Shields, S. A., & Harriman, R. E. (1984). Fear of male homosexuality: Cardiac responses of low and high homonegative males. *Journal of Homosexuality, 10*(1/2), 53-67.

Shilts, R. (1982). *The mayor of Castro Street: The life and times of Harvey Milk.* New York: St. Martin's.

Smith, K. T. (1971). Homophobia: A tentative personality profile. *Psychological Reports, 29*, 1091-1094.

Smith, M. B., Bruner, J. S., & White, R. W. (1956). *Opinions and personality.* New York: John Wiley.

Weinberg, G. (1972). *Society and the healthy homosexual.* New York: St. Martin's.

10

Kids Who Attack Gays

ERIC WEISSMAN

Maybe it was the heat, maybe it was just restlessness. Or maybe it was that certain type of craziness that attacks all of us at one time or another in our lives. Victor, Gerry, Carl, Allen, Mitch, and Sam had nothing to do, so they were driving around Manhattan. Finally they found themselves on Christopher Street, a few blocks from their home turf (despite the influx of gays, the old-time Italian presence remains strong in parts of Greenwich Village). They passed a deli; on the sidewalk outside lay a crate of oranges and a box of eggs, an after-hours delivery. Someone said, "Let's take them and throw them at the fags!"

Soon the eggs and oranges were in their possession. Tension was mounting, buzzing in the air; each guy felt it. Some of them were having second thoughts, but there could be no backing out now.

Gerry drove along under the West Side Highway and parked by one of the ramps. Once up on the abandoned roadway, they walked downtown a bit to a place just above West Street where the action occurred—faggots walking around, holding hands, even kissing openly on the promenade below. It was dark and hard for them to see; there were a lot of trees in the way. The

SOURCE: Reprinted by permission from *Christopher Street* (1978, August, pp. 9-13).

guys found a good spot, took up positions, and stood ready to fire. Each of them had two eggs.

They spotted a bunch of fags, threw the eggs, then ran like hell back to the safety of the car. They were sure they had hit someone. After driving past the scene to inspect the damage they let fly with the oranges, shattering a bar window as they sped off into the night.

That was a year ago. Since then I've had a chance to talk with these and other teenagers—all but one of them from middle or working-class Italian homes, all still living with their parents—about their reactions to homosexuality.

Victor, age seventeen, classifies his home-life as strict. A senior in a Catholic high school where his grades are low B's, he plans to go on to college and become an engineer. Victor spoke freely about what he and his friends had done last May; the memory of the incident remains fresh and clear in his mind. He also remembered another time when he and some friends went out searching for trouble:

"We were at the club [a private cellar club in the Village owned by the neighborhood kids], and we decided to go out and look for some kids who were bothering a local girl. We couldn't find them, so we started to hit these fags that were walking around the neighborhood. We were under the influence [of alcohol] at the time. There were five of them and the most they got was a black eye."

Would he do it again, I asked.

"No."

Why not?

"I have better things to do. Unless they did something to me or my friends. I wouldn't go looking for trouble."

Did Victor think what he had done was wrong?.

"Yes."

Did he feel guilty?

"No, but if I did it now I would feel guilty."

Why?

"I guess gay people do what they want to do and I do what I want to do. I don't think what they do is right. I can't see two guys making out. It goes against the Bible. All my life everyone told me it was wrong, and I guess that just sticks with you. But they have the same rights as I do and shouldn't be bothered."

Does Victor know any gay people?

"No."

I asked Victor what he thought of Mayor Koch's executive order banning discrimination against gay people in the police and fire departments.

"I don't know about that," he answered. "It doesn't seem right. I think that their homosexuality will get in the way of their job."

What would he do if he had a homosexual son or daughter?

"I would tell him that people would look at him as a different person, and judge him as a different person, that he wouldn't get anywhere in life, that he will be very unhappy. I would never hit him, and I wouldn't want anyone else to hit him either."

Although there were no real surprises in my talk with Victor, he seemed to me to have experienced a slight change of attitude, a small growth in character, since his escapade last May. A similar change became apparent in some of the other boys I questioned.

Eighteen-year-old Gerry comes from Mexican/Irish stock. He attends a college in upstate New York, is studying political science, and has a 2.6 index. (He had a B average in high school.) During vacation periods Gerry lives with his parents in a middle-income environment. He enjoys good health and a relatively carefree existence. I asked him to give me his account of the eggs and oranges caper.

"I don't really think about it much," he confessed. "In fact, I try not to think about things like that. It was a little game. We were trying to be tough to each other. It was like a game of chicken—someone dared you to do something and there was just no backing down. I wouldn't do it again. I'd be scared of getting caught.

"I knew it was wrong, but I wasn't going to be the one to say 'Don't do it.' We really didn't want to hurt anybody; at least I didn't. People do a lot of things that they know are wrong. I guess you're blinded at the moment the incident happens.

"It was a symbol of prestige. I don't think I was aware of anything that was going on that night. It was like being stoned; your perception of reality becomes warped. I was nervous, and while we were doing the throwing I was scared, both of getting caught and of really hurting somebody. After the incident I was relieved. We were all laughing and making a big joke of it. But there was an undercurrent of tension. I was also glad that we didn't get caught."

As I had with Victor, I asked Gerry what he thought about the mayor's executive order concerning gays.

"I don't really care," he said. "If gays can do the job it's all right with me. I'm not in the city much any more."

Gerry thinks that a cousin of his father's who is gay is "a nice guy." But he also thinks that gays are really different from other people:

"Mentally. Maybe they hate girls. I just can't accept what they do. If I had a gay kid I'd get upset. I'd try to talk them out of it and have them see a doctor. I'd tell them they'd be an outcast and persecuted by kids like me."

Would he ever hit them?

"Maybe. It would depend on whether or not they listened to me. I wouldn't hit him just because he was a homosexual."

Gerry has never read anything about homosexuality and denies ever having had a gay experience himself. (He seemed very uncomfortable when I asked him about this, and later admitted he had been "just a little" uncomfortable with the interview itself.) In reply to my request for a general statement summing up his feelings on homosexuality he said:

"Well, if they stay in the closet, I guess there's nothing much anyone can do about them. I really don't care one way or the other, as long as they don't bother me."

After talking with Gerry I felt that I was making progress, but I wasn't sure where. I next spoke with two boys who had nothing to do with the May 1977 incident.

Richie is fourteen years old, attends a Catholic high school, and does not plan to go on to college. His grades are low B's. He believes homosexuals are "a disgrace to mankind." Why?

"Because I don't think it's right that two guys get together and kiss and have sex together. It goes against the Bible and it just isn't natural."

Some of his teachers, he knows, are gay. They treat him nicely, but he always thinks twice before going anyplace with them. I asked him if he had ever attacked gay people.

"Not by myself," he answered. "My friends and I go 'fag-hunting' around the neighborhood. They should all be killed."

If, however, he had a homosexual son himself, he would "treat him like the rest of the family, under certain conditions— that he doesn't get out of hand. I wouldn't allow him to be seen with another homosexual and I wouldn't let him go out."

Would he want his child to be hurt by kids out "fag-hunting"?
"No."

In response to my question about Mayor Koch's executive order, Richie said:

"I couldn't care less if gays were in the fire department. It's the police that worry me. In the police department, I don't like it because
they can take advantage of the young kids in the neighborhood."

My interview with Richie came to a dead end when he answered my inquiry about whether he felt uncomfortable with a
flat "No."

Paul is seventeen and an A student. He plans to study business law in college. He feels that it is wrong of his friends to attack gay people:

"Gay people have rights like anybody else. No one should
have to worry about his safety because some stupid kid doesn't
like what he does in the privacy of his bedroom. I've been there
with my friends, but I've never participated. I would never do
anything like that. Peer pressure doesn't really affect me much.
If my friends start to get down on me I just go home. People
who do those things aren't really friends anyway."

Paul has a lesbian friend whom he characterizes as "a nice lady,
a good woman." About Mayor Koch's executive order he says:

"I think that gay people should not be judged by their sexual
preference. If they can do the job, they should have it. I do think
that this whole affair will bring more pressure on everybody,
gay and straight, and that the whole situation is going to erupt. I
guess there will always be people who are afraid of things that
they don't understand, that's only natural."

He admits that he doesn't "really understand" homosexuality
himself:

"Maybe it's just my upbringing. The church is against it, my
parents are against it, my friends are against it. It really is hard
to have a mind of your own. I hope I'll understand more as I get
older. If I had a homosexual son or daughter I would seek help
for them and try to understand their feelings. In any case I
would always love them."

Paul has read "some articles and a few books" on homosexuality and sums up his present feelings philosophically:

"Homosexuality," he observes, "has been around for a long,
long time, and it will continue to be around. I can't understand

their feelings, I can't put myself in their position, but I respect them as human beings. Other people should recognize the difference and try to understand it. Gay people should be free to live the way they choose. If they're happy, good for them."

He was "not at all" uncomfortable with the interview.

My next interviews were with two more boys involved in the eggs and oranges incident.

Allen is eighteen years old and attends a popular New York City business college. He was an A student in high school. Although he does not consider himself such, he is the acknowledged leader of the group involved in last year's attack. I asked him how many times he and his friends had assaulted gay people. "Only twice," he replied. Could he describe his feelings before, during, and after? He could:

"Before, there was a lot of anxiety. During I was really afraid, afraid of getting caught. And after there was just relief, a lot of joking around. We were getting high off our tension. I don't care what the others say, I know we were all scared; everybody was reluctant to throw their eggs."

How does he feel now about what he did?

"Maybe it was wrong."

Just maybe?

"Well, it wasn't right."

Allen has seen gays "where I work and in the streets" but does not personally know anyone who is gay. About Mayor Koch's executive order he says, "If a person can do a job, what difference should their sexual preference be? Homosexuality has nothing to do with one's job." He has read some literature on homosexuality—"Some of it was really garbage, but some of it made me think and question my attitude"—but still thinks homosexuality is "wrong."

Why?

"Because it wasn't meant to be. I can't relate to the concept of two men having sex together. Men and women have their own sexual roles to fill. The whole idea of men making love to each other sounds disgusting and immoral."

When I asked Allen what he would do if he had a homosexual child he exclaimed, "I knew you were going to ask me that question," and then proceeded to admit:

"I think I would take it pretty hard. I would always wonder what I had done wrong. But I would try to relate to him. If he had a strong will there would be nothing I could do. I would certainly tell him my feelings and let him know that I don't approve of his choice of lifestyle. But he would always be my son."

Would he want his son to get assaulted and possibly killed?

"Of course not! I would tell him, though, that that would be one of the hazards that he would have to face up to as a homosexual."

Does he think, then, that it's right that a person's sexual likes and dislikes should leave him open to attack by others who don't share them?

"No, that's wrong, no one should have to live like that."

Would he do it again, then?

"Under the same circumstances, yes. But today I hope I would react differently. Peer pressure has a lot to do with it. Sometimes you're forced into doing something to prove yourself to others. The guys consider me their leader, but I don't consider myself a leader. We usually do things by consensus. It was really just a joke. We didn't want anybody to get hurt.

"I think I'm a good guy. I always look to help people whenever I can, and I don't usually look for trouble. What we did was wrong. If I get into a situation like that again I hope I have the ability to walk away and not get caught up in the whole thing. I also hope my friends have the strength to walk away from it."

Does he think his attitudes will change?

"I hope so. I don't see myself making it with another man, but I can't really rule out the possibility. I don't mean I'm gay or anything, but who knows what the future will bring? I'm meeting so many new and different people every day and I really can't see too far into my future."

Seventeen-year-old Mitch is a straight-A student. He plans to go on to college to study business administration. His description of the events of last May varied somewhat from the others I heard:

"Before, we were in a joking mood. It was Friday and we were feeling good, and this seemed like a good practical joke. During, it seemed like a game—a little tense, but fun just the same. After, there were a lot of feelings. Relief. A kind of high. There was also a strong, close feeling that we were all in something together, you know what I mean.

"Everybody makes mistakes, and that night was my big one. Some of the guys do that kind of thing pretty regularly, but I'd never done that before."

Would he do it again?

"Never. It was wrong and stupid."

Does he know any gay people?

"Yes. Some of them are really nice people, they've tried to help me. That's why I've had a change of heart. I can begin to see their point of view. They have personalities and most of them are pretty smart.

"I've read some literature on homosexuality and that, too, has helped me to straighten out my head a little. Before, all I had were stereotypes; now I've got more understanding, but I still have a long way to go."

When I asked what he thought about the mayor's executive order, Mitch said:

"Gay people are already in the police and fire departments. If they qualify for the jobs and carry out their responsibilities, then what they do in their personal lives shouldn't matter."

Mitch admits that he's "a little confused lately" about homosexuality:

"I've just started to make it with girls and there are certain things I'd like to try before I'm ready to give up on sex. I guess I'll probably have a gay experience. I'm kind of free and easy about sex, and I'd like to try it out with another guy. Hey, no one's going to know my name, are they?"

I assured him that I would be changing the names in the article I was interviewing him for.

"Good," he said, relieved, "that would really be bad. The other guys would really get on me, although I think most of them feel the same way. They're just too afraid to admit it to anyone, even to themselves."

What would he do if he had a homosexual son or daughter?

"That's hard to say. I don't think I'd know how to face the problem yet, I'm still a little too young. Maybe people will be less uptight about sex. I hope I can be understanding, supportive, and helpful to my kid when the time comes.

"I've changed my mind about a lot of things in the past year. I guess the more I experience, the more my attitudes and ideas will change. What we did that night was stupid. We weren't trying to hurt anyone, we were just out for some fun. I don't go around looking for trouble. I like people. I only hope that my friends begin to grow up and change some of their attitudes. I really wish people could learn to live with each other instead of hating all the time."

Perhaps Mitch's last statement sums it up best. With hard work, and a lot of education, maybe, just maybe, there's some hope for these kids and thousands of others like them.

11

Gay-Bashing:
A Social Identity Analysis of Violence
Against Lesbians and Gay Men

KARL M. HAMNER

As has been documented throughout this book, anti-gay[1] violence and other forms of hate-motivated crimes are increasingly a problem for American society. Although some empirical data document the prevalence and nature of hate crimes (see Chapter 1), explanations also are needed for the motivations of perpetrators: why they commit hate crimes and why they victimize certain groups. In this chapter, I shall explore the usefulness of the social identity theory of intergroup behavior for answering these questions.

SOCIAL IDENTITY THEORY

According to social identity theory (Tajfel & Turner, 1986), individuals desire positive self-esteem, and their self-esteem is tied inextricably to the way their in-group is evaluated relative to other groups. Social groups or categories "do not merely systematize the world; they also provide a system of orientation for *self-reference*: they create and define the individual's place in society" (Tajfel & Turner, 1986, p. 16). Because an individual's self-concept is based on the image and evaluation of the group(s) with which he or she identifies, people can build up their own self-esteem by promoting their in-group's evaluation. This is accomplished by comparing one's in-group with and differentiating it from relevant out-groups.

An "in-group" is any group with which an individual identifies and feels a sense of membership. People often identify simultaneously with more than one in-group. Which in-group is the most salient at any one time depends partly on situational factors. For example, when he is in the presence of Black heterosexual males, a White heterosexual male may identify with other Whites as an in-group. He may, however, shift to identifying with heterosexual males as an in-group (including the Black men previously regarded as out-group members) when a White gay male comes on the scene.

"Out-groups" are any social groups with which individuals compare their own in-group to evaluate it and thus make judgments about themselves. Whereas the number of out-groups to which one might compare oneself is seemingly infinite, a relatively small number of out-groups are actually relevant at any time. As with in-groups, the salience of a particular out-group often depends on the situation. Certain out-groups are commonly relevant to many individuals, however, due to such sociohistorical factors as a history of conflict between two groups or dominance of one group by another. The ubiquitous heterosexism of American society, for example, makes gay people a potentially relevant out-group for everyone who identifies as a heterosexual, regardless of their membership in other in-groups (see Chapter 5).

Being able to establish and maintain a positive group image compared with that of an out-group leads to high in-group prestige and an accompanying increase in personal self-esteem among in-group members; the inability to do so leads to low group prestige and loss of self-esteem. This positive image is achieved through manipulating both symbolic and material capital. Manipulating symbolic capital involves elevating the in-group's status through positive labels and descriptions while denigrating the out-group through negative symbols. Manipulating material capital involves increasing the in-group's access to valued material resources while decreasing the out-group's access to them; violence against an out-group member is a drastic form of material discrimination.

What makes social identity theory particularly applicable to understanding anti-gay violence is its observation that establishing a positive differentiation from an out-group depends at least as much on denigrating that out-group as on lauding one's own in-group. Consequently, promoting one's in-group often includes discriminating against members of another group, including through violence.

That simple improvement of the in-group's position is not always a primary motivation has been demonstrated in experimental situations: In-group members have been repeatedly shown to discriminate against out-group members even when it has meant sacrificing their own overall gain (Brown, 1988; Hamilton & Trolier, 1986; Tajfel & Turner, 1986). Lemrye and Smith (1985) found that in-group members who were able to discriminate against out-group members scored higher on several measures of self-esteem than did either in-group members who were not allowed to discriminate or individuals who were not categorized in a group but were allowed to discriminate.

According to Tajfel and Turner (1986), differentiation of the in-group from an out-group both fosters and is generated by group conflict. Conflict prompts individuals to deal with each other not as individuals but as representatives of their respective groups. "The more intense is an intergroup conflict, the more likely it is that the individuals who are members of the opposite groups will behave toward each other as a function of their respective group memberships" (Tajfel & Turner, p. 8). At the same time, attempting to maintain a positive differentiation from an out-group promotes conflict over material and symbolic resources.

SOCIAL IDENTITY THEORY AND GAY-BASHING

On November 15, 1990, at 10:45pm, a gay man walking in the Silverlake area of Los Angeles [widely known as a gay neighborhood] was attacked by two White males in their late-teens or early twenties. The first assailant jumped the victim from behind and the

second assailant ran over from a group across the street and joined
in the attack, kicking and punching the victim, who attempted to
fight back. The assailants broke off the attack and fled when cars
and a pedestrian stopped at the scene. Nothing was stolen from the
victim, who received various cuts from the attack. The assailants
were unknown to the victim.[2]

According to social comparison theory, anti-gay violence and
other hate-motivated crimes can be understood to represent intergroup conflicts rather than simple interactions among a few
individuals. Heterosexuals use denigration and discrimination,
including violence, to create a negative evaluation of gay men
and lesbians and thereby to create a positive differentiation between the two groups; this results in increased personal self-
esteem for them. Thus the victims of anti-gay violence are selected
because they are members of a social category. As Berk, Boyd,
and Hamner point out in Chapter 8, victims of hate crimes are
chosen on the basis of their "symbolic status," which derives
from their perceived membership in particular social groups.
People become victims because of *what* they are (gay, Black, Jewish, and so on) rather than *who* they are.

The incident described above manifests several characteristics
common to many anti-gay street crimes, which suggest that, consistent with social identity theory, such violence serves social functions for the perpetrators. First, the victims and perpetrators are
typically strangers (see Chapter 1); even when a victim does know
his or her attackers, the acquaintance often is limited, such as being
neighbors (McDevitt, 1989). This suggests that the victims are being chosen because of their group membership more than their
personal characteristics. Although other crimes such as robbery
also frequently involve victims and perpetrators who do not know
each other, gay-bashing and other hate-motivated crimes are
unique because they often have no apparent intent other than the
infliction of injury on the victim. This lack of other accompanying
crimes further suggests that the social functions served by the attack are principal motivators rather than ancillary concerns.

Finally, the perpetrator-to-victim ratio in hate crimes typically
is high. Although Bureau of Justice statistics indicate that only
25% of recent violent crimes involved multiple perpetrators, 64%
of the hate-motivated crimes that McDevitt (1989) studied met this
criterion, most of them involving at least four perpetrators.

Similarly, 53% of the incidents reported to San Francisco's Community United Against Violence (CUAV) in 1989 involved more than one perpetrator (see Chapter 1). This pattern suggests that such crimes serve as a form of group affirmation. This also is evidenced in the statements of perpetrators themselves. In Weissman's interviews with a group of young men who had engaged in an incident of gay-bashing (see Chapter 10), the perpetrators reported feeling a kind of communal euphoria during the incident. As one of the youths put it, they all felt "a kind of a high. There was also a strong, close feeling that we were all in something together." In his discussion of anti-gay violence in Chapter 9, Herek notes that gay-bashing helps the perpetrators win approval from important others and thereby increase their own self-esteem.

Social identity theory also allows us to understand why lesbians and gay men are especially likely to be victims of hate-motivated violence. The theory posits that the ability of individuals to establish a positive evaluation of their own group vis-à-vis some out-group is strongly mediated by the relative social statuses of the two groups within the society's socioeconomic structure. Groups with high social standing can easily establish a positive identity because they have many lower-status groups with which to compare themselves favorably and against which to discriminate. A low-status group has less ability to manipulate either material or symbolic capital in its own favor, however, and so has fewer relevant out-groups with a lower social standing than itself. Because it is difficult to negatively evaluate an out-group that enjoys higher status than one's own in-group, groups with low social standing are disproportionately chosen as relevant out-groups for denigration and discrimination. As a group generally held in low regard by society, lesbians and gay men are likely to represent a relevant out-group for all quarters of society, particularly for individuals lower in the social system.

LIMITATIONS OF SOCIAL IDENTITY THEORY

Although social identity theory is useful for understanding anti-gay violence, it has several problems. First, the concept of in-group is ambiguous and circular. For example, Allport (1954, p. 37) defined *in-group* as any collection of individuals who "use the term 'we' with the same significance." Tajfel and Turner (1986, p. 15) provide a more elaborate but nevertheless tautological definition of *in-group*: "a collection of individuals who perceive themselves to be members of the same social category, share some emotional involvement in this common definition of themselves, and achieve some degree of social consensus about the evaluation of their group and their membership in it." Without a clearer definition, researchers have no choice but to base ingroup membership on an individual's professed identification with a particular group.

This raises the related problem that, although an individual can identify simultaneously with multiple in-groups, social identity theory does not offer a strategy for determining which one is most important to the individual. This is important because the centrality of an in-group to an individual's self-conception affects how important it is to his or her self-esteem (Gecas & Seff, 1990). Presumably, the importance of the in-group to the individual will determine which out-groups he or she is likely to use for social comparison.

This question becomes particularly relevant to anti-gay violence when the perpetrator and victim differ on more than one group identity. For example, when a heterosexual Black man attacks a gay White man, is he making a comparison between the victim and himself in terms of sexuality, race, or both? Although the end result is presumably the same for the perpetrator (increased self-esteem), his motives could be quite different depending on the relevant in-group and out-group. If the attack is primarily "heterosexual against gay," it may have been motivated by a sense of sexual superiority. If, however, it is "Black against White," the motivation may have been a sense of racial inequality. If both, the attack may have combined these motivations with a sense of personal inefficacy (for example, if self-comparison with all Whites results in lowered self-esteem, gay Whites might be used as an out-group instead).

Another major problem with social identity theory is that the criteria for a "relevant" out-group are entirely undefined. The definition of an out-group is simply any group that is not an ingroup. The usual method for determining a relevant out-group is circular. For example, because a teenage gang of White Skinheads is discriminating against gay people, gay people are the relevant out-group for the Skinheads. The question remains, however, *why* one out-group (e.g., gays) but not another (e.g., Blacks, disabled people) is relevant to this particular in-group?

A final weakness of social identity theory is that the link between personal self-esteem and group evaluation is poorly developed. Tajfel and Turner (1986) apparently assume that group identification is fairly uniform among members. A variety of factors affect an individual's self-esteem, however, and, consequently, the degree to which she or he identifies with the in-group. Although social identity theory takes into account the effects of differential status among groups, it fails to consider differential status among members within groups. Such variations can affect individual self-esteem and the likelihood that a given individual will engage in social comparison to boost his or her self-esteem. High status within the in-group would seem likely to lead to greater self-esteem, thereby reducing the need to denigrate out-group members. Conversely, low in-group status should cause lower self-esteem, creating a greater need to bolster the in-group's evaluation. This may help to explain the young age of many gay-bashers (and perpetrators of many other violent crimes). Whereas self-esteem depends on achieved rather than ascribed status (Wiltfang & Scarbecz, 1990), young people often have not yet had sufficient chance to achieve their own status. Consequently, they turn to group identification and social comparison to boost their self-esteem.

The problems discussed here can be addressed to some degree by complementing the social identity perspective with two more traditional approaches to prejudice. Societal-level theories explain prejudice as a justification for political or economic exploitation or as a consequence of the dynamics of intergroup contact (Allport, 1954; Cox, 1948; Dovidio & Gaertner, 1986; Sears, 1988). Societal-level theories allow us to begin addressing the question of salience for both in-groups and out-groups. Economic competition, or some other form of social conflict between groups, tends to make those groups relevant to each other for the purposes of social comparison. When one group exploits another, the subordinate group becomes a salient out-group for the dominant one. Cultural and economic change can make new groups salient, both as in-groups and as out-groups. The institution of a slave-based economy in the Americas, for example, ensured that in later years racial groups would become one of the most basic determinants of in-group identification and out-group saliency in the United States. In Chapter 5, Herek discusses some of the economic and social changes that made socioerotic identities the basis of important social categories and led to the stigmatization of nonheterosexual identities. These changes, along with the cultural linkage of socioerotic identities to gender roles (which resulted in the stereotyping of gay men and lesbians as having cross-gender characteristics), have resulted in gay people being generally held in low regard by society. This, in turn, has made them one of the principal out-groups in the United States today.

In contrast to societal-level theories, individual-level explanations of prejudice place the source within the individual (Adorno, Frenkel-Brunswick, Levinson, & Sanford, 1950; Aronson, 1980; Berkowitz, 1969; Brown, 1988). Whereas societal factors determine the general saliency of various groups as in-groups or out-groups, individual factors frequently determine whether or not an in-group member will use social comparison to boost self-esteem and will influence the degree to which an individual identifies with an in-group. Factors that prevent or undermine the formation of a personal sense of achievement (such as unemployment, youth, or some internal conflict) can lower self-esteem, frequently increasing the strength of identification with the in-group. As the result of psychological conflicts arising from doubts about one's own sexuality, for example, gay men and lesbians can be experienced as not only a particularly salient out-group but also a particularly threatening one. In Chapter 9, Herek suggests that some young males may seek to affirm their own masculinity by denying any nonheterosexual aspects of their socioerotic identity; their internal conflicts are externalized onto gays and lesbians in the form of violent attacks. This approach also helps to account for the young age of many gay-bashers.

IMPLICATIONS OF SOCIAL IDENTITY
THEORY

Despite its shortcomings, social identity theory shows great promise for understanding hate-motivated violence in general

and anti-gay violence in particular. It helps to explain the cognitive, motivational, and sociocultural aspects of this problem, especially when considered in conjunction with traditional approaches
to studying prejudice. Perhaps most important is that it suggests
several strategies for preventing anti-gay violence.

One strategy, aimed at deterring such crime, is to increase the
cost of gay-bashing to the perpetrator relative to its benefits. As
McDevitt (1989) pointed out, the return to offenders in hate crimes
already is relatively limited. The self-esteem they gain is fleeting
because the action does nothing to address the source of their low
self-esteem. If perpetrators believe that the criminal justice system
will take a strong stance against such crimes, the potential costs of
gay-bashing may outweigh its ephemeral gains. Thus the incidence
of hate crime might be reduced by dramatically increasing the penalties associated with it and by widely publicizing the commitment
of law enforcement agencies to pursuing and prosecuting gay-
bashers. This approach also might be effective because it would
convince perpetrators that they would be prosecuted and labeled
as criminals for engaging in hate crimes. For the many gay-bashers
who do not see themselves as "deviant" or "criminal" (e.g., see
Weissman, Chapter 10), such a possibility might be too much of a
threat to their self-concept.

A relevant strategy in this regard has been proposed by the
Los Angeles Police Department[3] and approved for implementation by the Los Angeles Mayor's Office. It entails the use of a
highly publicized reward system. An information hot line would
be established whereby someone calling in with any information
about people committing hate crimes would receive a reward
(tentatively set at $500) even if that information did not lead to
arrest and conviction. Although it is untested, this proposal
seems particularly promising because it strikes directly at the social nature of hate crimes: The very individuals who otherwise
would provide affirmation of the perpetrator's self-worth are
transformed into potential betrayers.

A second preventive strategy suggested by social identity theory is to design interventions to promote the self-esteem of those
groups who are identified as being "at risk" of becoming gay-
bashers. Rosenberg, Schooler, and Schoenbach (1989, p. 1016)
cautioned that we must better understand "the causal connections between self-esteem and the sociological and psychological

phenomena to which it is empirically and conceptually related" before implementing broad social policies designed to boost self-esteem as a means of preventing social problems. Although this is a valid warning, empirical evidence appears to warrant such interventions. Rosenberg and his colleagues (1989) themselves found a positive correlation between low self-esteem and delinquency in adolescents, indicating that promoting adolescent self-esteem might indeed help to reduce the incidence of gay-bashing. Given the youth of many perpetrators, such interventions logically should start with the school system; however, interventions to change adolescents' self-conceptions need to be systemwide, especially for minorities (Spencer & Markstrom-Adams, 1990). One strategy of particular importance for promoting minority self-esteem is to provide minority adolescents with a positive affirmation of their group identity, because group pride is positively related to self-esteem (Hughes & Demo, 1989; Spencer & Markstrom-Adams, 1990). Ideally, that affirmation should not occur at the cost of denigrating other groups.

Perhaps the most challenging preventive strategy is to eliminate gay men and lesbians as a negative out-group for heterosexuals by changing negative perceptions of them in our society. Although discussion of the difficulties of and means for changing intergroup stereotypes is beyond the scope of this chapter (see Herek, 1991; Stephan, 1985), the important point to be made here is that such change *can* be achieved. As one of Weissman's (Chapter 10) gay-bashers said, "Before, all I had were stereotypes; now I've got more understanding, but I still have a long way to go."

Such change is necessary if the problem is to be eliminated rather than merely suppressed. An analogy can be drawn to the fight against AIDS. Although treatments (such as AZT) for symptoms are important for combating the epidemic, the problem will not go away until a cure is found for the disease; people with AIDS will still die. Similarly, no matter what the effectiveness may be of measures aimed at responding to anti-gay violence, gays and lesbians will still be victimized until the root cause is addressed.

NOTES

1. *Anti-gay* and *gay-bashing* are used in this chapter to refer to violence directed at both gay men and lesbians.
2. The incident described here was reported to the Gay and Lesbian Community Services Center of Los Angeles on the day after the attack.
3. This strategy was described by Chief Frankel of the LAPD, Valley Division, at a hate-crime intake training session sponsored by the Los Angeles City Commission on Human Relations on October 31, 1990.

REFERENCES

Adorno, T. W., Frenkel-Brunswick, E., Levinson, D. J., & Sanford, R. (1950). *The authoritarian personality*. New York: Harper.
Allport, G. W. (1954). *The nature of prejudice*. Cambridge, MA: Addison-Wesley.
Aronson, E. (1980). *The social animal* (3rd ed.). San Francisco: Freeman.
Berkowitz, L. (1969). *Roots of aggression: A re-examination of the frustration-aggression hypothesis*. New York: Atherton.
Brown, R. (1988). *Group processes*. New York: Basil Blackwell.
Cox, O. (1948). *Caste, class, and race*. Garden City, NJ: Doubleday.
Dovidio, J. F., & Gaertner, S. L. (1986). Prejudice, discrimination, and racism: Historical trends and contemporary approaches. In J. F. Dovidio & S. L. Gaertner (Eds.), *Prejudice, discrimination, and racism* (pp. 1-34). Orlando, FL: Academic Press.
Gecas, V., & Seff, M. A. (1990). Social class and self-esteem: Psychological centrality, compensation, and the relative effects of work and home. *Social Psychology Quarterly, 52*, 165-173.
Hamilton, D. L., & Trolier, T. K. (1986). Stereotypes and stereotyping: An overview of the cognitive approach. In J. F. Dovidio & S. L. Gaertner (Eds.), *Prejudice, discrimination, and racism* (pp. 127-164). Orlando, FL: Academic Press.
Herek, G. M. (1991). Stigma, prejudice, and violence against lesbians and gay men. In J. Gonsiorek & J. Weinrich (Eds.), *Homosexuality: Research findings for public policy* (pp. 60-80). Newbury Park, CA: Sage.
Hughes, M., & Demo, D. H. (1989). Self-perceptions of Black Americans: Self-esteem and personal efficacy. *American Journal of Sociology, 95*, 132-159.
Lemyre, L., & Smith, P. M. (1985). Intergroup discrimination and self-esteem in the minimal group paradigm. *Journal of Personality and Social Psychology, 49*, 660-670.
McDevitt, J. (1989, November). *The study of the character of civil rights crimes in Massachusetts (1983-1987)*. Paper presented at the meeting of the American Society of Criminology, Reno, NV.
Rosenberg, M., Schooler, C., & Schoenbach, C. (1989). Self-esteem and adolescent problems: Modeling reciprocal effects. *American Sociological Review, 54*, 1004-1018.

Sears, D. O. (1988). Symbolic racism. In P. A. Katz & D. A. Taylor (Eds.), *Eliminating racism: Profiles in controversy* (pp. 53-85). New York: Plenum.

Spencer, M. B., & Markstrom-Adams, C. (1990). Identity processes among racial and ethnic minority children in America. *Child Development, 61,* 290-310.

Stephan, W. G. (1985). Intergroup relations. In G. Lindzey & E. Aronson (Eds.), *The handbook of social psychology* (3rd ed., pp. 599-658). New York: Random House.

Tajfel, H., & Turner, J. C. (1986). The social identity theory of intergroup behavior. In S. Worchel & W. G. Austin (Eds.), *Psychology of intergroup relations* (pp. 7-24). Chicago: Nelson-Hall.

van Dijk, T. A. (1987). *Communicating racism: Ethnic prejudice in thought and talk.* Newbury Park, CA: Sage.

Wiltfang, G. L., & Scarbecz, M. (1990). Social class and adolescents: Another look. *Social Psychology Quarterly, 53,* 174-183.

12

The Gay-Bashers

MICHAEL COLLINS

His name is Matt. He lives in the Valley and works as a mechanic. I was thinking of him as I climbed the stairs of the dingy apartment building in Glendale, one of those run-down box-type structures from the '60s, this one painted pukish orange. A true low-life, this Matt, he claims his hobby is "fag-bashing." He talks this way: "So this queer is talking and then he puts his hand on my thigh. He really freaked me out and I felt sick. I reached over the back of my seat, grabbed my baseball bat and cuffed him." This is Matt talking to me about a year ago. "As soon as I did, I realized that these guys are pervert degenerates. He's sitting there whining and crying just because a little blood is coming out of his head, so I reached across him, opened the door and pushed him out on the pavement. I wanged the fucking shit out of him and I'm not ashamed of it."

Now, with a surge of attacks on gays in Los Angeles in recent weeks, I'm trying to find out whether Matt and his friends are some of the men behind the bats and clubs being wielded in Hollywood, West Hollywood, and Silver Lake.

A man whose face I can't see is watching me from a window above as I go up the stairs. The apartment door opens and a rush

SOURCE: Reprinted by permission from the L.A. Weekly (1988, August 26), pp. 16-17, 20, 22.

of raging skinhead music washes over me. A painfully thin man in his 30s ushers me into a dimly lighted room. The music blasting at me is the neo-fascist rant of the British music group Skrewdriver's "Smash the IRA!" The thin man says, "We thought you'd appreciate that!"— a reference to past articles I'd written on Northern Ireland.

The man introduces himself as "Cap." He and his friends have agreed to talk to me because of Matt's assurances that I would protect their identities, as I had Matt's when I interviewed him last year. Matt has told Cap that I was a "right guy."

Cap motions to the group of seven other men behind him, who resemble a legion of equally disaffected younger Matts, a mini-army of self-professed or would-be bashers, mostly in their early 20s. We stare at each other for a moment. Having a symbol of the hated liberal media and a possible patsy for manipulation before them leaves them momentarily motionless and unsure of what to do.

We're introduced. These guys sport names like "Swat" and "D.H." (Designated Hitter). What at this point do I know about them? That they call themselves the Blue Boys. That they claim to roam the streets of Los Angeles' gay and lesbian neighborhoods seeking out "queers." That—or so Matt had informed me—they met at a local softball league in the San Fernando Valley two years ago. That the "club's" hard-core triumvirate includes an ex-Grateful Deadhead (Swat), a UCLA geology major dropout (D.H.), and Cap, who describes himself as a "pool-maintenance technician." Cap, Swat, and D.H. have organized our meeting to show me that there is "community support" for their malevolent endeavors, as well as to indoctrinate a new batch of young, white hoods. The five younger guys with them represent both the "community support" and the inductees.

The group around me doesn't fit the police profile of late-model gay-bashers. They aren't skinhead punks or Latino gang-bangers. They look like working-class yahoos, just this side of the KKK. To some degree they represent the latest misbegotten wave of right-wing hooliganism that has swept across America, reinforced by the wave of skinhead racism from Britain, embracing faded racist values and an old KKK-like indifference to the moral insanity of brute force, which is worshiped more than is intelligence. The Blue Boys may not be skinheads but are as ugly as any of the new rock & roll bad boys.

The apartment we're in is your basic beerhead single man's dive. There is a cheesed-out sofa and some beat-up chairs. A Formica table stands in one corner. The room is littered with pool-maintenance equipment from Cap's job and smells of chemicals. There are lots of socks and some Nazi and Klan memorabilia, lending an acid-crash-pad air. A cheap computer with broken keys sits in one corner.

We settle into conversational positions. Swat, a huge 30ish man with a bloated beer-belly, begins explaining, in response to my question, what "Blue" is about. "Blue is an identification color, like with the gangs," he says in a robotic tone. "We're not Crips or anything like that. We are white people. White people aren't these niggers and spics running around shooting each other or selling crack. We are out on the streets fighting for everyone's rights."

On the wall by a book shelf is a "Statement of Principals" [sic]. It is cheaply framed. I am informed that it has been signed in blood by at least eight members of the Blue squad. It reads:

1. We must reclaim the lives of our men and children from queerus Americanus.
2. Fairy-man is the inverse of true man and must be stomped.
3. That the active protection of these Holy Principals [sic] is invested in the sacred order of the Boys Blue.

I don't know whether to laugh at the absurdity of it or be outraged. But soon enough I get an answer as Cap, fondling a brand-new blue baseball bat, begins prattling to the mesmerized gang. Whether for my benefit or theirs, his tirade creates a surprisingly Mansonesque aura that suffuses the apartment. Cap's charges seem mesmerized. "We're not killing people, we're *maiming* them," Cap intones. "We're giving them a message *not* to go out there and spread their diseases. They should be quarantined, isolated." The young initiates stare vacantly back at him.

"The Blue Boys are *real* men searching for real solutions. We can't expect help from nobody but ourselves when it comes to cleaning the streets of the faggot and dyke scum. I mean, they had *queers* with AIDS sitting on the platform at the Democratic Convention. We're looking at a possible four years of homosexuals invading the White House! This is a serious problem here, and we aren't just going to sit back and watch the poisoning of America."

The other Blue Boys smile and "high-five" each other, yet are careful not to interrupt. Cap works himself into even more of a lather. "We appreciate this disease that has come down which has rained upon the fags [that] they rain upon themselves, yet we're [called] the homophobics. We don't want this plague that's been visited upon the planet. We just want it to finish its job that it hasn't been doing fast enough."

As surreal as this talk is, Cap is good at this stuff, modulating his tirade as effectively as the slickest TV preacher. He is really into it now, making it personal. "The first time is addictive. Then you get back [and] you think, what did I do? I cleaned up and I had a good time doing it. You know what, we're going to go back doing it because it felt so fucking good."

I glance at the "Hitler Is Alive!" clippings on the wall and wonder how seriously to take Cap, then I notice another posted clipping that says "Hitler Was a Woman." The room, I begin to see, is full of paradoxes. Next to an authentic "Fiery Summons" pamphlet from the Ku Klux Klan, for example, is a garish facsimile of Gainsborough's dainty *Blue Boy*. It seems to hang reverently in the corner. A Dodger baseball schedule is stuck in the picture's frame (the Dodger color is blue). Later, when I get the chance, I point out to Cap the irony of the choice of color—"Blue Boys" is a term usually reserved for men involved in homosexual pornography—and of the suggestively sexual painting, a favorite of older gays. Cap explodes, "That's a theory handed down by the fag culture we're growing up in, that everyone is a fag," he rants at me, missing the point. "Fags call each other fags, and a fag thinks that everyone is a fag. I tell you, [the] Blue Boys are male. We're heteros. We have girlfriends and wives. We're out there fucking chicks every night and we have nothing to do with any fag shit. So don't call me a fag or lay a fag trip on me, or we'll know where you're at."

Silence and stares at me from the other he-men. Defusing the situation, D.H. slips on a videotape of *The Many Faces of Death*. On the TV screen now appear nauseating scenes of people and animals being slaughtered in inconceivable ways. To my hosts this is infinitely more entertaining than even *The Morton Downey Jr. Show*, and the gleeful hoots from them all are typical of what Downey's crowd normally musters.

While this Riefenstahlish moment takes place, I wander over to
Cap's battered drafting table, on which lies an assortment of homophobic cartoons. Cap follows, explaining to me that he once dab-
bled in the arts. The sketches reveal a profoundly disturbed man.
One drawing shows the Grim Reaper bursting out of the buns of a
man. The caption reads, "Woe to the Queer to whom I appear, you
bugger and blow, and I reap . . . what you sow!"

By now the multimedia deluge of hate has me woozy (or is it the
pool chemicals?), and I have to fight back feelings of repulsion. I find
myself meditating on Cap's earlier and self-serving description of the
group: just red-blooded Americans "into" sports and chicks.

In the days that followed, as I gathered information about
gay-bashing in L.A., the Southland and the country, I had a lot
of occasion to reflect on the Blue Boys and the credibility of the
story they told me that night. After meeting through the softball
league two years ago, and finding they had a mutual interest in
the Dodgers' "Big Blue Wrecking Crew" and in hating homosexuals, Cap, Swat, and D.H. took to wearing blue baseball jackets, to worshiping the Dodgers as a group and—they
claimed—to terrorizing gays, usually disguised in eerie translu-
cent masks reminiscent of the Droogs in *A Clockwork Orange*.
Cap had boasted of their favorite weaponry—the blue bats. "We
chose the blue baseball bats because it's the color of the boy. The
man is one gender. He is not female. It is male. There is no confusion. Blue is the color of men, and that's the color that men use
to defeat the anti-male, which is the queer."

The group claimed (though they refused to give me precise
details—this, they said, to protect themselves from the law) that
they had initiated a campaign of savagery in the streets of Silver
Lake, Hollywood, and West Hollywood. Waiting at night along
darkened streets and stairways, they said, they stake out local
gay and lesbian bars, follow men and women home and record
surveillance information in one of their members' computer.
Later, they asserted, they would return and attack a targeted homosexual, threatening swift and extreme retribution against
anyone who calls the police. (Was this the product of Cap's
comic-book mentality?) Often, they said, they just assault an
easy mark rather than a predetermined target.

After the others had left that evening, filtering out in twos and
threes, Cap had expanded on the group's story. "We're doing

the work of Batman or some other masked avenger," Cap rationalized. "We're just doing 'social work'—that's what I call it. The
bat is a very efficacious way of getting your point across. It's
like when you hit a home run at a stadium—you get a message
across—and I think that's what people are doing sitting at home
reading about these so-called crimes. I think they are cheering it
on. One less faggot, what does that mean to the world?"

Would any new legislation against bashing have any effect on
these weeds blowing across Glendale into the gay neighborhoods
of Silver Lake and West Hollywood? Cap didn't think so. "All
these chumps passing this pro-fag stuff don't realize that we mean
business. They think that arresting us with a bat in hand next to
some butt-fucker spitting up teeth in the gutter will stop us because they can prove we're bashers and we'll get more jail time because it's a hate crime . . . but how are they going to prove that
some queer-bar was *burnt* down because the owner was a faggot?"

Vigilante groups and gay squads don't seem to faze the Blue
Boys either. The Guardian Angels' patrol of 1987 helped smooth
relations between Latino gangs and the burgeoning gay community in Silver Lake, but the watch soon disbanded and no one
has stepped in to fill the void, leaving anti-basher patrolling to
the understaffed LAPD. Cap dismissed the Guardian Angels
with his trademark racism: "All these niggers want is to be on
the cover of some magazine. They're nowhere to be found when
the real pounding begins."

I still wondered how much of this was chest-thumping. Had
Cap and the Blue Boys ever even hit anyone, or was the whole
thing a blustery show for their own diversion and egos? Had I
met the blowhard Morton Downey side of late-model American
fascism, or the real thing? Should I write about the Blue Boys as
the comic-book side of latent anti-gay sensibilities, metaphors
for the reactionary mind set behind violence against gays, or as
perpetrators of the violence itself? These doubts lingered for
awhile into my research, with me leaning toward the conclusion
that the Blue Boys were frauds. Then I learned from one of the
gay activist groups that on a Saturday night in July, three blue-
bat wielding men had stopped a man on a deserted Silver Lake
street; said, "Got AIDS yet, faggot?" and went to work on him
with bats. He suffered broken ribs and his teeth were knocked
out. The LAPD Rampart Division could not confirm this assault,

but I had already discovered that this was meaningless. Many gay-bashing incidents are unreported or are reported to the gay organizations and not the police, out of fear by the victims of disclosure of their identities, and of police harassment. Also, many officials of the LAPD, though not recently of the Sheriff's Department in West Hollywood, distinctly seem to have a policy of playing down "gay-bashings," this apparently to avoid criticism that the force is not doing enough by way of preventative patrolling. Some gay bashings reported in LAPD-patrolled areas have been described by detectives as "assault and batteries" without any homophobic motivations.

Then two weeks ago four "kids from deep suburbia" were picked up in West Hollywood for "menacing" a gay man. One of them carried a baseball bat. "Whoa! A . . . blue aluminum bat!" exclaimed Lt. Dan Mauro when interviewed for this article. "I will run right back and tell the detective assigned to this case that he probably needs to know that [about the Blue Boys]." Was the blue bat coincidence? Were the kids part of Cap's crowd? Or had blue bats already become fashionable in the yahoo world, without even the yahoos knowing why? One thing for sure: Cap would be pleased.

Sensing my contempt for him, Cap had sputtered, as I was leaving, a sort of justification. "They don't talk about the legality of going about in public infecting people with a fatal disease, now do they? These queers fucking deserve it. They are going around spreading their disease wherever they want under the rules of privacy given them by this fraudulent Constitution, with niggers in the Supreme Court saying what we can do and what we cannot do. This nation was built by white people for white people and is not to be confused with a bunch of faggots and niggers taking over." He sounded like a babbling speed freak.

During a recent 10-week period, April 16 to June 30, 33 assaults on gays and lesbians here were recorded by the Gay and Lesbian Community Services Center in Hollywood. It is axiomatic among gay activists that only a minute percentage of attacks are actually reported. Although not new to L.A., gay-bashing has taken on new and dangerous forms. In April two gay men were stabbed by bashers using anti-gay language outside a bar in Silver Lake. Both were seriously injured and refused hospitalization. On June 3, a group of four homosexual pedestrians in

West Hollywood were attacked by a gang calling themselves the AFL (Anti-Fags and Lesbians), who claimed to be "straights" protecting themselves against gays. They said "faggots" have no rights under the law and said they would "kill faggots and nothing would happen to them."

Three gay people have been beaten with tire irons on three separate occasions by unidentified bashers at the corner of Fairfax and Santa Monica Boulevards. A few weeks ago, in that same area at 2:30 a.m., two nongay rockers, Tim Ferris of the band Celebrity Skin and his roadie friend Gustavo X, were called "faggots" by some young men riding in two lowrider minitrucks with camper shelves, this even though the pair were accompanied by several women. Both trucks then stopped and eight or nine men—definitely not Blue Boys, as they were mostly black—climbed out and, according to one of the women, "just started hitting people" with long, heavy police-type flashlights. One of the victims got a plate number of the truck, which police traced to a Long Beach man known to be a member of a minitruck gang. A year ago *L.A. Weekly's* Gay Writes columnist, Doug Sadownick, was clubbed near the paper's Silver Lake offices by a bat-wielding assailant seemingly bent on killing him. And the *Los Angeles Times* last week reported an upsurge in gay-bashing by skinheads in Laguna Beach. (Also last week, a gay graphics designer, Jay Angel, was murdered on the street near a Silver Lake bar, the Detour. Typically, LAPD detectives have been claiming that the murder was not a gay-bashing, despite eyewitness evidence to the contrary).

Betty, a counselor at Open Quest Crisis Line, in operation since 1978 out of a Hollywood office, has fielded reports of attacks on homosexuals in L.A. in which the victims were grievously injured by men brandishing baseball bats and chains. However, she notes that the perpetrators of these incidents seem to come from a wide range of backgrounds and cannot be identified as Blue Boys. She also reports that two groups of skinheads wearing leather jackets emblazoned with the initials UAG (United Against Gays) and UAF (United Against Faggots) have been cruising Santa Monica Boulevard beating up gays. Vehicle licenses weren't taken by the victims due to the brutality and quickness of the attacks. According to eyewitnesses, a car being driven by an older man, around 60, has been stopping along

Santa Monica Boulevard as skinheads with chains and clubs jump out and assault their victims.

These incidents indicate an obvious pattern to the most serious gay-bashings here. Usually the victims are accosted on the streets by several assailants, who tend either to be hiding in whatever cover is available, or to leap out of vehicles. Bats and clubs are common weapons, though chains have been appearing recently. There is very seldom any warning—the victims are truly waylaid. The assailants tend to be in their 20s and, the Blue Boys notwithstanding, to come from every kind of ethnic background except Asian. Geographically, the assailants tend to issue from two distinct groups: the suburbs, including the deep reaches of both valleys and of Orange County, or from the inner city, meaning primarily gang members. Economically, these are mostly lower-class and lower-middle-class youths, though police have nabbed some middle-class suburban brats out on a lark, as if these were the '50s and early '60s.

The victims are usually white professionals. Many suffer serious trauma for some time afterward, including fear of public places. Commonly, as noted, they do not report the assaults to the police out of fear of public exposure and distaste for having to deal with hostile, indifferent, or insensitive police officers. Typically, the police, both LAPD and, until very recently, the sheriffs, treat these assaults as ordinary street crimes, quite deliberately—often rudely, some victims have said—debunking the notion that "gay-bashing" is involved, this to protect their departments from criticism and from pressure by the gay community.

A not uncommon bashing that foreshadowed the severe recent outbreak of attacks occurred in West Hollywood in August 1985. One of the victims was Gary Yettner, a vice president in the entertainment industry. Yettner is one of a few victims willing to talk. Walking with his lover, as they rounded a street corner adjacent to a large apartment complex, a group of eight bashers, each with a baseball bat, leaped from the bushes. "One mashed my friend in the face and broke his nose. Another hit me in the back of my head and it took 12 stitches to sew up the wounds," Yettner recalls. Fortunately, both men were in excellent physical shape. Yettner was able to block repeated blows with his forearm, and his roommate managed through quick footwork to evade others. At one point, down on the ground and fending off the bats, Yettner says, he managed to hurt one of the assailants. This gave him the opportunity to spring up and break through the pack and to run a distance. The assailants eventually fled in a pickup truck.

Battered and bleeding, the two men walked in a daze toward their nearby apartment. Units from the fire department and an ambulance arrived within minutes of their call and took the pair to the hospital. Only then, Yettner says, did he realize that he had wet himself during the attack, out of the fear that "they were going to kill me." There were no witnesses to the incident, he recalls, and West Hollywood sheriffs were "worthless. They tried to treat the whole thing as a robbery."

The suffering didn't end that night. Besides lost work and wages, Yettner's roommate, lacking health insurance, was overwhelmed by medical bills. Eventually, after struggling with a state bureaucracy for victims of violent crimes, which produces more traumatization, Yettner says, they received some payments to offset the bills. Some emotional scars remain three years later. "It's made me very paranoid about just walking the street," Yettner says. "I don't walk anymore. You just can't do it with this going on. It's just such a sick thing."

SURVIVOR'S STORY

Kathleen Sarris

In June of 1982, I appeared in a press conference as the representative of Justice, Inc [of Indianapolis, IN]. The news conference
was covered by all print and television media. The gay/lesbian
community was embroiled in conflict and controversy with members of several right-wing ministries because Justice, Inc., had
thwarted attempts by these individuals to block several of our
speaking engagements and our annual Brunch. The press conference was convened to delineate our success over the past year,
outline our future plans, and to counter the inflammatory statements being made about our community.

Within 24 hours of the aforementioned press conference, I began receiving threatening telephone calls and letters. The phone
calls and letters were religious in nature; they spoke of acting in
the name of God or Jesus and exacting retribution. They also
spoke of my leading people to become sodomites, and that this
person would put an end to my work. My initial response was
that it was an annoying hoax, and it would die down and go
away. Instead, the letters and telephone calls continued with
systematic regularity. I decided to move out of my home; I
moved in with a friend, and fellow Justice Board member, John
Tofaute. Within days, the letters and phone calls resumed. It
was very apparent that I was being tracked. John decided that I
needed help from the police. We took the most recent letter with
us and went to talk with the Indianapolis police. Their response

SOURCE: Excerpted from *Anti-Gay Violence* (Hearing before the Subcommittee on Criminal Justice of the Committee on the Judiciary, House
of Representatives, 99th Congress, Second Session on Anti-Gay Violence;
October 9, 1986; pp. 164-165). Washington, DC: Government Printing
Office, Serial No. 132.

was there was nothing they could do, and if I couldn't stand the heat, I should get out of the kitchen! After a couple of weeks, the letters and phone calls stopped. I assumed the person got tired of playing the game.

Then, approximately 2 weeks after the letters stopped, I was leaving my office and as I turned to lock the door, I felt the barrel of a gun in the back of my head. He pushed me back into the reception area. For the next three hours, he beat me with his fists, his gun, and his belt. I was sexually molested and, ultimately, I was raped. Throughout the assault, he talked about how he was acting for God; that what he was doing to me was God's revenge on me because I was a "queer" and getting rid of me would save children and put an end to the movement in Indiana.

At the end of his torture, he had me stand up; I was facing the desk in the reception area, and he again put his gun to the back of my head. I heard him draw back the hammer, and the chamber clicked into position. It was at that point it occurred to me that I had nothing to lose. I picked up an object from the desk and swung around and hit him in the head. While he was stunned, I kicked him and he lost the gun. We struggled for about 10 minutes until he finally knocked me unconscious. When I regained consciousness, about an hour later, he was gone. I called the Marion County Sheriff's department and then a friend. The deputies could not find the gun. They assumed that my attacker thought he had killed me with a blow to the head. One of the deputies took me to the hospital where I was met by detectives from the Sheriff's department. I was in the Emergency room for 8 hours; I suffered a concussion, hair line fracture of my right cheek bone, dislocation of my jaw, and damage to my left knee.

While I was in the Emergency room, the detectives were able to piece together the whole scenario of the past few months. It was then that I learned the Indianapolis Police department could have attempted to get fingerprints and conducted a paper and ink analysis on the letters; also, they could have ordered a tracer on my telephone. The Indianapolis Police chose not to give me any help.

I spent 4 weeks healing physically. For several months after the attack, I gradually isolated myself by choosing to work 16 hours per day. I lost 20 pounds and refused to see friends and family.

Eventually, I learned to cope with the pain, anxiety, and confusion, but I had damaged my relationships with people and had to spend time rebuilding my life.

It has been 4 years since the assault, and the pain is still very real.

I still do not have unrestricted freedom; my significant other and I live with constant fear that it will happen again. I also live with the knowledge that because of my orientation, because I chose to exercise what I believe are my constitutional rights, my life has no value to certain people.

PART IV

SURVIVING AND RESPONDING

13

Violence and Victimization of Lesbians and Gay Men: Mental Health Consequences

LINDA GARNETS
GREGORY M. HEREK
BARRIE LEVY

Like other survivors of the violence that pervades American society, lesbian and gay male crime victims must confront the difficulties created by victimization. And, as members of a stigmatized group, lesbians and gay men face numerous psychological challenges as a consequence of society's hostility toward them. When individual victimization and societal prejudice converge in anti-gay hate crimes, lesbian and gay male survivors face additional, unique challenges. Those challenges are the principal focus of this chapter.

Because of the widespread prevalence of anti-gay prejudice in the United States (see Chapter 5) and the large number of lesbian and gay male victims of hate crimes in this country (see Chapter 18; Herek, 1989), American gay people as a group might be expected to manifest significantly higher levels of psychological distress and impairment than heterosexuals. Yet this is not the case; the lesbian and gay male community does not differ significantly in mental health from the heterosexual population (Gonsiorek, 1982, 1991). Obviously, anti-gay victimization does not inevitably lead to psychological dysfunction.

This chapter treats anti-gay victimization as creating a crisis for the survivor, with opportunities for subsequent growth as well as risks for impairment (e.g., Caplan, 1964). This conceptualization does not deny or minimize the negative consequences of victimization—both physical and psychological, immediate and long term. But neither does it relegate lesbian and gay male targets of hate crimes to passivity. Instead, it should encourage researchers and mental health practitioners to view the survivors of anti-gay victimization as active, problem-solving individuals who are potentially capable of coping with the aftermath of the attack and using the experience as an opportunity for growth.

THE PSYCHOLOGICAL AFTERMATH OF VICTIMIZATION

In addition to dealing with the physical consequences of injury and the practical aftermath of having one's possessions stolen or damaged, crime victims often experience a variety of psychological symptoms. Common behavioral and somatic reactions to victimization include sleep disturbances and nightmares, headaches, diarrhea, uncontrollable crying, agitation and restlessness, increased use of drugs, and deterioration in personal relationships (e.g., Frieze, Hymer, & Greenberg, 1984; Janoff-Bulman & Frieze, 1983a). Victimization creates psychological distress for several reasons. First, it dramatically interferes with everyday processes of denial through which people are able to feel secure and invulnerable, that "it can't happen to me" (Janoff-Bulman & Frieze, 1983b). The world suddenly seems less predictable; people seem more malevolent. Because their victimization did not result from accidental or natural forces but was intentionally perpetrated against them, survivors are likely to feel a reduction in their previous level of basic trust (Bard & Sangrey, 1979).

Second, the experience of victimization interferes with perceptions of the world as an orderly and meaningful place. Survivors often try to restore some sense of meaning and predictability by asking "Why me?" and many respond to the question with self-blame. This is not necessarily maladaptive. Blaming specific behaviors related to the victimization (*behavioral self-blame*) may constitute an effective coping strategy because it helps survivors feel a sense of control over their own lives and provides strategies for avoiding revictimization (Janoff-Bulman, 1979, 1982). In contrast, blaming one's victimization on perceived character flaws (*characterological self-blame*) is associated with low self-esteem, depression, and feelings of helplessness (Janoff-Bulman, 1979). Although behavioral self-blame may sometimes be adaptive, observers may react more negatively to victims who blame themselves than to victims who attribute their circumstances to chance factors (Coates, Wortman, & Abbey, 1979), thereby exacerbating survivors' psychological distress.

A third reason that victimization creates psychological distress is that it often leads people to question their own worth. Survivors may devalue themselves because they perceive that they have been violated and because they experience a loss of autonomy, first at the hands of the perpetrator and subsequently as they must rely on others to help them recover from the victimization (Bard & Sangrey, 1979). Survivors also may internalize the social stigma associated with being a victim. Others often react negatively to survivors, seeing them as weak or inferior, as having failed in the basic task of protecting themselves, as somehow deserving their fate (Coates et al., 1979). Such social reactions may lead survivors to feel ashamed or embarrassed at their perceived "failure."

Severe psychological responses to victimization may be of short or prolonged duration and may be immediate in their onset or delayed by years after the victimization. Severe reactions are diagnosed as Posttraumatic Stress Disorder, or PTSD (American Psychiatric Association, 1987; Frederick, 1987), indicated by the persistence of three types of symptoms for at least one month consequent to victimization: (a) persistent reexperiencing of the victimization (e.g., via memories, intrusive thoughts, dreams, or intense distress from activities or events triggering recollection of the event); (b) persistent avoidance of trauma-associated stimuli or a numbing of general responsiveness (e.g., diminished interest in significant activities, feelings of detachment from others, restricted affect, sense of foreshortened future); and (c) persistent symptoms of increased arousal (e.g., sleep disturbances, exaggerated startle response, difficulty concentrating).

The crisis following victimization is likely to create different challenges as time passes (e.g., Tsegaye-Spates, 1985). Bard and Sangrey (1979), for example, highlighted three important stages: (a) an *impact* phase, when victims typically feel vulnerable, confused, helpless, and dependent on others for even the simplest decisions; (b) a *recoil* phase, characterized by mood swings and a "waxing and waning" of fear, rage, revenge fantasies, and displacement of anger (often onto loved ones); and (c) a *reorganization* phase, when survivors assimilate their painful experience, put it into perspective, and get on with their lives. Most victims successfully negotiate these stages of recovery, although not necessarily in a linear sequence and often only after a period of several years (Sales, Baum, & Shore, 1984). The victimization is not likely ever to be entirely forgotten, however; the self can no longer be regarded as invulnerable. Survivors must nevertheless reestablish a perception of the world as not entirely threatening, as a meaningful place in which most events make sense. Additionally, they must regain self-perceptions of being worthy, strong, and autonomous (Janoff-Bulman & Frieze, 1983b).

PSYCHOLOGICAL CONSEQUENCES OF HETEROSEXIST STIGMA

In addition to the victimization for which all Americans are at risk, lesbians and gay men are targeted for attack specifically because of their sexual orientation (see Chapter 1). The psychological consequences of anti-gay hate crimes must be examined against the background of cultural heterosexism, which is an ideological system that denies, denigrates, and stigmatizes any nonheterosexual form of behavior, identity, relationship, or community (see Chapter 5). American culture is pervaded by a heterosexist ideology that simultaneously makes lesbians and gay men invisible and legitimizes hostility, discrimination, and even violence against them. Heterosexist stigma also creates two interrelated challenges that lesbians and gay men must confront in the course of their psychosocial development: overcoming internalized homophobia and coming out.

Because most children internalize society's ideology of sex and gender at an early age, gay women and men usually experience some degree of negative feeling toward themselves when they first recognize their own homosexuality in adolescence or adulthood. This sense of *internalized homophobia* often creates a "basic mistrust for one's sexual and interpersonal identity" (Stein & Cohen, 1984, p. 61) and interferes with the process of identity formation (Malyon, 1982). Coming out[1] becomes a process of reclaiming disowned or devalued parts of the self and developing an identity into which one's sexuality is well integrated (Malyon, 1982; Stein & Cohen, 1984).

In the course of coming out, most lesbians and gay men successfully overcome the threats to psychological well-being posed by heterosexism. Psychological adjustment appears to be highest among men and women who are committed to their gay identity and do not attempt to hide their homosexuality from others (Bell & Weinberg, 1978; Hammersmith & Weinberg, 1973). As with other stigmatized minorities, gay men and lesbians probably maintain self-esteem most effectively when they identify with and are integrated into the larger gay community (Crocker & Major, 1989). Conversely, people with a homosexual orientation who have not yet come out, who feel compelled to suppress their homoerotic urges, who wish that they could become heterosexual, or who are isolated from the gay community may experience significant psychological distress, including impairment of self-esteem (Bell & Weinberg, 1978; Hammersmith & Weinberg, 1973; Malyon, 1982; Weinberg & Williams, 1974; see also Hodges & Hutter, 1979). Chronically hiding one's sexual orientation can create a painful discrepancy between public and private identities (Humphreys, 1972; see also Goffman, 1963), feelings of inauthenticity, and social isolation (Goffman, 1963; Jones et al., 1984).[2]

VICTIMIZATION OF LESBIANS AND GAY MEN

Consequences for the Victim

When people are attacked because they are perceived to be gay, the consequences of victimization converge with those of societal heterosexism to create a unique set of challenges for the survivor. Perhaps most important is that the victim's homosexuality becomes directly linked to the heightened sense of vulnerability that normally follows victimization. One's homosexual orientation consequently may be experienced as a source of pain and punishment rather than of intimacy, love, and community. Internalized homophobia may reappear or be intensified. Attempts to make sense of the attack, coupled with the common need to perceive the world as a just place, may lead to feelings that one has been justifiably punished for being gay (Bard & Sangrey, 1979; Lerner, 1970). Such characterological self-blame can lead to feelings of depression and helplessness (Janoff-Bulman, 1979), even in individuals who are comfortable with their sexual orientation.

The aftermath of victimization probably is affected by the survivor's stage in the coming-out process (Cass, 1979; Troiden, 1988). Those who have come out have already faced a major threat to their self-esteem and have emerged intact and possibly stronger for the experience. Additionally, lesbians and gay men in the course of coming out may develop coping skills (i.e., a "crisis competence"; Kimmel, 1978) that they subsequently can use when new life crises occur. Coming out does not "prepare" gay men and women for subsequent victimization, but it does provide them with tools that they can use in coping: supportive social networks, community resources, and nonheterosexist interpretations of the victimization experience. Lesbian and gay male survivors who are in the later stages of coming out prior to their assault have the benefit of being able to balance their victimization experience against many other positive experiences associated with being gay.

Women and men who are still in the early stages of coming out, in contrast, are unlikely to have the requisite social support and strongly developed gay identity that can increase their psychological resilience and coping skills (Miranda & Storms, 1989). Like closeted gay men with AIDS, closeted survivors of victimization face the prospect of a double disclosure—that they are gay and that they were victimized or have AIDS—with increased risks for stigmatization (Herek & Glunt, 1988). If the survivor's homosexuality becomes known, heterosexual family members or friends may blame the victimization on it. Lacking a more positive interpretation and feeling especially vulnerable to others' influence, the survivor may well accept this characterological attribution (Bard & Sangrey, 1979) and the attendant feelings of helplessness, depression, and low self-esteem. If closeted survivors can avoid public disclosure of their sexual orientation in such a potentially hostile setting as a police station, they are likely not to report the victimization. They may even minimize or deny its impact to themselves, a tactic that can intensify and delay the resolution of psychological and physical problems (Anderson, 1982; Koss & Burkhart, 1989; Myers, 1989).

Sexual Assault

Anti-gay sexual assault may give rise to unique problems in addition to the reactions described above. Lesbians may be directly targeted for sexual assault by anti-gay attackers or raped "opportunistically" (i.e., when the perpetrator of another crime inadvertently discovers that his victim is a lesbian).[3] Rapists often verbalize the view that lesbians are "open targets" and deserve punishment because they are not under the protection of a man. Because many lesbians are not accustomed to feeling dependent on or vulnerable around men, a sexual attack motivated by male rage at their life-style constitutes a major assault upon their general sense of safety, independence, and well-being. Any physiological response by the victim during the assault or the decision not to resist can raise doubts later regarding her complicity or her sexuality. Such doubts may be exacerbated by reactions from significant others when she describes details of or feelings about the victimization experience.

In addition to the humiliation and degradation that are common components of all sexual victimization, anti-lesbian rape may also include attempts by the perpetrator to degrade lesbian sexuality. For example, a lesbian couple sought counseling from one of the authors (Levy) after they were forced at gunpoint to engage in sexual behaviors together, then raped. When behaviors that formerly were expressions of love become associated with humiliation, violence, and victimization, lesbian partners can experience serious difficulty redefining their sexuality positively.

Male-male sexual assault is largely an invisible problem in contemporary American society, often assumed to occur only in prisons and similar settings. The few reports that have been published, however, indicate that it is a serious problem outside of institutions (Anderson, 1982; Kaufman, DiVasto, Jackson,

Voorhees, & Christy, 1980; Myers, 1989). As with rape of females by males, male-male rape is a crime of violence—often anti-gay violence—rather than a crime of sexuality (Anderson, 1982; Groth & Burgess, 1980; Kaufman et al., 1980). Contrary to popular stereotypes, the perpetrators of male rape often identify themselves as heterosexual (Groth & Burgess, 1980). Whereas the feminist movement has made important gains in sensitizing law enforcement personnel, caregivers, and society at large to the problems faced by female rape survivors, male rape survivors remain hidden and isolated. Although victims of male-male rape can be either heterosexual or gay, we focus here on the special mental health consequences for gay men.

Male gender role socialization creates distinct problems for gay male rape survivors. Because most men have internalized the societal belief that sexual assault of men is beyond the realm of possibility, the male victim's sudden confrontation with "his own vulnerability, helplessness, and dependence on the mercy of others" can be devastating (Anderson, 1982, p. 150). Men may have trouble accepting their rape experience as real, not only because it happened to them but because it happened at all. This may interfere with their subsequent recovery. If internalized homophobia resurfaces or is intensified, gay male survivors may interpret the rape as punishment for their sexual orientation, with all of the attendant problems detailed above. If a man did not resist, he may later blame himself and wonder whether he somehow was complicitous in the rape. Self-doubts are especially likely to follow when the assailant successfully forces the victim to ejaculate in the course of the assault (Groth & Burgess, 1980). The victim may retrospectively confuse ejaculation with orgasm and may interpret his own physiological response as a sign of personal consent to the rape. Paralleling the experience of some lesbian rape victims, gay men may experience their sexual assault as an attempt to degrade gay male sexuality, which may later give rise to fearful or aversive feelings associated with their normal sexual behavior.

Words Can Never Hurt Me?
Consequences of Verbal Victimization

Most discussions of anti-gay hate crimes focus on physical and sexual assaults. Yet verbal harassment and intimidation are the most common forms of victimization of lesbians and gay men; most survey respondents report that they have been the target of anti-gay verbal abuse (see Chapter 1). Although researchers, practitioners, and policymakers alike may be tempted to recall the children's chant, "Sticks and stones may break my bones," the potentially damaging effects of "mere" words should not be minimized.

Most people in American society find epithets such as *nigger* and *kike* to be offensive precisely because they convey raw hatred and prejudice. Such words have been used historically by oppressors to remind the oppressed of their subordinate status (Unger, 1979). Similar levels of hatred are conveyed by words such as *faggot, dyke,* and *queer* and the threats of violence (implicit and explicit) that accompany them. Such anti-gay verbal abuse constitutes a symbolic form of violence and a routine reminder of the ever-present threat of physical assault. Its "cost" to the perpetrator in time, energy, and risk is minimal, yet it reinforces the target's sense of being an outsider in American society, a member of a disliked and devalued minority, and a socially acceptable target for violence.

Like hate-motivated physical violence, anti-gay verbal assault challenges the victim's routine sense of security and invulnerability, making the world seem more malevolent and less predictable. The psychological effects of verbal abuse may be as severe as those following physical assaults and possibly more insidious because victims of verbal abuse may find its "psychic scars" more difficult to identify than physical wounds. It affects how one feels about oneself without a physical injury to which to attribute the feelings. Two of us (Garnets and Levy) have observed clinically that victims often minimize the impact of a hate-motivated verbal attack and subsequently do not understand the reason for their feelings of fear or self-hatred.

Because verbal abuse may be experienced as a near encounter with violence, it can seriously restrict day-to-day behaviors of lesbians and gay men. Most gay respondents to victimization surveys indicate that their public behavior is affected by their fear of physical attack (see Chapter 1). Verbal harassment and intimidation reinforce this climate of fear. Not knowing whether a specific instance of verbal harassment is likely to culminate in physical violence, many gay women and men probably follow the adaptive strategy of avoiding possible occasions of verbal abuse just as they avoid potential assault situations. Consequently, their day-to-day behaviors are restricted, and they lose considerable control over their lives. Victims who are more closeted may experience heterosexist verbal abuse as an involuntary public disclosure of their sexual orientation. They may respond by withdrawing even further into the closet.

Consequences of Victimization for Others

In the aftermath of anti-gay violence, victims turn to significant others for social support. A lover, family, and friends can greatly enhance a survivor's coping resources (Bard & Sangrey, 1979). Yet these others also must deal with the victimization experience. In cases of murder, they must cope with physical loss of the victim. With other crimes, they must deal with the survivor's immediate reactions (including her or his displaced feelings of anger). They must make sense of the event for themselves and deal with their own self-blame. Same-sex partners are at special risk for secondary victimization (see Chapter 18) as they assist the survivor in seeking services. They may be denied access to hospital visitation, for example, because they are not considered "immediate family." They are likely not to be eligible for or recognized by social workers or victim assistance agencies. Indeed, much of the postattack experience may serve to remind a gay couple that the larger society is hostile to them as gay people.

In addition to the victim's significant others, the entire gay community is victimized by anti-gay assaults. Hate crimes create a climate of fear that pressures lesbians and gay men to hide their sexual orientation. To reduce their own feelings of vulnerability, some members of the community are likely to blame the victims of violence, often focusing on "obvious" behavior, gestures, or clothing. Such victim-blaming reinforces key aspects of the cultural ideology of heterosexism, such as the prescription that men and women should conform to highly restrictive norms of gender-appropriate behavior[4] and the belief that being gay is wrong and deserves punishment (see Chapter 5). Victim-blaming also may discourage observers from taking precautions for reducing their risk of victimization—both personal precautions, such as taking a self-defense class, and community precautions, such as organizing neighborhood street patrols.

SUGGESTIONS FOR MENTAL HEALTH PRACTITIONERS

As a crisis, anti-gay victimization creates opportunities for growth, both at the individual and the community levels. Survivors who cope successfully may infuse their lives with greater meaning or purpose than before and enjoy a strengthened sense of self-worth. They may take control of parts of their lives that they previously had not been able to manage while at the same time accepting that some events are beyond their control (Burt & Katz, 1987). They may redefine previous setbacks they experienced as the result of prejudice rather than personal failings, thereby increasing their self-esteem (e.g., Crocker & Major, 1989). Previously complacent survivors may become outraged by the injustice of their victimization and may become politically militant (e.g., Birt & Dion, 1987), with a subsequent increase in feelings of self-efficacy and empowerment. Violence may shock community members into taking collective action that channels their feelings of helplessness and anger (for an example, see Chapter 14). Perhaps the most famous example of a positive community response to victimization was the 1969 "Stonewall Rebellion," which followed a police raid on a Greenwich Village gay bar and marked the beginning of the modern movement for gay rights (e.g., D'Emilio, 1983).

Mental health practitioners can help gay male and lesbian victims of hate crimes maximize the positive aspects of their response. Before working with lesbian or gay male victims, however, professional caregivers must be aware of their own heterosexist biases and assumptions and should be familiar with current and accurate information about gay male and lesbian identity, community, and mental health concerns. Among the basic assumptions to be avoided are that a homosexual identity or life-style is negative and unhealthy, that all clients are heterosexual unless they identify themselves as gay, and that biological family members necessarily constitute a client's significant others. In reality, homosexuality is not correlated with psychopathology;

many crime victims are gay but do not choose to come out; and gay clients may define their family in terms of a same-sex lover and gay friends (Cohen & Stein, 1986; Gonsiorek, 1991; Morin & Charles, 1983). Professionals should carefully respect confidentiality concerning clients' sexual orientation. In many jurisdictions, gay people whose sexual orientation becomes known to others can lose their jobs or apartments, lose custody of their children, and even be liable to criminal prosecution (see Chapters 5, 18). Professionals who fail to understand these potentially negative consequences can themselves become secondary victimizers (e.g., by inadvertently revealing a client's sexual orientation to law enforcement personnel).

Practitioners should be aware of the different needs and experiences of gay men and lesbians from different sectors of the gay community. Although space limitations do not permit its consideration here, the mental health consequences of anti-gay victimization are likely to vary according to the survivor's race, age, and social class, among other variables.

For heuristic purposes, mental health interventions with gay male and lesbian survivors can be conceptualized according to the *impact*, *recoil*, and *recovery* phases described by Bard and Sangrey (1979). Crisis interventions are necessary in the *impact* phase, when the first concern is whether the victim is safe from further attacks and whether she or he requires immediate medical care. The focus of the crisis intervention is assessing the meaning that the victim is deriving from her or his experience, feelings about the self, and the degree to which the victimization is equated with being gay or lesbian. Additionally, the mental health professional should assess internal and external coping resources: (a) learned coping skills; (b) support networks, such as a lover, family, or friends who can assist the victim in meeting immediate needs; and (c) existing or potential involvement in gay and lesbian community networks. Previously effective coping skills usually are not adequate to deal with the shock and fear of this stage of the reaction to physical or sexual violence. Assessment will suggest to victim and practitioner alike ways to build upon previous coping resources or the need to develop new ones.

In the *recoil* phase, mental health professionals can help greatly by allowing survivors to ventilate the horror and terror that the victimization evokes. By listening empathically, the professional can give the survivor who is feeling alienated and isolated a sense of connection to another person. The therapeutic goal at this stage is to support victims as they regain their self-confidence and sense of competence and wholeness while their feelings of guilt, shame, helplessness, and embarrassment diminish.

Reducing Negative Affect

Survivors should be encouraged to feel and express anger toward the assailant(s), especially survivors who are blaming themselves or are depressed (Bard & Sangrey, 1979; Bohn, 1984). Anger can be constructively directed, for example, by encouraging involvement in activist groups organized against anti-gay violence or in self-defense classes. Intervention to prevent self-blaming and guilt feelings involves helping the survivor to review decisions made before, during, and after the assault. To combat the distorted retrospective perceptions that lead to self-blame, survivors need to remember that their decisions were based on their perceptions and knowledge *at the time of the attack*, in a life-threatening situation. The aim is for survivors to see that they responded in the best way they could under the circumstances (Levy & Brown, 1984).

Victims who manifest the symptoms of Posttraumatic Stress Disorder may benefit from recently developed strategies that aim to reexpose the survivor to the memory of the traumatic event. These strategies include systematic desensitization, flooding or implosive therapy, and stress inoculation. Reexposure is accompanied by techniques of cognitive restructuring of false assumptions about oneself and the world (e.g., self-blame and the view of the world as malevolent; Fairbank, Gross, & Keane, 1983; Frank et al., 1988; Steketee & Foa, 1987). The cognition that "bad things happen because I am gay" can be reformulated to "bad things happen."

Gay male and lesbian survivors of hate violence often have to cope with negative feelings specifically about their sexual identity. If victimization has forced premature disclosure of the survivor's gay identity, it may have amplified the feelings of vulnerability, alienation, and exposure that often are part of the coming-out process. These feelings must be explored with the aim of separating the victimization experience from the coming-out experience. In addition, the survivor must be helped to feel the positive effects of disclosing her or his identity that also are part of coming out. When survivors who are in the later stages of coming out question their homosexuality as a result of the assault, the practitioner should review the bases for the client's coming-out decisions of the past, with the aim of reestablishing her or his positive identity as a lesbian or gay man.

Facilitating Positive Affect

Self-confidence can be mended through consciousness-raising, which can help survivors to locate their victimization in a social context. Understanding that the crime was based on global hatred that has its roots in a heterosexist society can relieve the survivor's feelings of being personally targeted and blameful. As Bohn (1984) noted, group work may be especially valuable for gay survivors because it permits identification with other lesbian and gay male victims and helps them to realize that they are not alone. Gay survivors in groups can share their reactions to victimization, express their anger, and develop analyses of their victimization that bond them to the larger gay community and its support systems.

Survivors inevitably are faced with the question of whether to report their victimization. At some point in the recovery process, this decision must be explored. In addition to its importance for the criminal justice system, reporting the incident has several potential benefits for the survivor. It can offer a constructive channel for anger, increase feelings of efficacy, and provide the satisfaction of helping to protect other members of the community from the sort of victimization one has experienced. At the same time, survivors should not be led to believe that reporting the crime necessarily will lead to arrest and prosecution of the attackers; indeed, such a result is unlikely in many cases (e.g., Bard & Sangrey, 1979). The practitioner assists the survivor in weighing the benefits and risks in reporting and ensures that the survivor makes her or his own decision. Because reporting also may lead to secondary victimization by insensitive or prejudiced criminal justice personnel (see Chapter 18), an increase in the survivor's sense of powerlessness can be prevented if the practitioner helps the survivor to become adequately prepared and to develop a good support system.

Working through these many issues and feelings eventually permits the survivor to integrate the experience of victimization into her or his larger worldview and to get on with life. This *reorganization* process may require considerable time to complete, especially if a victim denies or represses awareness of the victimization for months or even years after it occurs (Koss & Burkhart, 1989; Myers, 1989). Greater involvement with the gay community is likely to be particularly helpful in achieving reorganization.

Interventions After Sexual Assault

Survivors of anti-gay sexual assault need to separate the victimization from their experience of sexuality and intimacy and develop positive feelings about sexual expression that are not intruded upon by images of the assault. Gay male survivors are at special risk for phobic or aversive feelings toward male sexuality because their normal sexual behavior will superficially resemble the sexual assault (if for no other reason than that both involve another male). Lesbian survivors also may experience fear reactions and flashbacks to the assault triggered by normal sexual contact. Practitioners must support survivors (and their partners) to allow healing time for the fear to diminish. Survivors should be encouraged to initiate sexual contact in stages and to determine their own readiness for gradually increasing sexual involvement. The aim is to regain a sense of being in charge of one's own body, in contrast to the powerlessness and fear experienced during the assault.

Practitioners should be aware of the heterosexist bias that sexual assault survivors may experience if they come in contact with the criminal justice or medical systems. For example, police may not believe that male-male rape occurs; they may be hostile; or they may assume that, because he is gay, the victim deserved or brought on the attack (Anderson, 1982). Physicians and emergency room staff may assume that a lesbian rape victim is heterosexual and consequently display insensitivity in asking questions about previous sexual experience, contraception, and significant others (Orzek, 1988). Practitioners play an important role by advocating for survivors, helping them to advocate more effectively for themselves, and educating other professionals about sensitive responses to gay male and lesbian clients.

Interventions with Significant Others

Lovers, family, and friends also must deal with the losses and hardships imposed by the victimization, make sense of it, and regain a perception of the world as a stable and predictable place. Sometimes a lover or best friend will also have been victimized in the attack. In such cases where the victims cannot provide each other with primary support as they ordinarily would, both survivors may need assistance in expanding their support networks.

Mental health professionals must respond to the needs of significant others while at the same time helping them to respond, in turn, to the victim's needs. Professionals may need to educate significant others about the dynamics of violence, defuse their fears, and encourage their support for the primary victim. Significant others might benefit from exposure to educational materials (printed, audio, video) about homosexuality, victimization, and hate crimes. When internalized homophobia among significant others (gay and lesbian as well as heterosexual) makes it difficult for them to be supportive, professionals should assist the survivor in handling others' negative or nonsupportive reactions (e.g., through role-playing).

CONCLUSION

The trauma associated with anti-gay victimization may become linked to survivors' homosexuality. Although this often results in intensification of psychosocial problems associated with being gay or lesbian, it also may lead to further consolidation of the survivor's gay or lesbian identity and involvement with her or his community. Mental health practitioners can play an important role by assisting lesbian and gay male survivors, their significant others, and their communities in successfully reconstructing survivors' lives and mobilizing confrontation of hate crimes as a community problem. Researchers have an important role to play in filling gaps in information about the mental health consequences of anti-gay hate crimes and the effectiveness of individual and community-based intervention strategies. Most important, mental health practitioners and researchers should work with the lesbian and gay community to develop public awareness and comprehensive programs to prevent hate-motivated violence.

NOTES

1. *Coming out* (a shortened form of *coming out of the closet*) refers to the sequence of events through which individuals recognize their own homosexual orientation and disclose it to others. Conversely, being *in the closet* or *closeted* refers to passing as heterosexual (e.g., Dynes, 1985). Coming out is a continuous process: After coming out to oneself, one is continually meeting new people to whom one's sexual orientation must be disclosed. Consequently, different gay people are out to varying degrees.

2. Attempting to pass as heterosexual may increase some individuals' risk for victimization. Men who are hiding their homosexuality may be more prone to victimization when they seek sexual partners outside the relative safety of the gay community (e.g., Harry, 1982; Miller & Humphreys, 1980; for an autobiographical account, see Bauman, 1986). Additionally, because of the stigma attached to homosexuality and because discrimination against lesbians and gay men remains legal in many jurisdictions (see Chapter 5), closeted lesbians and gay men alike can be blackmailed with threatened involuntary revelation of their sexual orientation to family, employers, or others (Bell & Weinberg, 1978; Harry, 1982; Rofes, 1983).

3. Currently, operational definitions of hate crimes exclude male-female sexual assault unless the perpetrator can be shown to have attacked some aspect of the victim's identity other than her gender (e.g., her race, religion, or sexual orientation). Because space limitations prevent us from considering this definitional issue in detail, we focus here on the mental health consequences of male-female sexual assaults in which the victim is a lesbian and is targeted because of her sexual orientation (for more general discussions of the aftermath of sexual assault, see, e.g., Brownmiller, 1975; Burgess, 1985; Ledray, 1986).

4. Heterosexuals too are victimized by anti-gay hate crimes (see Chapter 1). The threat of victimization probably also causes many heterosexuals to conform to gender roles and to restrict their expressions of (nonsexual) physical affection for members of their own sex (e.g., Herek, 1986, 1991).

REFERENCES

American Psychiatric Association. (1987). *Diagnostic and statistical manual of mental disorders* (3rd ed., rev.). Washington, DC: Author.

Anderson, C. L. (1982). Males as sexual assault victims: Multiple levels of trauma. *Journal of Homosexuality, 7*(2/3), 145-162.

Bard, M., & Sangrey, D. (1979). *The crime victim's book*. New York: Basic Books.

Bauman, R. (1986). *The gentleman from Maryland: The conscience of a gay conservative.* New York: Arbor House.

Bell, A. P., & Weinberg, M. S. (1978). *Homosexualities: A study of diversity among men and women.* New York: Simon & Schuster.

Birt, C. M., & Dion, K. L. (1987). Relative deprivation theory and responses to discrimination in a gay male and lesbian sample. *British Journal of Social Psychology, 26,* 139-145.

Bohn, T. R. (1984). Homophobic violence: Implications for social work practice. In R. Schoenberg & R. S. Goldberg (Eds.), *With compassion toward some: Homosexuality and social work in America.* New York: Harrington Park.

Brownmiller, S. (1975). *Against our will: Men, women, and rape.* New York: Simon & Schuster.

Burgess, A. W. (Ed.). (1985). *Rape and sexual assault: A research handbook.* New York: Garland.

Burt, M. R., & Katz, B. L. (1987). Dimensions of recovery from rape: Focus on growth outcomes. *Journal of Interpersonal Violence, 2,* 57-81.

Caplan, G. (1964). *Principles of preventive psychiatry.* New York: Basic Books.

Cass, V. (1979). Homosexual identity formation: A theoretical model. *Journal of Homosexuality, 4,* 219-235.

Coates, D., Wortman, C. B., & Abbey, A. (1979). Reactions to victims. In I. H. Frieze, D. Bar-Tal, & J. S. Carroll (Eds.), *New approaches to social problems* (pp. 21-52). San Francisco: Jossey-Bass.

Cohen, C., & Stein, T. (1986). *Psychotherapy with lesbians and gay men.* New York: Plenum.

Crocker, J., & Major, B. (1989). Social stigma and self-esteem: The self-protective properties of stigma. *Psychological Review, 96,* 608-630.

D'Emilio, J. (1983). *Sexual politics, sexual communities: The making of a homosexual minority in the United States, 1940-1970.* Chicago: University of Chicago Press.

Dynes, W. (1985). *Homolexis: A historical and cultural lexicon of homosexuality.* New York: Gay Academic Union.

Fairbank, J. A., Gross, R., & Keane, T. M. (1983). Treatment of Posttraumatic Stress Disorder. *Behavior Modification, 7,* 557-567.

Frank, E., Anderson, B., Stewart, B. D., Danou, C., Hughes, C., & West, D. (1988). Efficacy of cognitive behavior therapy and systematic desensitization in the treatment of rape trauma. *Behavior Therapy, 19,* 403-420.

Frederick, C. J. (1987). Psychic trauma in victims of crime and terrorism. In G. VandenBos & B. Bryant (Eds.), *Cataclysms, crises, and catastrophes: Psychology in action* (pp. 59-108). Washington, DC: American Psychological Association.

Frieze, I. H., Hymer, S., & Greenberg, M. S. (1984). Describing the victims of crime and violence. In A. Kahn (Ed.), *Victims of crime and violence: Final report of the APA Task Force on the Victims of Crime and Violence* (pp. 19-78). Washington, DC: American Psychological Association.

Goffman, E. (1963). *Stigma: Notes on the management of spoiled identity.* Englewood Cliffs, NJ: Prentice-Hall.

Gonsiorek, J. C. (1982). Results of psychological testing on homosexual populations. *American Behavioral Scientist, 25,* 385-396.

Gonsiorek, J. C. (1991). The empirical basis for the demise of the illness model of homosexuality. In J. C. Gonsiorek & J. D. Weinrich (Eds.), *Homosexuality: Social psychological, and biological issues* (2nd ed., pp. 115-136). Newbury Park, CA: Sage.

Groth, A. N., & Burgess, A. W. (1980). Male rape: Offenders and victims. *American Journal of Psychiatry, 137*(7), 806-810.

Hammersmith, S. K., & Weinberg, M. S. (1973). Homosexual identity: Commitment, adjustment, and significant others. *Sociometry, 36*(1), 56-79.

Harry, J. (1982). Derivative deviance: The cases of extortion, fag-bashing, and shakedown of gay men. *Criminology, 19*(4), 546-564.

Herek, G. M. (1986). On heterosexual masculinity: Some psychical consequences of the social construction of gender and sexuality. *American Behavioral Scientist, 29*(5), 563-577.

Herek, G. M. (1989). Hate crimes against lesbians and gay men: Issues for research and policy. *American Psychologist, 44,* 948-955.

Herek, G. M. (1991). Stigma, prejudice, and violence against lesbians and gay men. In J. Gonsiorek & J. Weinrich (Eds.), *Homosexuality: Social, psychological, and biological issues* (2nd ed., pp. 60-80). Newbury Park, CA: Sage.

Herek, G. M., & Glunt, E. K. (1988). An epidemic of stigma: Public reactions to AIDS. *American Psychologist, 43,* 886-891.

Hodges, A., & Hutter, D. (1979). *With downcast gays: Aspects of homosexual self-oppression* (2nd ed.). Toronto: Pink Triangle.

Humphreys, L. (1972). *Out of the closets: The sociology of homosexual liberation.* Englewood Cliffs, NJ: Prentice-Hall.

Janoff-Bulman, R. (1979). Characterological versus behavioral self-blame: Inquiries into depression and rape. *Journal of Personality and Social Psychology, 37,* 1798-1809.

Janoff-Bulman, R. (1982). Esteem and control bases of blame: "Adaptive" strategies for victims versus observers. *Journal of Personality, 50,* 180-192.

Janoff-Bulman, R., & Frieze, I. H. (Eds.). (1983a). Reactions to victimization [Special issue]. *Journal of Social Issues, 39*(2).

Janoff-Bulman, R., & Frieze, I. H. (1983b). A theoretical perspective for understanding reactions to victimization. *Journal of Social Issues, 39*(2), 1-17.

Jones, E. E., Farina, A., Hastorf, A. H., Markus, H., Miller, D. T., & Scott, R. A. (1984). *Social stigma: The psychology of marked relationships.* New York: Freeman.

Kaufman, A., DiVasto, P., Jackson, R., Voorhees, D., & Christy, J. (1980). Male rape victims: Noninstitutionalized assault. *American Journal of Psychiatry, 137*(2), 221-223.

Kimmel, D. C. (1978). Adult development and aging: A gay perspective. *Journal of Social Issues, 34*(3), 113-130.

Koss, M. P., & Burkhart, B. R. (1989). A conceptual analysis of rape victimization: Long-term effects and implications for treatment. *Psychology of Women Quarterly, 13,* 27-40.

Ledray, L. E. (1986). *Recovering from rape.* New York: Holt, Rinehart & Winston.

Lerner, M. J. (1970). The desire for justice and reactions to victims. In J. Macaulay & L. Berkowitz (Eds.), *Altruism and helping behavior* (pp. 205-229). New York: Academic Press.

226   SURVIVING AND RESPONDING

Levy, B., & Brown, V. (1984). Strategies for crisis intervention with victims of violence. In S. Saunders, A. Anderson, C. Hart, & G. Rubenstein (Eds.), *Violent individuals and families: A handbook for practitioners* (pp. 57-68). Springfield, IL: Charles C Thomas.

Malyon, A. K. (1982). Psychotherapeutic implications of internalized homophobia in gay men. *Journal of Homosexuality, 7*(2/3), 59-69.

Miller, B., & Humphreys, L. (1980). Lifestyles and violence: Homosexual victims of assault and murder. *Qualitative Sociology, 3*(3), 169-185.

Miranda, J., & Storms, M. (1989). Psychological adjustment of lesbians and gay men. *Journal of Counseling and Development, 68*, 41-45.

Morin, S., & Charles, K. (1983). Heterosexual bias in psychotherapy. In J. Murray & P. R. Abramson (Eds.), *Bias in psychotherapy* (pp. 309-338). New York: Praeger.

Myers, M. F. (1989). Men sexually assaulted as adults and sexually abused as boys. *Archives of Sexual Behavior, 18*, 203-215.

Orzek, A. M. (1988). The lesbian victim of sexual assault: Special considerations for the mental health professional. *Women and Therapy, 8*(1/2), 107-117.

Rofes, E. E. (1983). *"I thought people like that killed themselves": Lesbians, gay men and suicide.* San Francisco: Grey Fox.

Sales, E., Baum, M., & Shore, B. (1984). Victim readjustment following assault. *Journal of Social Issues, 40*(1), 117-136.

Stein, T. S., & Cohen, C. J. (1984). Psychotherapy with gay men and lesbians: An examination of homophobia, coming out, and identity. In E. S. Hetrick & T. S. Stein (Eds.), *Innovations in psychotherapy with homosexuals* (pp. 60-73). Washington, DC: American Psychiatric Press.

Steketee, M. S., & Foa, E. B. (1987). Rape victims: Post-traumatic stress responses and their treatment. *Journal of Anxiety Disorders, 1*, 69-86.

Troiden, R. (1988). *Gay and lesbian identity: A sociological analysis.* New York: General Hall.

Tsegaye-Spates, C. R. (1985). The mental health needs of victims: An introduction to the literature. In A. W. Burgess (Ed.), *Rape and sexual assault: A research handbook* (pp. 35-45). New York: Garland.

Unger, R. (1979). *Female and male: Psychological perspectives.* New York: Harper & Row.

Weinberg, M. S., & Williams, C. J. (1974). *Male homosexuals: Their problems and adaptations.* New York: Oxford University Press.

Treatment and Service Interventions for Lesbian and Gay Male Crime Victims

DAVID M. WERTHEIMER

Although the concepts of *crime victim, victim assistance,* and *victim compensation* can be traced back to an early period in the Judaic roots of Western civilization (e.g., the Laws of Moses, *Exodus* 21:18, 22-25), the modern crime victims' movement has emerged in an identifiable form only in the second half of the current century. This contemporary manifestation of concern for crime victims springs from several significant and varied sources. Grass-roots organizing efforts during the late 1960s and 1970s, mostly within women's organizations concerned about violence against women, gave rise to community-based programs offering a modest range of services to survivors of domestic violence and sexual assault (Boston Women's Health Collective, 1984). Several state governments also initiated the earliest crime victim compensation programs during this time period and, after 1975, municipalities around the country began to fund programs providing crisis intervention services to a variety of crime victims (Stark & Goldstein, 1985). These "comprehensive" programs were often affiliated with municipal or county agencies such as local police departments and district attorneys. The federal government added its own voice to the growing expression of concern for the welfare of crime victims when the Justice Department established its Office for Victims of Crime in 1981. A Presidential Task Force on Victims of Crime studied the problem nationally, issuing its final report in 1982.

Today, grass-roots organizations throughout the nation continue to serve survivors of sexual assault, domestic violence, and other forms of victimization. Crime victim compensation is available in 39 states, the Virgin Islands, and the District of Columbia (Stark & Goldstein, 1985), and state funding for local delivery of crime victim services has enhanced crime victim programming in many areas. Municipal crime victim services exist in most large urban areas, often with scores of staff professionals and budgets in the millions of dollars. Federal funding under the Victims of Crime Act of 1984 has led to a modest expansion of the federal government's role in supporting efforts to deliver services to crime victims throughout the nation.

Despite these advances, many crime victim populations remain significantly underserved throughout the United States. More often than not, crime victims are members of groups that historically have been among the most vulnerable in our society—women, persons of color, children, the elderly, the disabled—populations whose disenfranchisement has resulted in, among other things, a minimizing of their social service concerns and needs. Lesbians and gay men are among these vulnerable and disenfranchised subsets of the general population. A largely invisible group, the membership of the lesbian and gay community cuts across all other socioeconomic, racial, ethnic, religious, and age lines. Although lesbians and gay men are prone to a level of victimization that far exceeds that of the nongay population (Philadelphia Lesbian and Gay Task Force, 1988), existing crime victim service networks have largely failed to acknowledge or address the existence and needs of lesbian and gay male victims of violent crime. Regardless of whether this failure has resulted from ignorance, neglect, or conscious hostility, its consequence is that lesbians and gay men still frequently suffer the often devastating consequences of victimization in isolation and silence. As a result, the initial physical and psychological injuries that follow an assault are compounded.

Because most crimes against lesbians and gay men are never reported to official authorities (see Chapter 18) and because heterosexism reinforces the invisibility and illegitimacy of lesbians and gay men generally (see Chapter 5), most established crime victim service providers remain unfamiliar with and insensitive to the needs of lesbian and gay crime victims. Consequently, lesbians and gay men who report crimes committed against them often must choose between hiding their sexual orientation from the service providers they encounter or disclosing it and thereby risking ridicule and revictimization.

In the past 10 years, the lesbian and gay community has taken upon itself the tasks of identifying and defining the problem of violence against its members, providing appropriate services to individuals in need, and working to heal the injuries that violence can create in the larger community. The community has, in short, decided that, if no one else cares enough to help us, then we must help ourselves. The remainder of this chapter presents a case study of how the lesbian and gay community in New York City developed its own response to anti-gay and anti-lesbian violence.

CASE STUDY: THE GROWTH OF
THE ANTI-VIOLENCE PROJECT

In 1980 a group of gay men and lesbians founded the New York City Gay and Lesbian Anti-Violence Project (AVP) in reaction to neighborhood incidents of anti-lesbian and anti-gay violence and the failure of the criminal justice system to respond to the problem. The project's staff and volunteers assist victims of anti-gay and anti-lesbian violence to regain their sense of control, identify and evaluate their options, and assert their rights. The project provides counseling, advocacy, and information for lesbian and gay crime victims, victims of anti-gay and anti-lesbian violence, and others affected by such violence. By documenting the existence and extent of these forms of violence and by educating the public, the project strives to reduce public tolerance of violence against lesbians and gay men. The project also seeks to hold governmental and social service agencies accountable to gay and lesbian people in the New York metropolitan area and to ensure sensitive and unbiased treatment for lesbian and gay crime victims. The project's mission is to provide these services as long as anti-gay and anti-lesbian prejudice and discrimination, and the violence they engender, exist (New York City Gay and Lesbian Anti-Violence Project, 1989).

In the early spring of 1980, lesbian and gay residents of the Chelsea neighborhood of Manhattan's West Side began hearing rumors about a significant increase in anti-gay attacks. It appeared that men walking in the evening, either alone or in pairs, were being attacked and beaten with alarming frequency by wandering groups of young White males who moved through the neighborhood either on foot or in cars. Many area residents had the impression that these young men had come to the neighborhood with the specific intention of harassing and assaulting gay men.

Because virtually none of these attacks was being reported to the Chelsea police precinct, there had been no official documentation of the problem and, accordingly, no official response. News of the assaults traveled by word of mouth, leaving community residents feeling highly intimidated, confused, and uncertain about exactly what was happening in the area. Members of the Chelsea Gay Association, a local lesbian and gay community organization, began to address the problem by sponsoring a number of well-attended town meetings. Numerous assault victims came forward publicly for the first time to report precisely what had happened to them. As a result of these meetings, two members of the Chelsea Gay Association placed a special telephone hot line in their own home to take reports from individuals who had been gay-bashed. Volunteers from the group were recruited and trained to respond to messages left on an answering machine, document incidents of violence, and provide basic crisis intervention services to callers. The group decided to provide volunteers who could accompany crime victims who wished to make police reports to the local precinct and to monitor the progress of any cases that resulted in arrests and entered the criminal court system. Palm cards with the new hot line number were distributed throughout the community. As word spread, calls came in to the hot line from all over the city. The project organizers quickly realized that anti-gay and anti-lesbian violence was not limited to any one neighborhood but was in fact present throughout every part of the region. Nevertheless, the organization remained a special interest program of the Chelsea Gay Association for the next three years.

In 1983 the Anti-Violence Project incorporated and, through the assistance of a local elected official, was able to receive its first grant of public monies from the New York State Crime Victims Board. This grant enabled the agency to open an office and hire its first paid staff: a full-time executive director and a part-time administrative assistant. The project continued to maintain a telephone hot line using an answering machine and a network of volunteers who responded to individual cases assigned to them by the paid staff. The organization provided short-term crisis intervention counseling, continued police advocacy and court monitoring, and developed an extensive referral resource listing to help crime victims identify various forms of assistance and victim entitlements. The presence of paid staff also enabled the organization to begin interacting on a more professional basis with other crime victim service providers as well as with the police and the offices of the various district attorneys. At this time, the organization's newly elected board of directors decided that the agency's mandate would be to provide crime victim services to clients throughout the New York City area.

As the organization became an established link in the network of crime victim services in New York City, its visibility increased among other service providers and within the lesbian and gay community. The agency's caseload grew steadily in the years following 1983; in 1989 the project served six times the number of crime victims served during its first year of operation.[1] Since 1985 the Anti-Violence Project has expanded its services to meet the varied needs of lesbian and gay crime victims who request the agency's assistance. Its annual budget has increased from $35,000 to more than $250,000 and has been augmented by specialized grants from private foundations and no fewer than five government agencies as well as by regular contributions solicited from the community. Five full-time and several part-time staff now are assisted by student interns and a corps of 25 trained volunteers. The services originally offered by the community-based hot line have been expanded to meet the full range of needs presented to the agency by its clients, as described below.

TREATMENT AND SERVICE INTERVENTIONS

Crisis Intervention

The core of the Anti-Violence Project's services remains the telephone hot line. The hot line responds to crime victims on a 24-hour basis: The phones are answered by professional counselors during regular working hours and by an answering service during evening and weekend hours, when AVP staff and volunteers are on round-the-clock call. Additionally, the agency's office location in New York's Lesbian and Gay Community Services Center results in a regular flow of walk-in clients.

Immediately upon initial contact, a trained project counselor assists the caller in assessing any immediate safety and urgent medical needs to which the client may not yet have attended. Once these primary issues have been addressed, the project counselor begins to help the caller to ventilate feelings about the attack and to identify and evaluate the various response options available. They may review the decision about whether or not to report the crime to the police, as well as whether or how to tell family members, lovers, employers, and others about the crime. Within this context, the counselor begins to assess the affective impact of the incident on the crime victim and helps the client to identify and express feelings and reactions to the incident. Exploring the choices facing the crime victim is an essential component of helping the survivor deal with the affective impact of the crime. Simply identifying decisions that crime victims can make themselves is an essential first step toward helping them to return to a sense of control over their lives and safety. It also is an opportunity for the counselor to provide information about resources with which clients may not be familiar, such as hospital-based crime victim programs with emergency room components and the availability of crime victim compensation.

During the initial telephone contact, callers often choose not to identify themselves to the counselor, except by first name. AVP counselors are trained never to demand this information but to leave the decision about disclosing identity to each caller. This procedure is, in and of itself, an important clinical intervention that enables callers both to remain anonymous if they are concerned about disclosure of their sexual orientation and to retain control over a situation at a time at which they may be feeling considerably out of control.

By the end of the initial client contact, the counselor and the client usually have identified a plan for steps that can be taken immediately to ensure safety, to receive needed medical attention, and to deal with the criminal justice authorities. They also have determined what type of follow-up services, if any, are indicated. Some clients wish no further contact with the agency and have called simply to talk about what happened and to encourage the AVP to document the incident for its own records. Others continue to have contact with the project; they schedule an in-office appointment with a mental health professional, arrange to be contacted by one of the agency's trained volunteer peer counselors, or ask the project to provide follow-up or advocacy services.

FOLLOW-UP SERVICES

Short-Term Professional Counseling

Clients frequently request or are encouraged to consider scheduling an appointment for in-office counseling by one of the agency's social workers or psychologists. Following an initial clinical assessment, the client and counselor may contract verbally to enter into a counseling relationship for a limited time period. This counseling follows a short-term crisis intervention model, with the goal of returning the client to a sense of control and power. Counseling follows a structure that incorporates ventilation, exploration of affective contents, and extensive psychoeducation.[2]

The trauma of victimization and the realities of its aftermath are the usual focus of this crisis intervention counseling rather than the issues surrounding the victim's actual or perceived sexual orientation. Matters relating to sexual orientation are not excluded from the counseling arena, however. Victims' sexual orientation can be directly relevant to their counseling. In one case, for example, two women were attacked precisely because they were perceived to be lesbians; they had been walking arm-in-arm when they first were spotted by their assailants. One not unusual result of their assault was that it left the women uncomfortable demonstrating any affection for each other at all, even within the privacy of their own home. Their counselor helped them to understand that one impact of the anti-lesbian attack against them was both to challenge their individual self-identities and to threaten their shared life-style. As the women decided that the hate crime perpetrated against them would not succeed in intimidating them, they were able to resume normal physical interactions.

Internalized homophobia may enter into a victim's reactions to a given incident, especially when addressing feelings of guilt and self-blame that often accompany an attack. As with many rape survivors, the lesbian or gay victim may feel that she or he either asked for or deserved the assault. As with the two women described above, the circumstances of an assault may result in survivors who give the appearance of being uncomfortable with their underlying sexual orientation. It is important in these situations to reaffirm the positive value of a gay or lesbian sexual identity while at the same time facilitating an understanding of the way in which victims can internalize the hatred manifested by an assailant (see Chapter 13).

Counseling at the Anti-Violence Project usually continues until both the client and the counselor determine that termination is appropriate. Cases also are discussed regularly by counselors in clinical supervision. Counselors may resume their work with clients on a periodic basis, as, for example, when a case becomes active in criminal court or around the anniversary of a given assault.

Peer Counseling

Trained volunteer peer counselors are able to provide ongoing emotional support for crime victims when professional crisis intervention counseling is not indicated. Peer counselors are trained to listen, reflect back feelings that are expressed, and provide emotional support in a lesbian- and gay-sensitive context. Some peer counselors are former AVP clients who have gained sufficient time and distance from their own assaults to provide appropriate services to others. Clients often ask if the peer counselor assigned to them also has been a crime victim, and some prefer a peer counselor who has experienced victimization firsthand. The counselors are trained in appropriate use of self when disclosing this type of information; although it is inappropriate for peer counselors to use the counseling setting to dwell upon their own victimization experience, their experience help to inform their empathic interaction with clients. Discussion of common cognitive and affective experiences (and the differences in these experiences) can be a critical tool in reducing the feelings of isolation, guilt, and worthlessness that frequently accompany victimization.

Peer counselors stay in contact with their clients on a weekly basis in the period immediately following an incident, providing emotional support while monitoring recovery. During this period, the peer counselors also stay in frequent contact with the mental health professionals on staff who supervise volunteer activities. Peer counselors can refer clients back to staff professionals if more extensive interventions are indicated. Similarly, staff professionals can refer clients to peer counselors after a period of crisis intervention counseling as part of the process of monitoring recovery while facilitating termination from the agency. As with the professional counseling services, the duration of peer support counseling varies from case to case. It rarely lasts more than six weeks, although peer counselors frequently remain in regular contact with clients whose cases have entered the court system.

Group Counseling

The AVP also on occasion offers group counseling using a time-limited, 12-week model in which two professional cotherapists work with a group of crime victims who all have experienced a specific type of violence. During the past several years, group services have been offered for male survivors of sexual assault and lesbians who have been battered in primary relationships. Clients are selected for groups after screening by a staff mental health professional. Group members frequently are clients who have received either professional or peer counseling from AVP staff or volunteers. Referrals for groups are also accepted from other crime victim service providers in the New York City area.

ADVOCACY SERVICES

Virtually all crime victims experience some form of trauma subsequent to victimization, regardless of their sexual orientation. Much of what the Anti-Violence Project offers is quite similar to the activities of other small crime victim programs, with the difference that the services are offered in a lesbian- and gay-sensitive, lesbian- and gay-identified setting. The AVP works with other human service providers assisting victims of violent crime, for example, by assisting individuals in securing crime victim compensation and related entitlements and securing timely referrals for clients to other social service agencies that are sensitive to lesbian and gay concerns. These advocacy efforts frequently involve taking the time necessary to educate service providers about the specific concerns and needs of lesbian and gay crime victims. The AVP also offers services that are not traditionally associated with crime victim counseling programs. These advocacy services have been developed specifically in response to the criminal justice system's failure to respond to the needs of the lesbian and gay community.

Police Advocacy

Precinct accompaniment. In the trauma that immediately follows an assault, many crime victims are not prepared to interact with police officers who may consider the extreme situation the victim has encountered to be just one more assignment in the course of a busy tour of duty. Crime victims often are surprised that the police remain so emotionally detached and apparently uninterested in the violent event that has just transpired.

Lesbian and gay crime victims who decide to make formal police reports of an attack against them often articulate the additional, legitimate concern that their complaint either will not be taken seriously by the local precinct or will be met with disdain or hostility. Although lesbian and gay community-police relations in New York City have improved during the past few years, many lesbian and gay male New Yorkers remember the police harassment and violence that occurred on a regular basis before the state's sodomy statutes were declared unconstitutional in 1980. Raids of bars, harassment on the street, and unprovoked police violence were not only tolerated but at times condoned. This history, combined with lingering uncertainty regarding current police attitudes and occasional acts of police brutality, leaves many lesbians and gay men uncomfortable at the thought of entering a police facility and filing a police report by themselves. In fact, only half of the crime victims reporting attacks against them to the Anti-Violence Project file formal complaints with the police.

In an effort to monitor and improve case-by-case police response, the AVP trains volunteers to escort crime victims to the police and to facilitate the filing of a police report. These advocates are trained in how the police are instructed to interact with crime victim complainants. When the use of an advocate is requested by a client or recommended by a project counselor, the advocate and client usually meet prior to going to the precinct to file the report. They review what the procedure will be and what the crime victim should anticipate. The advocate then accompanies the crime victim to the precinct and monitors the process of filing the complaint, asking to review relevant documents to ensure that an anti-gay or anti-lesbian crime is correctly documented.

Advocates are trained not to engage in hostile or argumentative interactions with the police but to remind the police in a professional fashion of proper procedures when they are not being followed. Continuing police disinterest or hostility in the presence of an advocate is not challenged but reported back to the project staff after the advocate leaves the police precinct. Although individual police officers often initially are wary of having a third party present during the process of filing a complaint, they usually become cooperative and responsive when they determine that the advocate is there as a facilitator and monitor rather than as an adversary.

Local police liaison. The Anti-Violence Project has established productive working relationships with a number of local police precincts. These relationships have resulted from regular contact with individual police officers, representatives of the community affairs office based in the local precinct, and ranking or commanding personnel. These relationships enable project staff and volunteers to make direct contact with a sympathetic local police representative after a crime has occurred within a given jurisdiction but before formal police contact has been made. A specific case can be discussed with the project's police contact and arrangements can be made for the crime victim to speak directly with the AVP police contact at the time the formal police report is filed.

Liaison with specialized units. The police department maintains a number of specialized units that can be of great assistance to lesbian and gay crime victims. The AVP has worked on a case-by-case basis with the Sex Crimes Unit, the Senior Citizen Unit, the Major Case Squad, and various homicide bureaus. The most notable specialized unit is the Bias Incident Investigations Unit, which investigates crimes motivated by a victim's race, religion, ethnicity, or sexual orientation. Referral of a case to this unit greatly augments the ability of the department to respond to both a particular crime and the needs of that crime's victim(s).

Standard police procedure requires the local precinct to notify the bias unit when a bias crime has occurred within its jurisdiction. Many bias crimes, however, are not correctly identified at the local level, and clients of the Anti-Violence Project who have been victims of anti-gay and anti-lesbian violence frequently report that the responding police officers failed to identify and document the bias-related nature of the assault against them.

To facilitate the proper reporting of bias crimes, the Anti-Violence Project maintains regular communication with the bias unit and forwards cases directly to the unit for investigation, bypassing what may be an unresponsive local precinct. From time to time, the project receives referrals from the bias unit of cases of anti-gay and anti-lesbian violence that have moved through established police channels without coming to the AVP's attention.

Project staff also work with the bias unit to improve the police department's ability to correctly identify and classify bias-related incidents. The result of these efforts is reflected in the police department's statistics: Since the bias unit first began accepting anti-gay and anti-lesbian cases in 1985, the number of such cases handled by the unit has virtually doubled each year. Whether or not this increase reflects a rise in the actual number of anti-gay crimes being committed, it clearly indicates the success of continuing efforts to train police personnel to identify and classify anti-gay and anti-lesbian crimes.

COURT MONITORING

Advocacy with Prosecutors

The New York City criminal courts are so overwhelmed with cases that individual crime victims' concerns and needs often are minimized or ignored. The process of seeking justice for them requires strong advocacy by crime victim service providers. Anti-Violence Project staff and volunteers are trained in the structure and function of the criminal court system and do not hesitate to communicate regularly and assertively with prosecutors to make known the concerns and needs of a crime victim in a given case. Advocacy with the criminal court system usually commences shortly after the project learns of an arrest in a given case and proceeds through case evaluation, processing, plea bargaining, jury selection, trial, and sentencing. The project takes an aggressive role in contacting prosecutors to ensure that a victim's concerns are communicated and understood. Project staff also assist prosecutors in understanding and preparing for the various strategies employed by defense attorneys, such as the "homo-sexual panic" defense (see Chapter 18).

Anti-Violence Project representatives also work with the crime vic-tim to explain the criminal court process and her or his role in the criminal proceedings. Central to this task is helping the client to main-tain an accurate understanding of the limited nature of the victim's role in a criminal trial and a realistic expectation of what may or may not be the outcome of a given case. Project staff also assist clients in preparing victim impact statements and assist in communicating rele-vant concerns to the court at the time of sentencing.

Court accompaniment. Trained volunteer court monitors are available to escort victims and witnesses to required court appearances. These monitors also can attend court proceedings at which the victim is not present. The purpose of this monitoring is twofold. First, the monitor provides a supportive presence in the courtroom for the victim. The monitor is often the only person in the courtroom who is there entirely and solely for the purpose of providing this type of support to the victim. Second, the monitoring process puts the prosecutor, the defense attorney, and the court on notice that the lesbian and gay community is watching as a given case moves forward and will not hesitate to communicate the mishandling of a case directly to the community. To this end, a monitor will frequently announce his or her presence to the prosecutor and the court and will report extensively to AVP staff on the progress of given cases. Monitors also can serve as a conduit to the media for information about cases that are a matter of public record. Court monitors are encour-aged to monitor an assigned case until it reaches final court disposition, which sometimes can take several years.

CONCLUSION

The emergence of the lesbian and gay crime victim's move-ment is an affirmation of the rights, concerns, and needs of a his-torically underserved community that experiences an alarming level of violence directed against its members. The strength of this movement, with new community-based crime victim agencies serving lesbian and gay crime victims emerging throughout the na-tion, indicates that the lesbian and gay community is committed to addressing the needs of individual victims even as the larger soci-ety continues to marginalize the gay and lesbian population. Cur-rently, lesbians and gay men have more crime victim services available to them than at any time in the past. Yet even the available services are totally insufficient to meet the needs of the thousands of lesbians and gay men who become crime victims each year. The vast majority of incidents still go unreported; an overwhelming number of lesbians and gay men continue to suffer the trauma that follows a violent crime in isolation and silence.

Not every community can create and fund services for lesbian and gay crime victims following the model that has been described above. All communities, however, can still respond. For example, professional crime victim service providers and criminal justice system employees can be trained about lesbian and gay crime victim issues and the impact of homophobia on the delivery of services to lesbians and gay men. Few mainstream service providers recognize the extent to which their caseloads include lesbian and gay male clients with concerns that are different than those of nongay victims. Training curricula should include not only concrete clinical issues and case management strategies but also more general training on how to create a nonprejudiced agency environment in which lesbians and gay men will feel safe requesting assistance.

Once trained in gay and lesbian crime victim concerns, mainstream victim service organizations can engage in outreach to inform the lesbian and gay community of available services. Agency publications should contain explicit reference to the services available for lesbians and gay men. Speakers from mainstream service agencies can offer presentations and information to lesbian- and gay-identified organizations (e.g., human service providers, religious organizations, social clubs, and recovery groups).

Finally, mainstream service agencies can issue nondiscrimination policies that explicitly include sexual orientation. Such policies communicate important information not only to potential clients but also to existing and future employees. An agency with a work environment in which lesbian and gay staff members feel comfortable with publicly identifying themselves to their colleagues will also be more responsive to the needs of the lesbian and gay clients who seek services.

Services provided by and for lesbian and gay male crime victims will remain necessary as long as the needs of those victims are misunderstood, underfunded, and neglected. Someday, when lesbians and gay men no longer face prejudice and discrimination and when every crime victim has his or her needs met in a sensitive and caring fashion, the question of whether or not specialized social services for lesbian and gay crime victims are necessary or even valid can be addressed. Until that day, lesbians and gay men must have resources to which we can turn when the crisis of victimization strikes our individual lives and tears at the fabric of our community.

NOTES

1. Not all of the gay men and lesbians who came to the AVP for assistance had been victims of anti-gay or anti-lesbian violence. The agency's increasingly visible profile in the community resulted in the identification of lesbian and gay crime victim populations that previously had been largely unrecognized. They included survivors of sexual assault and survivors of domestic violence in lesbian and gay relationships. A small number of agencies serving female crime victims had begun to acknowledge the problems faced by lesbian rape survivors and victims of domestic violence in lesbian relationships. A handful of battered women's shelters were responsive and sensitive to self-identified lesbians who requested their assistance. Other shelter facilities provided assistance without knowing their client's lesbian orientation; the survivors simply changed the pronoun used to describe the batterer, thereby receiving services ostensibly as a heterosexual client. Gay men, however, lacked even these limited services. Virtually no sexual assault programs at that time provided crisis intervention services for male survivors of sexual assault (whether gay or heterosexual), and no resources whatsoever were available to gay men battered in their relationships.

2. *Psychoeducation* refers to the presentation of cognitive material and exploration of its affective content and impact. Psychoeducational interventions might include statistical and anecdotal discussion of violence against lesbians and gay men, information about the nature of psychological reactions to an assault, and examination of the range of lesbian and gay crime victim concerns.

REFERENCES

Boston Women's Health Collective. (1984). *The new our bodies, ourselves.* New York: Simon & Schuster.

New York City Gay and Lesbian Anti-Violence Project. (1989). *Statement of purpose.* (Available from the New York City Gay and Lesbian Anti-Violence Project, 208 West 13th St., New York, NY 10011)

Philadelphia Lesbian and Gay Task Force. (1988). *Violence and discrimination against Philadelphia lesbian and gay people.* (Available from 1501 Cherry Street, Philadelphia, PA 19102)

Stark, J., & Goldstein, H. W. (1985). *The rights of crime victims.* New York: Bantam.

15

The Community Response to
Violence in San Francisco:
An Interview with Wenny Kusuma,
Lester Olmstead-Rose, and Jill Tregor

GREGORY M. HEREK

One of the oldest and most successful community organizations for responding to violence against lesbians and gay men is San Francisco's Community United Against Violence (CUAV).[1] CUAV's beginnings can be traced to many events, including the organization of neighborhood "Butterfly Brigades" as a response to increasing anti-gay violence in the late 1970s, the protests that followed the murders of Harvey Milk and George Moscone in 1978, and escalating anti-gay violence and harassment by the San Francisco police. By the mid-1980s, CUAV was incorporated and had become a viable service agency. Today, CUAV is an important community organization, based in San Francisco's Castro district.

On November 18, 1990, I spoke with Jill Tregor, Wenny Kusuma, and Lester Olmstead-Rose. Jill is CUAV's program coordinator. Wenny was a client advocate at CUAV. Lester is a former CUAV community organizer; he is currently an aide to San

AUTHOR'S NOTE: I thank Kevin Berrill for his generous assistance in preparing this chapter.

Francisco Supervisor Angela Alioto. We discussed CUAV, the nature of violence against lesbians and gay men, and how communities can respond to it.

GMH: *Could you give a quick rundown of how CUAV is set up as an organization?*

Jill: CUAV has eight paid staff people: an executive director, two client advocates who work both with domestic violence and anti-gay/lesbian violence, a hot line coordinator, a community organizer, a Speakers' Bureau coordinator, a fiscal coordinator, and a program coordinator. We have a budget of about $250,000. Our funding comes from United Way, of which we are a member agency; from the city and county of San Francisco through the District Attorney's office; and from the Office of Criminal Justice Planning, a state agency that distributes V.O.C.A. funds, which are Federal Victim funds. Then we have some private donations and small private foundation grants.

GMH: *How does CUAV organize its activities?*

Wenny: I look at antiviolence work as being both preventive and responsive. On the one hand you address the trauma of violence after the fact, but on the other hand, you take a proactive approach in preventing what's happening. I see this in CUAV, where we have two client advocates who address, after the fact of trauma, the aftermath of hate violence and also the aftermath of domestic violence in the lesbian/gay community. But we also have proactive efforts through community outreach and the Speakers' Bureau.

In the larger context, I also see what we do with the community as being important. That's what Jill does, that's sort of a third arm of CUAV's work. It's not necessarily dealing with actual victim survivors or potential victim survivors of violence but working with the external system, the police and community groups. They are external to CUAV, external to our community, but certainly interactive with our community.

Another thing that CUAV does that needs to be done is documentation. It is very important to document what's happening, not only to get the attention of mainstream America for our community's needs, but also to empower our own community. By offering this information to gay and lesbian citizens, we are giving gay men and lesbians the information to make informed choices about what it is that they do.

Jill: We do education in several different areas. First, we have the kind of education that we do with mainstream communities about demystifying homosexuality, or through showing our *Bashing* video. It's education that says "There's a problem that exists, and it's called anti-gay violence," or "Here's who we are, and, if you realized how human we are, we believe you'd never come out and beat us up."

We also do education inside our community about self-defense and carrying a whistle. The denial among lesbians and gays about the extent of the problem is amazing. I know it's a coping mechanism but it's scary to know just how many people think, "Oh, that doesn't happen in San Francisco, does it? Maybe it happens in some other horrible place but not here." And when we say to people that there are more incidents of anti-lesbian and anti-gay violence here than anywhere else in the country, they are shocked. Even if they have been in incidents themselves, they are shocked to hear that. A phenomenal number of people don't even carry a whistle, which for a buck or two is really the simplest thing you can do to take a proactive stance.

Another thing we're doing is outreach within the lesbian and gay communities to raise awareness about the importance of reporting. People think, "Well, haven't you already proved there's a problem?" But until everybody reports every incident of violence and harassment, I think there's some way in which we're failing to do our job completely. We have to let people know that (a) it's safe to report, and (b) there's something to talk about. Too many people have taken in the idea that "Violence is so much a part of my life that I don't even need help dealing with it." It's really important to say to them: "This is horrible each and every time it happens. It's OK to need to talk about it with your friends, with a counselor, or at an agency. You're not weak." I think that's a particularly big issue for gay men who are dealing with violence. That's part of what we're doing also.

The last part of what we do is training related. We say to police, "We hope you're not homophobic. But here, bottom line, is what we expect from you as professionals when you're dealing with us." The same with Muni bus drivers; I've done countless trainings with Muni bus drivers. The same with fire fighters. We say: "All right, first we're going to give our best shot at changing how you think about us. But then we're going to tell you what we expect and what we'll go by in the future. And if you don't come up to these standards, we'll have something to talk or yell about."

Wenny: One of the things that keeps coming up is education. Our frustration is that it's so easy to document victimization; that's in the statistics. It's so difficult to document prevention. How do you document the success of your preventive work? Yet it's one of the things that we need to be so vigilant about. People don't call up to say they were *not* bashed. I would love to hear success stories more often.

One of the things that education points to is not only the education of our mainstream culture, but also the education of ourselves in terms of breaking silence. This is especially true around domestic violence in the lesbian and gay community. Of course, each domestic violence situation has its own specific dynamics. But on top of that the issue of oppression and internalized oppression—internalized homophobia—adds another dimension to domestic violence situations. Educating our own community members about domestic violence is something that needs to be done and I think it's something that's picking up.

Lester: In the years that I talked publicly on a regular basis about CUAV's work, I broke it down into prevention and response. It's useful for people to hear that there are different pieces, especially if someone's interested in starting a local group. It's important to start with just one piece and not try to do everything that needs to be done at once. But we shouldn't forget just how interrelated the pieces are. I know that counselors at CUAV and New York's Anti-Violence Project do a lot of preventive work. For example, David Wertheimer [former Executive Director of the AVP] talks a lot about the client advocacy aspect of their program. Strictly speaking, that's a part of responding to a specific incident. When you do advocacy for individual victims, part of what you're doing is changing the system. You're educating judges, prosecutors, and defense counsels to the reality of violence against lesbians and gays, and to the realities of heterosexism. In educating people to those issues you are actively trying to prevent future cases of either victimization or revictimization.

Likewise, the prevention and public education efforts can have an effect on the organization's response to individual incidents. I was responsible for statistics when I was with CUAV and whenever we would release statistics and talk about broad issues of violence, we also would have an immediate increase in clients. They learned through our public education work that there was a place for them to come and deal with their individual personal situation. The statistics and the media weren't used just to change that hateful world out there that's coming at us; they also were able to reach and impact individuals who had been assaulted. And every time we released reports and got a round of media, there would be an increase in the number of people coming in to CUAV with their individual stories for the next two or three weeks. Suddenly they saw that there was a place they could go for help personally. So prevention and response are very interactive that way.

Jill: I also want to mention the education that happens in individual counseling. One thing that our counselors do in terms of helping our clients look at their options is to have them do things like think about taking a self-defense class or think about carrying a whistle. That's an important cornerstone of the work that we do with individuals.

GMH: *Could you talk about how CUAV responds when an individual is assaulted? Suppose that someone is victimized and they call CUAV. What happens next?*

Wenny: The specific services that we offer depend on where the client is at in the context of his or her trauma. The typical victim who calls CUAV is an adult White male. What I might do first is quickly assess his needs. I always start with medical needs. "Where are you? Are you OK? Are you physically all right now?"

GMH: *I'm imagining this happening at midnight on a Saturday night. Is someone on call? Is there a hot line?*

Wenny: We have a 24-hour hot line that's staffed during the day by client advocates at CUAV. After office hours and on weekends we have a volunteer corps of trained hot line advocates who take shifts one week at a time. And we have staff on backup to those volunteer advocates.

GMH: *So someone is victimized in the middle of the night, the police give them CUAV's card and say, "You might want to call this number." And they do so and they're in touch with someone from CUAV. Is that how it works?*

Wenny: That's a good scenario. Unfortunately, depending on the nature of the assault, the police may or may not respond immediately. San Francisco currently is suffering a shortage of approximately 200 patrol officers. So people are calling 9-1-1, and they're making a point of saying an assault is in progress, and still some responses are taking up to half an hour. If it's not in progress you can be waiting 3 to 6 hours, or 24 or 36 hours.

GMH: *What happens once the client gets in touch with you?*

Wenny: When we provide crisis intervention services or short-term counseling, our focus is on exploring options with our clients. When a person is victimized, they frequently feel like they have fewer options than perhaps they really have. It can be because of lack of knowledge of the system, or lack of real support, or a perceived lack of social support. We try to offer options. For example, where you go for help, who you might call in crisis, where you might go for training in self-defense or self-empowerment. Or what options are available in terms of the legal process, or in terms of criminal justice advocacy. We work on options counseling.

GMH: *What are some of the mental health needs of people who get in touch with CUAV?*

Wenny: Different individuals who experience hate violence or domestic violence have different needs when they come to CUAV. At the simplest level, some need to make a report as a form of personal empowerment. "This is what has happened to me and I would like it known." At the more complex end, an individual might be seeking counseling because of the postassault trauma in terms of flashbacks, in terms of shock.

One thing that I see consistently is the challenge to one's worldview and the challenge to one's denial. I really associate that with the shock that's experienced in the aftermath of a hate crime. And that's what I hear a lot of, "Yes I knew that this was going on. Of course I've been victimized in the past where I've been called faggot or dyke but I never knew it went on to this extent. I didn't know that this was happening." I also hear a lot of disillusionment.

I focus a lot on hope. I know that sounds vague, but it's really an important issue in victimization, especially in violence against gays and lesbians, which can be so very hateful and so really hurtful. I'm not even talking about verbal abuse, although that's very common, but the daily occurrences of physical assaults against gay men and lesbians. What's hard for me is seeing clients who were already victimized in other ways, whether because of AIDS or the generalized homophobia, and here they are, above and beyond all of that, sitting in front of me with crutches, with a leg in a cast, with stitches across their head because of a recent assault that was hate motivated.

So their needs go all the way from report-making to counseling. I offer them information about breaking out of isolation. It's very important that they get the message that they're not the only ones who experience this, that they can find some common issues to identify with others. Going back to the choice issue, I provide them with information not only about hate violence but also about systems. About what can be done through the criminal justice system; through the social services system; what can be done to meet their medical needs, their work-related needs, and so on.

GMH: *Are there differences between lesbians and gay men in their needs after they have been victimized?*

Jill: I think that there are. I think women have less experience in general with dealing with being angry, so we are challenged to help our lesbian clients to be angry in appropriate ways. Not by going out with an Uzi, but in fact they do need to express it and deal with it.

Another difference that we see consistently is that lesbians tend to use their own support groups, their friends and what they consider their extended family. They don't have the same desire or comfort as men do for using an institution to get support. We have men who will be coming back to CUAV long after an incident. I can think of one man in particular who was victimized two years ago and still shows up on a fairly regular basis to talk about the incident again or whatever has come up for him in relation to it. We never see lesbians on that sort of long-term basis. We might help them to remember or identify their own support system, but then that system is what they're going to go back to, that's what they are going to use. We're still working hard to get more women to come to us. When I started, lesbians were barely 3% of our client population. It's almost 20% now, but 20% is still nothing compared to the San Francisco population.

Lester: Women who are victimized often are not sure whether it was an anti-lesbian or antiwoman attack. The issue of women not going to Community United Against Violence is directly related to making that distinction. I think by and large women are much more likely to go to a rape treatment center, or rape peer-counseling group, or some sort of organization that's specifically for and by women, rather than to a more mixed locale.

GMH: *What about your clients who are people of color?*

Jill: About 14% of our clients have been people of color—5% were African American, 5% Latino or Latina, 2% Asian or Pacific Islanders, 1% identified as American Indians, and another 1% identified as multiracial. Eight percent of our incidents contained identifiable racial dynamics. Those are the cases in which the victim reported during the intake interview that, along with some specifically anti-gay or anti-lesbian element, there had been a racial dynamic as well. There were racial epithets of some kind or some other element to the attack that made the victim believe that it was not solely motivated by homophobia.

GMH: *Are there racial differences in the ways that your clients are victimized?*

Jill: One difference is that the majority of people of color who report to us say that they find it difficult to separate the anti-gay or anti-lesbian element of the attack from the elements that are racial. The incidents seem to be motivated by both for a lot of the people reporting.

Once they have been victimized, I think it's important that people of color be able to report to somebody who is able to understand the complexity of their victimization. Someone who will not try to focus just on the anti-gay or anti-lesbian element of the incident as though it's the only important element. So I think there's a need for greater sensitivity in that regard on the part of people taking reports.

GMH: *When people of color have been victimized by a White attacker, is it difficult for them to go an agency where White people are present?*

Jill: I think that it could be. It can create a situation where it's hard to trust the person that you're reporting to. Historically, I think that CUAV was perceived as a place that wasn't available for anybody other than White, gay men. I think that people often simply didn't report at all if they believed that they were going to be reporting to members of the perpetrating group. It wasn't even a conscious thing like "Gee, I won't go to CUAV because they'll rebuff me." I think it was much more subtle.

GMH: *Has CUAV changed in that respect?*

Jill: I know for sure that the number of lesbians and gay men of color who report to us has increased. Although our numbers are still low, they've increased significantly. I'm pretty confident that the numbers will continue to increase if we continue to do the kind of work that we've been doing. The number one thing that we did was to change the racial composition of our staff. We now have a multiracial, multiethnic staff, with people of all races, backgrounds, classes and ages. We have differently abled people on staff. All of that has significantly changed the image of CUAV. It also has changed what is important to CUAV.

CUAV's direction has changed in some ways over the last three years in a way that reflects the changes in staff. Our executive director is a person of color, which I think is a very strong message about how the agency's goals have changed in different ways. Almost all of our outreach resources go into doing outreach to lesbians of all races, and particularly to lesbians and gay men of color. That means we don't put out a lot of money to have a booth at an event where we don't think we'll be able to reach people of color. In the last three years we also have started working much more seriously than ever before to work in coalition with other groups concerned about hate crimes.

GMH: *A question I'm often asked is whether anti-gay violence is on the increase. What is your sense?*

Jill: I always answer that in several different ways. One answer is that we don't really know, although we do know that reported attacks are increasing. I usually follow that up by saying that it is my strong feeling that it is increasing. Open sentiment against us has definitely increased. We could measure that if we just looked at newspaper articles. And that is not unconnected to the move of our government to the right, to resentment at the increase in our community's visible political power, and to the use of AIDS as an excuse for openly venting that sentiment. If you put all of those things together, you get a climate where it's permissible to express your hatred against lesbians and gay men.

There is a theory that for every reported victimization, at least ten others go unreported. The victim either didn't know about the resources, or didn't think it was important enough to report, or was afraid to report. If that theory is true, then there's not anybody in this community who hasn't dealt with victimization.

You also have to recognize the degree to which we are all victimized by anti-gay and anti-lesbian incidents that we hear about. Two nights ago, the Metropolitan Community Church in San Francisco was firebombed at two or three in the morning. The next morning, when I heard about it, I went over to remind the folks that CUAV was there for them if they needed counseling or advocacy, or if they wanted us to help with press, or whatever. I am not a member of that church, and I feel no particular connection with them. I sometimes think I'm immune to it, but when I saw what that firebomb had done, I felt scared. And that was precisely the intent of that kind of attack. To the degree that there are more people who identify as lesbian or gay, there are more people to feel victimized by that sort of event. In that way, if in no other, violence has certainly increased.

Lester: When I worked at CUAV, I did a lot of work trying to put together intercommunity responses to hate violence. Trying to get lots of different kinds of people together working on hate violence: women, straight and gay; Black people, straight and gay; Latino people, straight and gay; and so on. One of the lessons I learned is that the sense of victimization does not only result from violence. For Black individuals and communities in this country, there is widespread educational and economic victimization. And that victimization is every bit as real and hateful and painful as a physical assault on the street.

So one of my feelings when people ask, "Is violence on the increase?" is to say that I think the type of victimization of lesbian and gay people maybe has changed to a certain extent. In the 1950s, different tools were used to keep us in the closet—economic pressures or political witch hunts. For example—you wouldn't go anywhere in a corporation unless you were married so we had to stay invisible. You couldn't go anywhere in government unless you weren't a homosexual and swore you weren't a communist. As the community has coalesced, become more visible and more self-conscious about our existence and more outspoken about what's happening to us, there may be more physical violence. But in no way is there more victimization. I cannot believe that we are more victimized today than, say, Del Martin and Phyllis Lyon were in the 1950s. I just can't believe that.

I think it's important to remember this as those of us in the lesbian and gay communities who are White go out and try to interact with other communities. When I was trying to do broader work with other communities, I found that we weren't always speaking the same language. I was concerned about being bashed on the street at 18th and Castro, but other people were concerned about no housing or about Black students dropping out before they finished high school. Those are horrible situations that need to be addressed, and both of them stem from the same causes. That's why I always come back to context, the whole contextual picture of why these things are happening.

GMH: *I think that physical bashing of gay men and women was expected in the 1950s; it wasn't even defined as violence or a crime. If two men were walking down the street holding hands or two women looked "queer," of course they'd get bashed. It must have seemed almost like a law of nature.*

Jill: That's a very important point and it connects with what I've been seeing lately. I recently named for myself something that I think has been happening for a long time, which is an enormous age gap within our community. It's best described by looking at the differences between the lesbians and gay men who are active in the gay democratic clubs versus those in Queer Nation or ACT UP. I think some of what that is about—a very powerful part—is the younger generation's level of expectations about what is right, what are their options for living. Their expectations are different from those of people who are 40 or older, those who had very different experiences as young lesbians and gay men and who developed very different expectations about what they could expect from living in this country. These young folks notice the violence and think, "I can't believe that we're sitting around and not fighting back and shooting back and bashing back and arming ourselves." It's a whole different level of response and some of it is because the younger lesbians and gay men live in such a different context today.

Lester: Jill referred earlier to San Francisco being the location with more hate attacks against lesbians and gays than any other place. CUAV is often asked, "Why does it happen in San Francisco, which is a gay mecca and socially tolerant?" And that raises the

whole question of visibility and whether it's better or worse to
be visible, to be "out there." A lot of people think that if we
would just stay quiet that we wouldn't be bashed. My grand-
mother, who is 87 and who thinks my lover is great, really
hasn't any problem with me being gay. But she doesn't want me
on TV because she thinks that's dangerous. I agree with Jill that
it's largely generational, although certainly not completely.

   Jill: A lot of gay people say "Why don't you just behave? We
haven't been doing so badly just being polite."

   Lester: I think we have to be careful not to buy into that argument. In San Francisco more than any other place in the country,
the lesbian and gay community is ghettoized. There are certain de-
finable, distinct neighborhoods that are predominantly lesbian and
gay. And in fact, those areas do become targets for people who
want to come and bash us; they know where to go to bash a queer.
That's also true in other urban areas of the country but my sense is
that it's more true in San Francisco. That is partly why we have
such a large number of violent acts in San Francisco.

   But that doesn't mean that in a small town you don't have victimization. It may be like in Maine, where one murder of one
youth—throwing him off the bridge to let him drown—serves as
a message to the whole state: "You—don't be queer." You just
need one example rather than thousands of examples. Of course
Maine has more than just one example. But in places like that,
other tools of oppression and violence are still in place more
completely, be they economic pressures or family pressures or
religious pressures or whatever. In San Francisco, a lot of those
other tools have broken down because we have some economic
protection, some political protection. It's limited, but it's there.
So, as those other tools of keeping us in the closet break down,
our antagonists have to revert to the violence.

   GMH: *We've talked about the cultural context of victimization.
What do you think are some of the causes for violence at the individual
level? What are the motivations of perpetrators?*

   Wenny: My personal feeling is that a lot of anti-gay and anti-
lesbian violence has its basis in misogyny. Time and again, I
meet one-to-one with male clients who have been victimized by
other males. These are gay male clients who have been sexually
assaulted by straight, heterosexual males. They are reporting to
me what was being said to them during the assault, which I feel

is very important in terms of revealing motives. Time and again the sentiments in those assaults are misogynist.

GMH: *What do you mean by "misogynist"?*

Jill: It is so much related to the hatred of women. And it's true not just for men, but also for women. And it goes to what I believe is the essence of homophobia: The perception that gay men are acting like women and lesbians aren't acting enough like women, so nobody's doing it right in terms of gender roles.

Wenny: You hear this in the graphic descriptions of gang rapes and, I'm not sure why, but more gang rape victims are coming to us lately. I have a client who was gang-raped by three or four men. He wasn't sure because at different times he was beaten during the assault by different people who held him down. He was sitting in my office crying, and he was saying, "You know, the hardest thing to get out of my head is what they were saying to me as they were holding me down and fucking me from behind. They said, 'Oh, haven't we got a pretty one this time. Yes it's the prettiest one of them all. Isn't he pretty. He's so cute.' And they were saying this as they were fucking me and I just can't get that out of my head, how pretty I was." And the assault was anti-gay. That scene is remarkable for not being remarkable; other clients have revealed the same sentiments to me.

Jill: We've done a lot of work at CUAV over the last three years to connect the issue of anti-gay violence to other types of hate violence. But a lot of times the conversation about what causes hate violence against other groups is very much an economic discussion. The violence is based on the concept of "if you get some of the pie, I won't have any," particularly in relation to anti-immigrant sentiment. The escalation of anti-gay violence is certainly connected with the escalation of those other forms of hate violence in some ways. Since gays and lesbians are growing in political power, they are probably seen as having greater access to economic resources. But the other forms don't have at their root that millennia-old hatred of women. In this way, we stand very separate from other forms of hate violence.

Lester: This conversation reminds me of Greg's article on the context of hate violence [*Journal of Interpersonal Violence, 5*, 316-333, 1990]. You also talked about the gender roles that are expected of people. I think the violence is based on those roles. It's directed at men who don't act enough like men and at women

who don't act enough like women. When you talk about hate violence in general, it often involves people who don't act the way
they're supposed to act. Whether it's immigrants who don't stay in
their own country, Blacks who don't stay in their own ghetto, lesbians and gays who don't stay in their closets. It's people who don't
act like they're supposed to act. In this sense, I agree that there's a
very close relationship between anti-gay violence and the gender
roles that are expected of people. The homophobia comes from the
perception that we're not playing the correct gender role. Whether
you're a straight woman who is strong, active, and out there; or
whether you're a gay man who doesn't want to have 3.4 children
and live in the suburbs and marry a woman. Whatever you're doing, it's not what you're supposed to be doing.

Wenny: And these feelings exist in our own community as
well. As gays and lesbians living in this country, how can we
help but not be affected by the generalized homophobia? One of
my biggest disillusionments since I've been working with
CUAV has been discovering how much hate violence was also
being perpetrated by citizens of our own community on ourselves. We hear comments like, "That queen deserved it." Or
"Look at that dyke; she needs a dick between her legs." We're
hearing this from gay people.

GMH: *If you could talk to the perpetrators, what is going on in
their heads? Is it really an articulated misogyny?*

Jill: I don't think it's misogyny on the level of, "Gee, I woke up
this morning and I remembered that I hate women and I'm going
to do something about it." But I do think it's conscious. I know,
just because of my own experience as a lesbian and what straight
men have said to me. I think it's conscious to them that people living without needing them are more than just a threat; something
needs to be done about them. It's almost a cliché for lesbians, when
we're talking to each other, to talk about all the straight men who
think all we need is to be fucked. And rape is the natural extension
of that belief; it's a statement that "I'm going to show you that all
you need is to be fucked." So I do think there's a way in which it is
a quite conscious belief that we aren't doing what we're supposed
to. What's being said is either, "You are not a woman if you don't
act like my idea of one," or "If you're a man you shouldn't act like
a woman." They just wouldn't use the term "misogyny" for it;
they'd say they're putting us where we belong.

Lester: You can pick up a newspaper any day of the week and see the underpinning of the violence, going back to your article on the context. Everything we're taught by different institutions about who we're supposed to be is right there. The particular person who believes himself to be heterosexual and who is gang-raping a man is not necessarily going to say, "You're not playing the role you ought to be playing." But he might have come just that morning from a church that preached, "Well, you can be a homosexual, but don't act on it because that's sinful and horrible and you'll go to hell." Or he might belong to the Catholic church and have heard a sermon about the recent American Bishops' statement on homosexuality. Or he might have just been watching television and seen [U.S. Representative William] Dannemeyer or [California State Senator James] Neilson saying that AIDS is God's punishment. Every day you can see the cultural underpinnings for homophobia. It's a message that people then act upon in an extreme form, a more violent form, a more active form. But it's the same stuff, it's part of the same continuum. To me that's very clear.

Wenny: I just wanted to add one more thing about how prevalent this antiwoman sentiment is. When we keep statistics at CUAV, we ask victims to define the incident as they experienced it, what they feel motivated it rather than putting words in their mouth. Very frequently, the antiwoman sentiment is expressed. If it looks like the victim is going in this direction, I say, "Well here is our list of categories" for motivations, and I will read off a few. Lo and behold, there are male victims who say, "Well yeah, this was definitely antiwoman."

Lester: CUAV had a researcher, Beatrice von Schulthess, who was working on her Ph.D. with us and she interviewed 400 lesbians. The most consistent issue for lesbians who had been victimized was that they were hard pressed to say whether the assault was anti-lesbian or antiwoman. It became so mixed up whether she was being assaulted because she was a dyke or because she was a woman [see Chapter 6].

GMH: *What is your advice for people in small communities who are trying to deal with anti-gay violence? What priorities should they set?*

Lester: When I worked at CUAV we were asked that fairly often. People would call up and say, "How can I get a project going?" and usually they don't have the resources to staff seven people right off the bat. But there are so many pieces that even one person who's volunteering their time can begin to put something together. You can start a reporting project to develop statistics, with basic peer counseling or even without peer counseling. You can put together a resource guide of where people can go. You can put together a training program with nonprofit social service agencies so that they are prepared either to report or to have staff who are sensitized to the issues. You can put together a program where you educate the police. Or you can organize a police reporting program, where you work on getting the police to recognize hate violence. If you do that, you would want to work with other communities that are victimized by hate violence; so you could start pulling together coalitions around the issue of different types of hate violence. You can create speakers' bureaus and basic educational programs in the schools or in other settings. Any one of those pieces is going to move the agenda forward. It's going to take on a life of its own and snowball in the response that it generates to hate violence and general discrimination against lesbians and gays. I think it's important for people with limited resources to start with one piece. Start that and then let it move on its own. The rest can be added later.

GMH: *Of all those different components, do you think one or two of them are most important?*

Lester: I'm always biased toward a reporting system. For better or worse, people look at numbers in this country. When you have some documented numbers, two things will happen. First, when you have some numbers you can go to people and say, "Here is a demonstrable problem. These are individuals who came and took the time to talk, the time to write down their experiences." It gives you background, substance you can use to go out and look for more resources and for more help. And at some point, the pressure of having people call you up and say, "I was victimized," will be an impetus to learn the skills of peer counseling and to set up resources for the victims. So when you set up that basic reporting, which can be low intensity to start with, it lays the groundwork to move onto more things. Another suggestion I'll add is that working with police departments is important: sensitizing police, setting up hate crime units, doing lesbian and gay sensitivity training.

Jill: I agree that if we were to prioritize, the one thing that you might do first is documentation. If you are overwhelmed by all the things you feel need to be done in your community, buy a $49 answering machine; put it in somebody's bedroom; print up some stickers that say "Report anti-gay assaults" and the phone number; slap them all over town, in every bathroom, in every rest room that's used for cruising and sex and every rest stop that is on the freeways near that community; and sit back and you'll have a project. You don't have to do counseling at the beginning if nobody feels that they know how. Don't tell anybody that you are providing counseling; just say you're a reporting system and you will have the beginnings of something. The fact is that we live in a time now when right-wing people like to talk about victims' rights. There's money for victims, and there's actually money for lesbian and gay victims. And once you have proved that you have some victims, you can do something.

GMH: *What future directions do you see for CUAV and for other groups working against anti-gay violence? What should people do next?*

Lester: I think it's essential that we develop intense educational programs. This needs to be done as a community, not just in San Francisco, but everywhere. There are lots of ways to do that, whether it be advertising on TV, educational programs in the schools, or whatever. We need to tell people who we are in a very intense, well-focused way. We need to do it in a way that's not attached to any political movement or issue or candidate. We need to be out there spending money, time, and resources to tell people who we are. It should be, in a sense, a continuation of Harvey Milk's admonition to come out. Everybody come out, now, in a bigger way. The mother whose son committed suicide because he was gay, and she rejected him, have her come out and say what happened to her. The man who was not allowed to take bereavement leave when his lover died, have him come out on TV and talk about his experience and his relationship and how the company he worked for refused to give him three days bereavement leave, incidentally pre-AIDS. Real hard-hitting, basic stuff about our families, our jobs, our lives and the whole sexual and cultural mixture of people who are lesbian and gay and bisexual. To me that's essential work and we have to do it.

Jill: This bashing-back movement is very much on my mind right now. There is a whole segment of our community that's struggling with feeling disempowered because of hate violence and feeling that the current responses to hate violence are inadequate. They're advocating not just defending themselves through self-defense or whistles, but actively fighting back. Hunt down the attackers at their homes, if you know where they live. That kind of thing. I have a lot of concern about it, so it's made me focus my attention on what I think is the real solution. And I think that's the form of education that comes from really knowing lesbians and gay men.

It's amazing to me that coming out is so undated as a concept, that it's as radical an idea today as it was 20 or 30 years ago. It is radical for two reasons. One, I do believe that knowing somebody well who is lesbian or gay changes how heterosexual people think. When someone from our Speakers' Bureau goes out to a group of young people, we just see those kids one time; six months later, I don't know what effect that one 50-minute visit still has on them. But actually having someone in their life on a regular basis changes how a young person thinks. To have an uncle or an aunt, or a cousin, or a godmother who is openly lesbian or gay has an enormous effect on that young person.

Two, I don't underemphasize the effect it has on ourselves in our own ever-evolving coming-out process. To let other people see all of who we are is, I think, a much more important and permanent way of bringing true radical change to this country than punching somebody or shooting somebody ever could be.

NOTE

1. Readers can obtain more information about Community United Against Violence by writing to CUAV, P.O. Box 14017, San Francisco, CA 94114.

Organizing Against Hate on Campus: Strategies for Activists

KEVIN T. BERRILL

On college and university campuses across the United States, lesbian and gay students, staff, faculty, and alumni/ae are more visible and vocal than ever before. In recent years, dramatic increases in both the number and the activity levels of lesbian, gay, and bisexual campus groups have led hundreds of colleges and universities to adopt policies prohibiting discrimination based on sexual orientation. Some institutions have taken other affirmative measures, such as extending spousal benefits to gay couples (e.g., Stanford University), offering lesbian and gay studies courses (e.g., Vassar College), sponsoring task forces to counter anti-gay prejudice and improve the quality of life for gay and bisexual students (e.g., Rutgers University), and establishing offices to address the needs of lesbian, gay, and bisexual students (e.g., the University of Michigan).

Although increased lesbian and gay visibility on campus has brought about positive institutional changes, it also appears to have triggered an unprecedented level of anti-gay harassment and violence. Thousands of incidents, including threats, vandalism,

AUTHOR'S NOTE: I thank Todd Clark, Howard Ehrlich, Curtis Shepard, and Richard Wood for assisting me in the preparation of this chapter.

assault, and arson, have been reported by campus groups to the National Gay & Lesbian Task Force (NGLTF) in recent years (NGLTF, 1990). At several colleges, prevalence studies of anti-gay violence and other victimization also show the problem to be alarmingly widespread (see Chapter 1 by Berrill).

The following are just a few of the anti-gay episodes that have occurred in recent years:

- University of Delaware (Newark): A chalk outline of a body, with raw meat splattered on the head, was found outside a university building with the written message, "Another dead faggot." The "Homophobic Liberation Front" claimed responsibility (NGLTF Policy Institute, 1991).
- Mt. Vernon College (Washington, DC): An African American lesbian student was repeatedly subjected to racist and anti-gay harassment, including notes left on her door that read "Die Dyke!" and "You Need Dick" (NGLTF, 1990).
- University of Akron (Ohio): At a campuswide festival, several male students approached a woman who staffed the lesbian/gay information booth and smashed eggs in her face (NGLTF, 1990).
- Columbia University (New York): During a rash of anti-gay incidents, two leaders of the Gay and Lesbian Alliance received death threats in the mail. Taped to one of the letters was a .38 caliber bullet (NGLTF, 1990).
- University of California (Los Angeles): During a UCLA football game, a mob of fraternity brothers taunted members of a lesbian sorority and threw ice, beer, and paper cups at the women (NGLTF, 1990).

That such victimization occurs alongside increasing attacks against people of color, women, and Jews suggests that bigotry is gaining ground on many campuses. Indeed, slurs and offensive jokes, ugly graffiti, hate mail, sexual harassment, and physical assaults are becoming an all too familiar, and sometimes accepted, part of college life (e.g., Tift, 1989).

Perhaps even more disturbing than the attacks themselves is the lack of reaction to them by many college and university officials. Although some administrators have forthrightly confronted the problem, most still deny or ignore its existence or respond in a manner so tepid as to be ineffectual. Such was the case in 1989 at Pennsylvania State University, where a student sent out a message on the university computer bulletin board calling for the extermination of homosexuals. Despite appeals to the school's president that he condemn the episode, he remained silent. Only after a sustained lobbying campaign by concerned members of the Pennsylvania State community did he issue a statement that, instead of condemning the bigotry in the message, denounced misuse of the computer system.

In many cases, administrators dismiss incidents as "isolated" or argue that drawing attention to them would only "make matters worse." Sometimes they have gone so far as to blame the victims, suggesting that they keep a lower profile or else transfer to another school.

STRATEGIES FOR ACTIVISTS

Although there is no single formula for countering hate, the following are some suggestions that gay and lesbian students, staff and faculty, and their allies can use in organizing an effective response.

(1) Support the victims. When responding to hate-motivated harassment or violence, make the welfare of those victimized your paramount concern. Any decisions about whether to publicize or organize a response to an incident directed at specific individuals always should be made in consultation with the victim(s). It is inappropriate and potentially very damaging to victims for others to speak or act on their behalf without their knowledge and consent.

Acts of anti-gay bigotry violate and isolate not only the individuals who are targeted but all gay and lesbian people. Because the impact of such incidents is widely felt, it may be helpful to create an opportunity for all concerned to share their feelings and discuss a possible response (e.g., a facilitated discussion or a speak-out).

The aftermath of bias incidents often leaves victims feeling profoundly isolated (see Chapter 13 by Garnets, Herek, & Levy). It is important, therefore, that they receive emotional support. Let them know you care. Listen to them. Inform them about counseling and other support services that are available. Affirm the choices they make.

Victims may choose not to report harassment for a variety of reasons, including fear of publicity, fear of revictimization, or a desire to put the incident behind them. Whatever the reason, a victim's decision not to go to the authorities always should be respected.

If, on the other hand, victims decide to report, get behind them. Find out what the official channels are for reporting harassment and help them through the process. It may be appropriate to go to campus police, resident advisers, a campus ombudsperson, or the dean of students.

Reporting harassment to the authorities is often an intimidating experience, especially for gay and lesbian people. It can be enormously helpful to victims if others accompany them when they make a report. Choose one or more persons who can assist in making the report and in monitoring the school's handling of the case.

(2) Document anti-gay harassment and discrimination. By keeping detailed information on incidents that occur, you can establish that they are not isolated and strengthen your case for official action. Therefore, whenever harassment or discrimination occurs, document everything. Write down exactly what, when, and where incidents happened. Record the names or descriptions of perpetrators. Make photocopies of hate mail. Never give away your only copy, even to the authorities. Keep a careful log of hate calls and make a tape of hate calls recorded on your answering machine. Photograph physical injuries, offensive graffiti, and evidence of vandalism. This information may prove useful as evidence in court proceedings. When compiling documentation, keep confidentiality in mind. Do not include victims' names or other identifying information in your records unless you have their permission, preferably in writing.

At several colleges, supportive social science faculty members have conducted surveys of lesbian, gay, and bisexual people on campus to gauge levels of harassment, discrimination, and fear. The data from these surveys have been useful in advocating for official action (see Chapter 17 by Herek & Berrill).

(3) Set your agenda. Your efforts to counter bigotry will be most effective if you develop clear goals and strategies and if all the members of your group have had an opportunity to participate in decision making. Such input expands the range of ideas and

options and gives members an opportunity to get excited about, and invested in, any proposals that are made to the administration. It is also important for those who will be negotiating with the school to make sure that they agree on the agenda, goals, and tactics.

Acts of bigotry are ugly, offensive, and sometimes dangerous and therefore require a strong response. They also afford opportunities, however, to expose and challenge the prejudice and institutional neglect that facilitate attacks. It is not enough that administrators discipline individual perpetrators or otherwise react to a specific incident. Systemic problems require a systemic response from the administration and the entire campus community. (See Appendix 16.A in this chapter for a list of recommended measures.)

In calling for a response to anti-gay bigotry, be wary of "quick fix" remedies, such as policies to limit and punish offensive speech. Such restrictions initially may seem attractive but they can lead to limitations on other forms of expression. In the long run, it may be more productive for campus officials and the larger campus community to condemn rather than censor bigoted speech. Some hate speech, however, including libel and threats of violence, is not legally protected and warrants punitive action.

(4) Build awareness and coalitions. Negotiation inside is helped by agitation outside. The administration is likely to take acts of bigotry more seriously if the problem is widely publicized and if your proposed solutions are widely supported. Accordingly, you and your allies must be seen and heard. Inform the campus media about the problem. Hold a forum or speak-out. Ask the student and faculty governing bodies to pass resolutions condemning acts of hatred and to support your agenda. Circulate petitions. Ask students, parents, faculty, and influential outsiders to write letters to key officials. In short, create a climate of moral outrage that will facilitate moral action.

Before developing your agenda, consider meeting with groups representing other minorities and women to find out whether they are interested in working together with you. Bias-motivated harassment is a natural issue around which to build coalitions. Because bigotry in all its forms has similar dynamics and expressions, it makes sense to promote comprehensive solutions.

Building coalitions can be difficult work, especially on campuses where gay people are perceived as marginal and powerless. Lesbian and gay organizers often choose not to reach out for support from other groups because they expect to be rebuffed, ignored, or shunted aside. They may also fear that a broad-based coalition would be fragile and move too slowly.

When diverse groups come together to meet these challenges, however, they often succeed in bringing about significant change. The result can be enormously rewarding. At their best, coalitions and alliances can accomplish far more than any individual group that goes it alone. Working together with other groups that are the targets of hate not only increases your collective power, it also creates goodwill and solidarity. By working with and standing up for each other, coalition partners may eventually become allies and friends who are deeply committed to each others' issues.

(5) *Meet with the administration.* Do your homework before meeting with campus officials. Start with a thorough investigation of your university administration. Who is responsible for setting policy on harassment and related matters? Request a meeting with the appropriate officials to discuss the problem and how they can best respond to it. Bring along statistical and anecdotal documentation you have compiled, a list of proposed remedies, positive examples of how other colleges have responded, influential allies (e.g., representatives of other student groups, parents, alumni/ae, respected faculty), and, if possible, one or two victims who are willing to share their experiences.

During meetings with administrators, it helps to stress how your interests converge with theirs and how implementation of your proposals will lead to a more open, less oppressive, and safer campus environment. Listen carefully to what they say in response to your requests. If you are not sure how to answer their proposals, ask for time to think them over and consult with others. Ask that they make their commitments in writing, including target dates for implementation.

(6) *When you get the runaround.* If you have been negotiating in good faith and your key requests are unanswered or refused by the administration, it may be necessary to take a confrontational approach.

One strategy is legal action. If your school fails to adequately protect its members from abuse and harm, it might be liable for civil damages. Contact national gay and lesbian legal advocacy groups or your state chapter of the American Civil Liberties Union (ACLU) for advice, assistance, and referrals (see "Resources" below). Sometimes all it takes is a call from an attorney to persuade reluctant administrators to take appropriate action.

A second option is to bring bias-related incidents on campus to the attention of the gay and mainstream media. Call reporters individually or hold a press conference. College officials hate negative publicity and tend to act more quickly and responsibly when reporters begin to call or appear on campus.

A third option is direct action. Identify the administrators who are obstacles and plan an action that attracts their attention as well as that of the media and the community. Choose an action that fits your resources and objectives (e.g., a teach-in, demonstration, or a sit-in). Have a clear set of demands, always keep channels of communication open, and agree in advance among yourselves what minimum demands must be met for you to end the action. Remember that confrontational tactics—especially acts of civil disobedience—are most appropriate after you have exhausted other means of persuasion and are willing and prepared to accept the possible consequences of violating campus regulations or the law.

In the coming years, it is likely that lesbians and gay men on campus will experience increased acceptance and empowerment, on the one hand, and increased harassment and violence, on the other. In the face of rising abuse, academic institutions have a responsibility to address not only specific anti-gay incidents but also the prejudice that motivates them. Lesbian and gay activists and their allies must play a key role in fostering official action to counter hate and create a safe and affirming campus environment for all those who are the targets of bigotry.

RESOURCES

The following is a list of organizations that can assist campus organizers in countering bigotry and violence.

National Gay & Lesbian Task Force Policy Institute, Campus and Anti-Violence Projects, 1734 14th Street N.W., Washington, DC 20009 (202) 332-6483: monitors anti-gay incidents, provides technical assistance on countering anti-gay bias on campus.

National Institute Against Prejudice and Violence, 31 South Greene Street, Baltimore, MD 21201 (301) 328-5170: monitors hate-motivated incidents, provides technical assistance.

Center for Democratic Renewal, P.O. Box 50469, Atlanta, GA 30302 (404) 221-0025: monitors and promotes responses to bias incidents and hate-group activity.

Anti-Defamation League, Department of Campus Affairs, 823 United Nations Plaza, New York, NY 10017 (212) 490-2525: monitors anti-Semitic incidents; provides technical assistance.

Lambda Legal Defense and Education Fund, 666 Broadway, New York, NY 10012 (212) 995-8585: provides legal advocacy and referrals for the lesbian and gay community.

ACLU Lesbian and Gay Rights Project, 132 West 43rd Street, New York, NY 10036 (212) 944-9800, ext. 545: provides legal advocacy and referrals for the lesbian and gay community.

APPENDIX
Responding to Bias Incidents on Campus:
NGLTF Policy Institute Recommendations for Action

College and university administrations have a legal and moral obligation to counter bias-motivated harassment. They should take a comprehensive rather than piecemeal approach, addressing underlying causes as well specific incidents. The following recommendations, many of which have been adopted by colleges across the country, are offered to facilitate positive action.

(1) Enact a policy addressing bias-related harassment. Every academic institution should adopt a policy that condemns and prohibits harassment and violence based on prejudice. To underscore the university's commitment to protecting individuals of different identities, backgrounds, and beliefs, such a policy should specifically name the categories that are protected. These should include, but not necessarily be limited to, sexual orientation, race, religion, ethnicity, gender, and disability. Furthermore, harassment policies should explain the process by which victims may file complaints against perpetrators.

Antiharassment policies have little or no deterrent effect unless they are widely publicized. They should be brought to the attention of the campus community regularly: at orientation, at campuswide meetings, in the student handbook, and on campus bulletin boards. When a serious episode occurs or pattern of bias incidents emerges, special efforts should be made to publicize the policy.

In recent years, extensive debate has occurred on college campuses about whether and to what extent offensive speech should be regulated. These guidelines do not attempt to delineate the boundaries of acceptable speech and behavior. Such complex matters require careful study and debate not only among administrators but in the entire campus community. If proposals to impose sanctions on offensive speech are considered, such discussions should take into account the serious consequences such restrictions might have on other forms of expression.

Whether or not hate speech is punishable, it should always be condemned. If administrators and others in the campus community remain silent merely because such speech is legally protected, their silence can be easily interpreted as acceptance of or agreement with such expressions. Because many forms of bigoted speech cannot be *censored*, it is all the more important that they be *censured*.

(2) *Prohibit discrimination based on sexual orientation.* It is inconsistent to prohibit anti-gay harassment while permitting the targets of such abuse to suffer discrimination. When they fail to protect individuals from discrimination based on sexual orientation, academic institutions relegate lesbian and gay students, staff, and faculty to second-class status. Such unequal treatment encourages expressions of anti-gay bigotry while at the same time discouraging gay and lesbian people from reporting harassment and receiving the education to which they are entitled.

(3) *Establish formal procedures for handling harassment.* Every college and university should have clear procedures for handling complaints of bias-related harassment. To minimize confusion about where to report, certain offices (e.g., the dean of students, campus police, office of human relations) should be designated to receive and respond to such reports.

Because of their volatility and serious consequences, investigation of bias incidents and response to them should receive high priority. Top-level administrators should monitor the handling of each case and give special attention to developing strategies for averting additional outbreaks of prejudice or violence. Tensions can be calmed and further incidents deterred by prompt official statements that vigorously condemn acts of bigotry and assure a thorough investigation. When appropriate, administrators should call on local or federal law enforcement agencies to assist in the investigation of bias crimes.

Plans also should be in place for rumor control, external publicity, and prompt removal of offensive graffiti (after it has been photographed and inspected for evidence). Furthermore, campus officials should have a policy for dealing with the hate-mongering presence of extremist speakers.

(4) Encourage reporting of bias incidents. Unless episodes of harassment on campus are reported, college officials can do little about them. Because victims of bias incidents fear discrimination and revictimization, they seldom inform the authorities. Their reluctance is often reinforced by confusion about where to go and how to proceed with a complaint. Establishing a special harassment telephone hotline (with great emphasis placed on confidentiality and anonymity) can help victims to take the first step. Victims will be more likely to report bias incidents if information is disseminated through brochures, posters, and videos that encourage them to step forward and that explain how to proceed.

(5) Establish a task force to discourage bias and promote appreciation of diversity. Levels of awareness and reporting can be increased by creating task forces to counter intolerance and encourage appreciation for diversity. Such task forces should be composed of students, staff, faculty, and administrators. They can monitor and guide the university's response to bias incidents, provide advocacy for victims, develop publicity materials to encourage reporting, and sponsor educational programs aimed at reducing prejudice and increasing tolerance. To be effective, task forces must reflect the diversity of the campus community (especially those groups targeted for harassment) and receive sufficient financial resources to carry out their mission.

(6) Collect data on bias incidents. A system should be established on every campus to identify, classify, and compile information on bias-related incidents. Data on such incidents can be evaluated during regular assessments of the campus environment and the possible need for interventions. By sharing these data with the campus community, the administration can show its ongoing commitment to dealing with the problem. Periodic reports also signal to minorities and women that their victimization is a matter of official concern. Victims thus feel encouraged to report, even when their perpetrators cannot be identified.

(7) Provide assistance to victims. To minimize the potential trauma of anti-gay and other hate incidents, support services should be made available to victims. These should include advocacy, counseling, and peer support. Training should be provided to resident advisors, campus security, student life personnel, and other staff to help them to respond sensitively to needs of victims and their loved ones.

Victims, like defendants, deserve the right to participate in the judicial process and to make a "victim impact statement." Such statements, which are presented orally or in writing to the offender and those who will administer discipline, allow victims to express their feelings about the incident and how they wish punishment to be imposed. Although some victims may choose not to make such a statement, it is nevertheless important that the option be available to them. Organizations representing communities affected by the incident should have an opportunity to be heard as well.

(8) Discipline perpetrators of bias incidents. Treating bias-motivated incidents as "childish pranks" trivializes the incidents and their profound impact on both the victims and the larger community. Individuals found to have engaged in such incidents should therefore be disciplined appropriately. Moreover, the results of disciplinary hearings ought to be made public. As the New York State Task Force on Bias-Related Violence stated in its report, "Bias violence cases affect a community that has a right to knowledge of the outcome" (Governor's Task Force, 1988, p. 63).

(9) Educate the campus community about prejudice and violence. As the only known means of overcoming the prejudice that leads to harassment and violence, education must be a high priority on every campus. From orientation onward, students should receive clear and repeated messages that encourage appreciation for diversity and discourage acts of intolerance. Toward that end, the university should sponsor speakers, cultural events, and other types of affirmative programming. Moreover, the curricula should be carefully evaluated and reformed so as to include perspectives relating to cultural, racial, and sexual diversity.

Faculty and staff also should receive training to help them recognize and overcome their biases. This should extend to campus security, career planning, counseling, residence life, student activities, campus ministries, financial aid, health services, and the dean of students. Although such training obviously cannot require individuals to change their attitudes, it must establish norms of appropriate behavior. Finally, training for both faculty and staff should focus on what must be done when bias-related incidents are brought to their attention.

REFERENCES

Governor's Task Force on Bias-Related Violence. (1988). *Final report.* New York: State of New York, Division of Human Rights.

National Gay & Lesbian Task Force. (1990). *Anti-gay violence, victimization & defamation in 1989.* Washington, DC: Author. (Copies of this and other NGLTF publications may be obtained from the NGLTF, 1734 14th Street N.W., Washington, DC 20009)

National Gay & Lesbian Task Force Policy Institute. (1991). *Anti-gay/lesbian violence, victimization & defamation in 1990.* Washington, DC: Author.

Tift, S. (1989, January 23). Bigots in the ivory tower. *Time,* p. 56.

17

Documenting the Victimization of Lesbians and Gay Men: Methodological Issues

GREGORY M. HEREK
KEVIN T. BERRILL

Accurate information concerning the victimization of lesbians and gay men is of considerable importance for researchers, service providers, policymakers, and community organizations. Researchers need to understand the parameters of the problem of anti-gay violence to study it effectively in its many manifestations. Service providers need to know how victimization occurs and how it affects a variety of subpopulations to design targeted interventions and to conduct community outreach. Policymakers need data with which to determine needs for policies and legislation and to identify areas for funding. The lesbian and gay community needs to know the scope and extent of the problem for all of the same reasons (research, services, policy) as well as for effectively organizing its members to prevent and respond to anti-gay attacks.

As with other types of crime, three principal strategies exist for documenting anti-gay hate crimes, each of which has both strengths and limitations (O'Brien, 1985). One source frequently used in research on criminal victimization is information collected by law enforcement agencies (e.g., police reports). In the past, anti-gay crimes were rarely identified as such in official statistics. The newly enacted Hate Crimes Statistics Act, however, requires the federal government to collect data on hate crimes based on race, ethnicity, religion, and sexual orientation. Although this data collection holds promise for a better understanding of the extent and nature of anti-gay hate crimes, nonreporting of victimization no doubt will remain a problem for the immediate future.

A second data collection strategy is to survey perpetrator populations. Self-report studies of perpetrators can take two forms. One approach is to interview convicted or admitted perpetrators; these respondents, of course, are not necessarily representative of all anti-gay victimizers. Alternatively, groups of potential perpetrators (e.g., adolescent and young adult populations) can be surveyed about their past anti-gay behavior. Neither of these approaches has yet been used in published empirical research on anti-gay hate crimes, although some journalistic accounts follow this model (see Chapter 10).

Surveys of victim populations are a third source of data. Currently, victimization surveys conducted with samples from lesbian and gay communities are the most common source of data on anti-gay hate crimes (see Chapter 1). Because documenting anti-gay victimization has not been a high priority for criminal justice personnel or for individual researchers, activists within the lesbian and gay community often have found it necessary to conduct their own community surveys. The quality of these surveys has varied widely. Lacking adequate training, some researchers have produced surveys of limited usefulness because of flaws in question construction, sampling, methodology, data analysis, or reporting. Surveys also have been hindered by financial constraints and time pressures. Given these problems, the fact that survey results can be used to paint a fairly coherent picture of victimization (see Chapter 1) is a credit to the researchers who have conducted the surveys.

This chapter is intended to provide practical suggestions and resources for researchers and community activists planning to conduct a survey of their local gay and lesbian community. In this chapter, we point out some difficulties with previous surveys and suggest ways to overcome these problems. Recognizing the value of community surveys, we hope to assist in improving them and in making surveys conducted in different regions more comparable. Obviously, this chapter cannot present a thorough discussion of survey methodology; for more information in this regard, see Fowler (1984) and Rossi, Wright, and Anderson (1983).

PLANNING THE SURVEY

Identifying Goals

The first step in the research process is to determine what kind of data are desired and how they will be used. Which items are most appropriate for inclusion in the questionnaire will depend upon how the survey results eventually will be used (e.g., for lobbying legislators or for designing community programs). Community groups that ultimately will use the survey results should be involved in this stage. If the survey is being planned by a community group, social scientists from a local college or university should be asked to assist at this stage, even if only in an advisory capacity. If community researchers are concerned about the survey's ultimate credibility, they might also wish to seek sponsorship or endorsements for the survey from "mainstream" churches or political organizations.

Prioritizing

Researchers usually want to take full advantage of their survey effort by asking as many questions as possible about as many topics as possible. Although this desire is understandable, other considerations also are important. First, from a respondent's perspective, shorter surveys are better surveys. A sure strategy for increasing the rate of response is to develop an attractive, one-page survey that can be completed in less than five minutes. Second, including additional questions requires additional pretesting and analysis, both of which are discussed below. Third, adding items to the survey increases costs of photocopying, postage, data analysis, and the like. For all of these reasons, questions should be included only when they are directly related to the goals of the survey and fit clearly into the overall data analysis plan.

Considering Resources

Directly related to identifying and prioritizing goals, community researchers must consider their resources. At a minimum, funds will be necessary for photocopying questionnaires, distributing them (which may include postage costs), and analyzing the data (which can best be done with a computer equipped with statistical software). Another resource to consider is time. Immediate deadlines (e.g., the data are needed for legislative hearings in the near future) may result in a costlier survey because time is not available to find the least expensive strategy. Under extreme time limitations, researchers should consider alternate strategies for documenting victimization (e.g., obtaining personal testimony from several victims).

SAMPLING

A *sample* is a subset of the entire group about which information is sought; the larger group represented by the sample is the *population* or *universe*. In survey research of the sort described here, the population might be all lesbian and gay male Americans or the lesbian and gay male residents of a state, county, city, or neighborhood. The sample is the group of men and women who actually are asked to complete questionnaires or to be interviewed.

Samples are used primarily when contacting every member of the population is not feasible. The goal is to obtain a sample that is representative of the larger population (i.e., that will yield results similar to those that would be obtained from the population as a whole). Samples are evaluated less by their final characteristics than by the process through which their members were selected. Simply knowing that both the population and a sample drawn from it are 50% female and 15% African American, for example, does not indicate that the sample is representative. Instead, the technique through which the sample was selected must be examined. In brief, the sample is representative only when all members of the population had a chance of being included in it and when the probability of any member's inclusion can be calculated (for further discussion of sampling theory and procedures, see Sudman, 1976).

Because of its high cost and methodological complexities, obtaining a representative sample of lesbians and gay men will not be a realistic possibility for most readers of this chapter. Researchers unable to draw a representative sample should try to collect data from as diverse a group of respondents as possible and should try to identify the subgroups that they failed to reach. They are likely to get the widest and most varied sample when the research team itself is diverse (e.g., when it includes men and women from different racial backgrounds and age groups). Data should be collected in as many places as possible (including sites that are not gay or lesbian identified) to recruit as many different kinds of respondents as possible. Questionnaires can be reprinted in lesbian or gay publications (although this makes calculation of response rate difficult; see below) or, alternatively, a phone number can be disseminated for potential respondents to call to receive a questionnaire. Questionnaires distributed to different groups should be identified unobtrusively to permit later calculation of response rates (e.g., by using different colors of paper or by writing codes on the questionnaires themselves).

As much as possible, researchers should avoid biasing their sample (i.e., they should not recruit respondents in such a way as to overrepresent or underrepresent important subgroups; see Harry, 1986). For example, collecting survey responses at a rally against anti-gay violence or at a self-defense class could bias the sample (and discredit the results) by including a disproportionately large number of victims. The sample also can be biased simply by labeling the survey. A survey with the words *gay* or *lesbian* in its title, for example, may discourage closeted respondents from participating. Even such a straightforward label as "Survey on Victimization" may bias the sample by discouraging respondents who have not themselves been victimized (they may perceive that the survey is not aimed at them). (For an example of a creative approach to sampling, see Martin & Dean, 1990.)

THE SURVEY INSTRUMENT

A good survey is sufficiently interesting and attractive that respondents *want* to complete it. Assuming that most readers of this chapter will use a written survey that respondents will complete themselves (rather than, for example, a telephone survey or face-to-face interview), several basic rules are described here for layout, appearance, and question wording. The survey should be easy to read, simple, and attractive. The pages should not be cluttered or crammed with questions (it should not resemble a bus schedule). A generous amount of blank space should be included on each page to make the survey appear "cleaner" and less intimidating. At the same time, the survey should not have so many pages that it resembles a small telephone directory. Every item should be numbered to prevent inadvertent skipping.

Writing survey questions is considered by many to be an art. Nevertheless, several basic rules can be articulated (for a very useful discussion of question wording, see Sudman & Bradburn, 1982). A basic consideration for researchers is whether to use closed- or open-ended questions. *Closed-ended* items provide an exhaustive list of alternative responses from which respondents choose. *Open-ended* items ask for more general information and then several blank lines are provided on which the respondents write an answer. The following is an example of a closed-ended item concerning the nonreporting of an assault: "Did you decide *not* to report the attack to the police because (a) you feared they would be hostile; (b) you didn't feel it was important enough to report; (c) you feared further reprisals from your attacker; or (d) some other reason?" The following is an open-ended question: "Why did you decide *not* to report the attack to the police?"

Each type of question has advantages and disadvantages. Closed-ended questions allow respondents to complete the questionnaire fairly quickly and are easy to tabulate and analyze; they do not allow respondents to tell their story in their own words, however. Open-ended questions permit respondents to answer from their own frames of reference, uninfluenced by the researcher's response options, and they reveal what is foremost in respondents' minds. But they also have problems. Open-ended questions lengthen the time required to complete the questionnaire, often yield irrelevant material, pose difficulties for respondents who are not verbally skilled, and elicit responses that are difficult to analyze. A frequent strategy is to use open-ended questions in the pretesting stage to define appropriate response alternatives for closed-ended questions in the final questionnaire. A few open-ended questions, however, may be desirable in the final questionnaire, depending upon the researcher's goals (Sheatsley, 1983).

With both closed and open questions, researchers should be careful that only one topic is covered by each question. Short, simple words should be used wherever possible; long or technical words should be avoided unless absolutely necessary, in which case they should be defined for the respondent. Although the matter of question wording might seem simple enough, the same question often can be interpreted very differently by different respondents. For this reason, a survey instrument should always be *pretested* on a small group of people who are similar to those who will receive the final survey. Respondents should be interviewed after they complete the pretest. Researchers should ask about interpretations of each question, which questions were the most difficult to answer, which the easiest, which the most interesting, which the most boring, and why. This information then can be used to revise the survey questions. If necessary, another pretest can be administered to a second group. This process should be repeated until the survey questions are interpreted uniformly by all respondents, and all questions identified by respondents as "bad," "confusing," or "boring" have been revised.

During the pretesting, the survey should be timed to assess whether it is of appropriate length. The more time required for the survey, the more difficult it will be to get respondents to complete it. Respondents' willingness also will vary, of course, according to where the survey is conducted. Someone completing the survey at a dance or party probably will want to finish it quickly, whereas someone standing in line for a concert or movie might be willing to give it more time. Even the most patient and generous respondents experience fatigue, however; consequently, surveys should be as short as possible. A suggested maximum length for a self-administered community victimization survey is three to five pages.

Whenever possible, researchers should try to use items from other surveys. This strategy provides questions that already have been pretested and have been found to be valid (assuming that the items were appropriately evaluated for the original survey). Borrowing from other surveys also allows the results of the two surveys to be directly compared. To encourage the use of similar items across surveys, a set of basic items for assessing victimization are presented in the Appendix in this chapter. Depending on their own research goals, readers can select from these items and supplement them with additional questions.

Demographic Data

All surveys should include items to assess relevant demographic data. Information about sexual orientation, sex, race/ethnicity, and date of birth or age on last birthday always should be collected. Depending upon the study's goals, other relevant demographic information might include highest educational level attained, approximate income last year, degree of "outness" (e.g., has come out to parents, coworkers, employer, heterosexual friends), degree of integration into the gay/lesbian community (e.g., reads community newspapers, goes to community events), current relationship status, home zip code (indicates geographic residence), and whether or not registered to vote (relevant for legislative advocacy). Sample formats for assessing some of these variables are provided in the Appendix.

COLLECTING THE DATA

Standardized techniques should be used when collecting the data: Each survey should be completed under conditions that are as nearly identical as possible. All respondents should receive the same instructions, background information, and assurances of confidentiality before completing the survey.[1] They should each have as private and quiet a setting as possible in which to complete the survey. The persons administering the survey must all be trained to provide the same instructions to respondents and must be prepared to answer questions in a uniform manner (for example, definitions of words or concepts in the questionnaire). Some of these questions will have been raised in the pretest, but new questions often arise in the field. Researchers therefore should agree on general guidelines (e.g., "Don't interpret questions for respondents; tell them to answer as best they can"). Anticipating various logistical problems can make data collection proceed more smoothly.

For example, each researcher should be equipped with extra pencils (short, eraserless pencils can be bought cheaply by the gross) and, if appropriate, several clipboards so that respondents will have a flat writing surface.

DATA ANALYSIS

In earlier times, data analysis required a devoted researcher to sort through questionnaires with a sharp pencil and an adding machine or calculator. Today, personal computers and statistical software have made fairly sophisticated data analysis possible for most researchers. Data analysis should proceed in three stages. First, the *response rate* should be calculated: the ratio of (a) the number of questionnaires completed and returned to (b) the total number of surveys that were distributed. Knowledge of the response rate permits evaluation of how the sample might possibly have been biased. When surveys are distributed in a variety of settings, calculation of the response rates for each setting permits assessment of whether certain groups were more likely than others to respond.

Second, the sample should be described. For example, the number of males and females, their mean (average) ages, and their racial background should be tabulated. Third, the responses to individual items should be analyzed. For each item, the number of people who answered in each response category (e.g., yes or no, agree or disagree) should be calculated. Appropriate cross-tabulations should be conducted. Cross-tabulating simply means tabulating two or more items simultaneously (e.g., number of males and females who did and did not report an attack). Because even a small survey contains a vast number of possible cross-tabulations, researchers must decide which tabulations are most relevant to the survey goals and priorities. At a minimum, each item should be broken down according to respondents' gender, race, sexual orientation, and age group.

REPORTING THE RESULTS

Unfortunately, the findings of anti-gay victimization surveys sometimes are rendered largely unusable by the inadequacy of the written report. Results from some surveys have been disseminated without any accompanying information about the survey methodology, wording of questions, or administration techniques. In some cases, even information about the sample size has been omitted. The absence of such information lowers the credibility of the survey considerably because it prevents readers from evaluating the adequacy of the researchers' methods.

A good research report provides enough information about the survey and the data collection procedures to enable a trained reader to duplicate the study. As a general guide, researchers should explicitly describe how they handled each aspect of the survey described in this chapter, beginning with goals. One strategy for producing a document that is both readable and thorough is to include an Executive Summary at the beginning of the report in which the procedures and major findings are described briefly; this can be followed by a longer report thoroughly describing the survey. Along with other information, the final report should describe how the sample of respondents was obtained as well as the response rate. A copy of the survey instrument should be included.

The responses to each substantive question should be thoroughly described. Although percentages may be reported, the raw frequencies on which the percentages are based should always be included in the report as well. Reporting the actual numbers in conjunction with percentages is important for at least two reasons. First, the numbers can clarify the meaning of percentages by making explicit how they were computed. This is especially important when only a portion of the sample responded to a particular item (e.g., the percentage of respondents reporting a victimization to the police will be based only on the portion of the sample that experienced victimization). The second reason for reporting raw frequencies is related to the actual meaning of survey results. Because most victimization surveys are not based on a representative sample, the findings cannot be assumed to describe the entire lesbian and gay male population. The fact that, say, 50 out of 200 survey respondents (25%) had been assaulted, for example, cannot be assumed to mean that 25% of all gay people in the community have been assaulted. Yet, the fact that 50 lesbians and gay men have been violently attacked because of their sexual orientation is itself important.

Focusing on percentages can lead researchers and activists into a "numbers game" whereby they begin to believe that anti-gay hate crimes are not a significant problem unless they can be shown to affect a large proportion of the gay community (what constitutes "a large proportion" is always a matter of debate). In reality, the existence of *any* anti-gay victimization should be regarded as a serious problem warranting immediate attention.

In addition to quantitative data, the survey may have yielded personal stories and anecdotes from people who have been victimized. These should be included in the final report to illustrate the quantitative findings. After reporting their results, researchers should evaluate the overall survey findings and offer policy recommendations. In addition to providing copies of the report to policymakers, criminal justice personnel, and the press, copies should be distributed to the local gay community whose members provided the data. Additionally, researchers should consider sending a copy of their report to a central clearinghouse, such as the National Gay & Lesbian Task Force, for use by other researchers. Some reports from victimization surveys have even been published in academic journals (e.g., Comstock, 1989; D'Augelli, 1989).

CONCLUSION

Documenting the extent of anti-gay hate crimes is of critical importance in responding effectively to them and preventing them. The task of documentation is difficult and time-consuming but is tremendously valuable if done correctly. By using the guidelines and resources provided in this chapter, researchers can conduct better surveys that will be more useful for the community.

APPENDIX
A Sample Survey of Anti-Gay Violence and Victimization

ANONYMOUS QUESTIONNAIRE

Please answer all questions, even if you have not experienced the incident described. Your responses are completely anonymous. If you wish to make more detailed comments, please write them on a separate page and fold it into this questionnaire.

1. How often have you experienced the following kinds of incidents *because someone presumed you to be a lesbian or gay man?* Please tell us how often you have experienced each incident during the past year and since you reached age 16. Use the following scale:

> 0 = Never
> 1 = Once
> 2 = Twice or More

	DURING PAST YEAR	SINCE AGE 16
a) Had verbal insults directed at you?	____	____
b) Been threatened with physical violence?	____	____
c) Had your personal property damaged or destroyed?	____	____
d) Had objects thrown at you?	____	____
e) Been chased or followed?	____	____
f) Been spat upon?	____	____
g) Been punched, hit, kicked, or beaten?	____	____
h) Been assaulted or wounded with a weapon?	____	____
i) Been sexually harassed (without assault)?	____	____
j) Been sexually assaulted?	____	____
k) Been harassed by police (without assault)?	____	____
l) Been beaten or assaulted by police?	____	____

2. *FOR EACH OF THE ABOVE ITEMS TO WHICH YOU RESPONDED WITH A "1" OR "2":* Did the person make references to AIDS in any of the incidents? *IF YES,* please circle your response for that item (if you wish to describe the incident, please do so below or on the back of this page). *IF NO,* please go on to Question #3 (next page).

Anonymous Questionnaire Continued

If you experienced any of the incidents described on the previous page, please use this section of the survey to tell us about the person(s) who attacked you. If you experienced more than one incident or attack, please describe only the perpetrator(s) of the most recent incident. If you have not experienced an incident, please skip to item #13 on page 4.

3. As far as you know, how many people attacked or harassed you? (Write the actual number or your best guess; if you don't know at all, please write DK)

_____ attackers (total)

How many of them were men?   _____ men

How many were women?   _____ women

For how many were you unsure of their gender?   _____ unsure

4. As far as you could tell, how many of the attackers fit into each of the following age groups? (please write the actual number or your best guess; if "none," please write 0)

_____ Younger than 13   _____ 26 - 40

_____ 13 - 18   _____ Older than 40

_____ 19 - 25   _____ Don't know

5. As far as you could tell, how many of your attackers fit into each of the following racial groups? (please write the actual number or your best guess; if "none," please write 0)

_____ White, not Latino   _____ Asian or Pacific Islander

_____ Black or African American _____ Native American or American Indian

_____ Latin or Hispanic   _____ Don't know

6. As far as you know, how many of the attackers were people whom you know and how many were strangers to you?

_____ Strangers

_____ Person or people I knew

_____ Don't know

7. Did you try to get medical care after the incident? (circle one)

YES   NO   WASN'T NECESSARY

8. In what city, town, or other location did the incident occur? _____

9. Please describe in a few words the place where the incident or attack occurred. If it was in a public setting, please tell us whether it was a setting where lesbians or gay men are known to gather (for example, a gay-identified neighborhood, outside a bookstore or bar or social center).

10. Did you report the incident to the police? (check one)

___ YES, I REPORTED IT

___ NO, I DIDN'T REPORT [*IF NO, WHY DIDN'T YOU REPORT THE INCIDENT? (use the back of this page if needed)*]

11. If you *did* report the incident to the police, how would you describe their overall response to you? Please circle YES or NO for each of the following (*Remember: If you have reported more than once, please describe your most recent reporting experience*)

IN GENERAL, WERE THE POLICE:

SENSITIVE?	yes	no	ABUSIVE?	yes	no
INDIFFERENT?	yes	no	EFFICIENT?	yes	no
HOSTILE?	yes	no	HELPFUL?	yes	no
THREATENING?	yes	no	HOMOPHOBIC?	yes	no
PROFESSIONAL?	yes	no			

If you wish to describe the police response further, please do so here or on the back of this page.

12. Regardless of whether you reported the incident to the police, did you report it to a community organization, a lesbian or gay violence project, or a similar agency?

YES   NO

Anonymous Questionnaire Continued

13. *Whether or not you yourself have been attacked*, has the possibility of anti-gay/lesbian harassment or violence affected in any way how you yourself act or behave? (circle one)

              YES   NO

IF YES, how has it affected the way you act? (*Please use the back of this page*)

14. How many people do you know *personally* who have been verbally harassed, threatened with violence, or physically attacked because they were assumed to be lesbian/gay?

NONE   ONE   TWO OR THREE   MORE THAN THREE

15. Please indicate the extent to which you have experienced each of the following during the past year and since your 16th birthday *because someone presumed you to be a lesbian or gay man.* Use the following scale:

              0 = Never
              1 = Once
              2 = Twice or More

	DURING PAST YEAR	SINCE AGE 16
a) Been denied employment or fired from a job?	____	____
b) Been denied a promotion or salary increase?	____	____
c) Received an unfair work evaluation?	____	____
d) Been evicted or denied housing?	____	____
e) Been refused services in a bar, restaurant, club, or similar establishment?	____	____
f) Been refused services in a hotel, motel, or similar establishment?	____	____
g) Been refused other services or accommodations?	____	____
h) Been denied insurance?	____	____
i) Experienced other discrimination?	____	____

16. How many people do you know *personally* who have been discriminated against in housing, employment, or some other area because they were assumed to be lesbian/gay? (circle one)

NONE   ONE   TWO OR THREE   MORE THAN THREE

17. Has the possibility of anti-gay/lesbian discrimination affected in any way how you yourself act or behave? (circle one)

              YES   NO

IF YES, how has it affected the way you act? (*Please use the back of this page*)

BACKGROUND INFORMATION

18. Please indicate your gender (circle one):   FEMALE   MALE

19. What is your date of birth (month/day/year)?   _____

20. What is your racial/ethnic background (Asian, Black, Latin/Hispanic, Native American, White, etc.)?

_____

21. What is the highest level of formal schooling that you have completed?

_____

22. To give us an idea of the area where you live, what is your home zip code?   _____

23. Please indicate your sexual orientation (circle one):

    GAY/LESBIAN   BISEXUAL, PRIMARILY GAY/LESBIAN

    HETEROSEXUAL   BISEXUAL, PRIMARILY HETEROSEXUAL

24. *If you are gay, lesbian, or bisexual,* how much would you say you are "out" to your friends and acquaintances? Please circle a number on this scale, where 0 indicates that you are not out at all (no one knows you are gay, lesbian, or bisexual) and 9 indicates that you are completely out (everyone knows).

        0   1   2   3   4   5   6   7   8   9

Not Out At All   Completely Out

25. *If you are gay, lesbian, or bisexual,* how much would you say you are "out" to your blood relatives?

        0   1   2   3   4   5   6   7   8   9

Not Out At All   Completely Out

26. *If you are gay, lesbian, or bisexual,* how much would you say you are "out" to your supervisor, colleagues, and the people with whom you work?

        0   1   2   3   4   5   6   7   8   9

Not Out At All   Completely Out

If you would like to describe in detail one or more of your experiences with harassment, discrimination, or violence, please do so on a separate page and enclose with this questionnaire. Or write to: Dr. G. Herek, Psychology Department, University of California, Davis, CA 95616.

NOTE

1. Most community questionnaire studies are conducted anonymously. If respondents' names (or other identifying information) are obtained, however, extensive steps must be taken to ensure that their survey responses remain confidential. Access to identifying information should be limited to one or two members of the research team. Such information should be kept locked in a secure location. All members of the research team should be thoroughly trained in procedures for safeguarding respondents' privacy, and these procedures should be explained to all participants.

REFERENCES

Comstock, G. D. (1989). Victims of anti-gay/lesbian violence. *Journal of Interpersonal Violence, 4,* 101-106.

D'Augelli, A. R. (1989). Lesbians' and gay men's experiences of discrimination and harassment in a university community. *American Journal of Community Psychology, 17,* 317-321.

Fowler, F. J., Jr. (1984). *Survey research methods.* Beverly Hills, CA: Sage.

Harry, J. (1986). Sampling gay men. *Journal of Sex Research, 22,* 21-34.

Martin, J. L., & Dean, L. (1990). Development of a community sample of gay men for an epidemiologic study of AIDS. *American Behavioral Scientist, 33*(5), 546-561.

O'Brien, R. M. (1985). *Crime and victimization data.* Beverly Hills, CA: Sage.

Rossi, P. H., Wright, J. D., & Anderson, A. B. (Eds.). (1983). *Handbook of survey research.* New York: Academic Press.

Sheatsley, P. B. (1983). Questionnaire construction and item writing. In P. H. Rossi, J. D. Wright, & A. B. Anderson (Eds.), *Handbook of survey research* (pp. 195-230). New York: Academic Press.

Sudman, S. (1976). *Applied sampling.* New York: Academic Press.

Sudman, S., & Bradburn, N. M. (1982). *Asking questions: A practical guide to questionnaire design.* San Francisco: Jossey-Bass.

PART V

IMPLICATIONS FOR POLICY

18

Primary and Secondary Victimization in Anti-Gay Hate Crimes: Official Response and Public Policy

KEVIN T. BERRILL
GREGORY M. HEREK

Lesbian and gay male targets of hate crimes face multiple levels of victimization. First, they face *primary victimization* by their assailants. Second, as crime victims, they are likely to experience indifference, rejection, or stigmatization from family, friends, community agencies, and society in general (Coates, Wortman, & Abbey, 1979). Additionally, gay people face the possibility of still further victimization because of American society's willingness to condone prejudice, discrimination, and violence against them (see Chapters 5 and 9). If their sexual orientation becomes publicly known as the result of a crime, lesbians and gay men risk the loss of employment, eviction from housing, denial of public accommodations, and loss of child custody. We refer to such consequences of heterosexism[1] as *secondary victimization*. Secondary victimization occurs when others respond negatively to a crime survivor because of her or his homosexual orientation. In contrast to discrimination based on a victim's race or ethnicity or religion, discrimination on the basis of sexual orientation is prohibited by law in only four

states and several dozen municipalities (National Gay & Lesbian
Task Force [NGLTF], 1988a). Additionally, in approximately one
half of the states and the District of Columbia, gay crime victims
risk prosecution under state sodomy statutes, some of which
carry prison penalties in excess of 10 years.

Secondary victimization is one form of what Harry (1982, p. 546)
labeled "derivative deviance": victimization of people such as
lesbians and gay men "who, because of their deviant status, are
presumed unable to avail themselves of civil protection." Whereas
Harry (1982) emphasized forms of victimization that are officially unacceptable (bashings, extortion, and police shake-
downs), we use the term *secondary victimization* to highlight
negative treatment of gay people that is legal and widely condoned. Although gay victims can seek legal remedies for violent
assaults, for example, they often have no legal recourse if, because they report the attack, their employers learn of their homosexuality and fire them.[2]

The threat of secondary victimization shapes the way lesbian
and gay male survivors respond to the primary victimization of
hate crimes. To respond effectively to anti-gay hate crimes and
their victims, public policy must address both forms of victimization. In this chapter, we describe some manifestations of secondary victimization and offer policy recommendations for an
approach to anti-gay hate crimes that addresses all levels of victimization associated with them. We begin by briefly describing
how governmental nonresponse fosters primary and secondary
victimization of lesbians and gay men.

GOVERNMENT RESPONSE
(AND NONRESPONSE)
TO ANTI-GAY HATE CRIMES

Although various levels of government have begun to address
crimes motivated by racial, ethnic, and religious prejudice, the
official response to anti-gay crimes lags far behind. For example,
28 states and the District of Columbia have enacted laws that
monitor crimes motivated by prejudice or enhance the penalties
attached to them, but such laws specifically address anti-gay
violence in only 20 states and the District of Columbia. In recent

TABLE 18.1 Laws that address hate crimes based on sexual orientation. (Prepared by the National Gay & Lesbian Task Force Policy Institute)

	Statistics Collection*	Provisions Criminal Penalties	Civil Penalties	Injunctive Relief
Federal	1990	—	—	—
State				
Arizona	1991	—	—	—
California	1989	1987	1984	1987
Connecticut	1987	1990	—	—
District of Columbia	1990	1990	1990	1990
Florida	1991	1991	1991	—
Illinois	—	1990	—	—
Iowa	1990	1990	1990	1990
Maine	1991	—	—	—
Maryland	1991	—	—	—
Massachusetts†	1990	1979	1979	1979
Michigan	1991	—	—	—
Minnesota	1988	1989	1989	—
New Jersey	—	1990	—	—
New Hampshire	—	1990	—	—
Nevada	—	1989	1989	1989
Oregon	1989	1989	—	—
Rhode Island	1991	—	—	—
Texas	1991	—	—	—
Utah	1992	1992	—	—
Vermont	—	1990	1990	—
Wisconsin	—	1988	1988	—
Local				
Atlanta (GA)	1989	—	—	—
Burlington (IA)	—	1989	—	—
Chicago (IL)	1990	1990	—	—
Columbus (OH)	—	1988	—	—
El Cerrito (CA)	1991	—	—	—
Louisville (KY)	1990	1990	—	—
Montgomery County (MD)	—	—	1989	—
Oklahoma City (OK)	—	1988	—	—
St. Louis (MO)	1989	1989	1989	—
Seattle (WA)	—	1984	—	—
Wichita (KS)	—	1990	—	—

† Massachusetts laws guaranteeing freedom of movement, speech, and association protects lesbians and gay men and other groups included in state civil rights laws from bias-motivated harassment and violence.
* Although not mandated to do so by law, police departments in several U.S. municipalities, including New York City, currently gather data on crimes based on sexual orientation and other characteristics.

Figure 18.1. Hate Crimes in the United States
NOTE: Some state laws prohibit specific types of hate motivated acts (e.g., cross burnings, institutional vandalism), but do not address crimes motivated on the basis of specific characteristics (e.g., race, gender, sexual orientation). Such laws are not indicated on this map. Artwork by Ann Rall.

years, moreover, hate crime legislation has been blocked, defeated, or amended to delete "sexual orientation" in at least nine other states (Georgia, Maine, Maryland, Michigan, Missouri, New York, Pennsylvania, Texas, and Washington) where legislators objected to any form of statutory recognition or protection for lesbian and gay male citizens.

At the federal level, congressional passage of the Hate Crime Statistics Act was repeatedly delayed because of fierce opposition by Senator Jesse Helms and other outspokenly anti-gay members of the House and Senate (see the Introduction to this volume; Harding, 1990). An exploratory report on the criminal justice system's response to bias crime (Finn & McNeil, 1987) was suppressed by the Justice Department shortly after the news media reported on its conclusion that "homosexuals are probably the most frequent victims" of hate violence in America today (Committee on the Judiciary, 1988).

Given the widespread resistance to addressing the primary victimization of gay people, it is perhaps not surprising that efforts to eliminate secondary victimization have been practically nonexistent. Federal legislation to protect lesbians and gay men from discrimination has languished in Congress since 1974, with no immediate prospects for passage. State sodomy laws remain in effect, providing legal justification for viewing gay people as criminals and deviants.

Such governmental action (and inaction) clearly conveys the message that lesbians and gay men do not deserve full legal protection and justice. It also signals to perpetrators, criminal justice personnel, and the rest of society that anti-gay hate crimes will not be punished and that secondary victimization of gay people is acceptable. As a consequence, lesbian and gay male victims of hate crimes generally do not report to the police and, when they do enter the criminal justice system, are subject to various forms of secondary victimization.[3]

The Criminal Justice System as Victimizer

Crimes in general, and hate crime in particular, are underreported in the United States.[4] Among those victimized by hate crime, lesbians and gay men are especially reluctant to report to the police and seek redress through the criminal justice system (Finn & McNeil, 1987; Governor's Task Force, 1988). For example, in Chapter 3, von Schulthess found that only 15% of the 226 lesbians in her sample who had experienced victimization reported the incident to the police. In Chapter 2, Dean, Wu, and Martin found that only 13%-14% of violent incidents were reported to police in each year of their five-year study. Among the gay men and lesbians surveyed by Platt (1990) and Comstock (1989), 89% and 73%, respectively, declined to report an incident to police. Similarly, 71% of Pennsylvania residents (excluding Philadelphia) who had experienced anti-gay criminal victimization did not report it to the police; rates of reporting were considerably higher in Philadelphia, where "only" 56% of gay men and 52% of lesbians who had suffered criminal violence did not report to the police (Gross, Aurand, & Addessa, 1988). The situation is similar in New Jersey (almost 80% did not report at least one incident; New Jersey Lesbian & Gay Coalition, 1984), Massachusetts (86%; LeBlanc, 1991), Baltimore (87%; Morgen & Grossman, 1988); Minneapolis (91%; Anderson, 1982), and San Francisco

(82%; Winslow, 1982). Campus victimization also is largely unreported. Surveys of gay men and lesbians at Yale (Herek, 1986),
Rutgers (Cavin, 1987), Pennsylvania State (D'Augelli, 1989),
Oberlin (Norris, 1990), and the University of Oregon (Task Force
on Lesbian and Gay Concerns, 1990) revealed that 81% or more
of those who had been victimized declined to report at least one
incident to the police or campus authorities (see Chapter 1).
    One of the reasons most frequently cited by lesbian and gay
male victims for not reporting a crime is their fear of secondary
victimization. Comstock (1989), for example, found that 67% of
those who had declined to report had experienced or perceived
the police to be anti-gay; 14% feared abuse from the police; and
40% feared public disclosure of their sexual orientation.[5] Similarly, fear of the police was among the principal reasons for not
reporting by respondents in Baltimore (Morgen & Grossman,
1988) and Pennsylvania (Gross et al., 1988). The fear and distrust of
law enforcement personnel among gay people are amply justified:
Police abuse of lesbians and gay men appears to be widespread
(see Chapter 1, Tables 1.1 and 1.2). The few gay victims who report
often find the police to be unprofessional, indifferent, or even hostile (Committee on the Judiciary, 1983; Comstock, 1989; District of
Columbia Lesbian and Gay & Anti-Violence Task Force, 1988;
Gross et al., 1988; LeBlanc, 1991; Morgen & Grossman, 1988; Vermonters for Lesbian and Gay Rights, 1987).
    Like victims of rape, the victims of anti-gay hate crimes often are
blamed for the incident by police, prosecutors, judges, and jurors.
Dallas Judge Jack Hampton, for example, justified his lenient sentence for a man convicted of murdering two gay men by stating, "I
put prostitutes and queers at the same level. . . . And I'd be hard
put to give somebody life for killing a prostitute."[6] In another 1988
case involving the beating death of an Asian American gay man, a
Broward County (Florida) Circuit Judge jokingly asked the prosecuting attorney, "That's a crime now, to beat up a homosexual?"
The prosecutor answered, "Yes, sir. And it's also a crime to kill
them." To this the judge replied, "Times have really changed"
(NGLTF, 1989a, p. 25). Other criminal justice officials who recently
engaged in public displays of bigotry include a New York district
attorney who described lesbians and gay men as "queers" and
"sick people" (NGLTF, 1990); a Montgomery, Alabama judge who

called gay people "flaming queens" and "volunteers for AIDS" (NGLTF, 1990); and a Washington, DC, district judge who referred to a gay plaintiff as a "homo" (York, 1991).

Another form of secondary victimization occurs in the courtroom when a gay victim is accused of provoking or inviting the attack. The most dramatic example of such victim blaming is the "homosexual panic defense." This defense, which has prevented the successful prosecution of numerous anti-gay violence cases, alleges that the defendant's violent actions were committed in self-defense against the victim's unwelcome and aggressive sexual overtures or were part of an acute psychological panic resulting from those overtures (Berrill, 1986; Chuang & Addington, 1988; Gonsiorek, 1982). In shifting responsibility from the perpetrator to the victim, the homosexual panic defense appeals strongly to the cultural stereotype of gay people as sexually predatory (e.g., Herek, 1991). Further, it is based on the assumption that murder is an appropriate response to a sexual advance by one man to another (assuming that such an advance even occurred; the homosexual panic defense has been used most successfully when victims were dead and unable to respond to the defendant's allegations).

The homosexual panic defense and similar tactics have resulted in lenient sentences and even acquittals for those charged with assaulting or murdering gay people. For example, Terry B. Kerr, a defendant charged with the brutal murder of Harry Wayne Watson, a gay man, was alleged by the prosecutor to have "kicked [Watson] mercilessly until blood sprayed from his face" and then later to have returned to the crime scene and struck him with a sledgehammer. The defense countered that Watson had attempted to assault Kerr sexually and that Kerr had reacted in self-defense. Kerr was acquitted by the jury. Responding to the verdict, presiding Judge Robert Borsos said, "I would have found first degree murder if it had been a bench trial" (Pierce, 1986). Similarly, when a jury accepted the defense assertion that James Lee Oliver's murder by stabbing of Bruce Mulgrew, a gay man, was justified by an alleged sexual advance, Common Pleas Judge John E. Corrigan called the verdict "absolutely inappropriate. . . . I cannot in my wildest imagination believe that a jury could come up with a verdict as shocking as this" (NGLTF, 1988b, p. 13).[7]

POLICY RECOMMENDATIONS

With this brief discussion, we wish to illustrate the need for governmental responses to anti-gay hate crimes to address secondary as well as primary victimization of lesbians and gay men. Such a broad-based response must include enactment of appropriate legislation, reform of the criminal justice system, and widespread establishment of community education programs.

Federal and State Legislation

Congress and state legislatures can take three major actions to address the problems of anti-gay hate crimes. First, statutes should be enacted that facilitate arrest and prosecution of hate-crime perpetrators, enhance criminal penalties, and authorize victims or their survivors to file civil suits against their assailant(s). These statutes might also require convicted perpetrators of hate crimes to receive education that promotes understanding, tolerance, and respect for gay people, members of other minorities, and women. Such laws will send a clear message to victims, perpetrators, and law enforcement personnel that crimes of violence based on prejudice are especially repugnant to society and will not be tolerated.

Second, legislative bodies should facilitate research on the extent and nature of anti-gay hate crimes. State and federal agencies (e.g., the National Institute of Justice, the National Institute of Mental Health) should receive funding specifically designated for empirical studies of anti-gay and AIDS-related bias crimes. An immediate priority for Congress and the administration should be implementation of the Hate Crime Statistics Act, which mandates the collection of statistics on bias crimes (including those motivated by anti-gay prejudice) by the Department of Justice. Because of substantial underreporting by victims of anti-gay hate crimes, the data initially collected no doubt will represent only the tip of the iceberg. Nevertheless, the legislation constitutes an important first step toward increasing official awareness and response to the problem, which, in turn, will foster the development of policies and procedures designed to encourage reporting.

Third, legislation is needed to eliminate the institutional barriers that discourage reporting and foster secondary victimization. All Americans should be protected from discrimination based on sexual orientation in employment, housing, and services. Further, laws that criminalize consenting sexual conduct between adults should be abolished.

The Criminal Justice System

To respond effectively to primary victimization of lesbians and gay men, the criminal justice system must first enact policies that clearly communicate to law enforcement personnel that such victimization is a crime. Local departments should prepare to respond vigorously to reports of anti-gay violence. Model procedures and programs should be developed for training officers to recognize and respond to acts of anti-gay violence and other hate crimes. Police department activities should be coordinated with those of community organizations to prevent and respond to outbreaks of crime. Incidents that appear to have been motivated by bigotry should be closely monitored and the likelihood of further violence continually assessed. Additional police should be deployed in areas where anti-gay hate crimes are concentrated. In communities where hate crimes are particularly serious or frequent, special units should be established to prevent, investigate, and respond to such incidents. Such units already function in Boston, Chicago, New York City, and San Francisco.

Further, official policies and regulations must be changed so that denigration, harassment, and abuse of lesbian and gay male crime victims by criminal justice personnel is explicitly condemned. Allegations of anti-gay abuse by police must be vigorously investigated and, when substantiated, followed by prompt and appropriate disciplinary action, counseling, and retraining.

In conjunction with these institutional changes, criminal justice personnel (including police, district attorneys, and judges) will need training in how to be sensitive to the needs of survivors of anti-gay hate crimes. In-service and academy/professional training programs should include mandatory education about the gay community and why anti-gay bias crimes are serious as well as training in how to identify and report hate crimes and how to work with their victims. In particular, training is needed in methods for sensitively interviewing survivors of anti-gay violence, similar to those that have been developed for rape victims. Prosecutors also should receive training in selecting jury members in gay-related cases and countering the homosexual panic defense.

Even when a particular police force or district attorney's office has taken positive steps such as those outlined above, residual distrust is likely to remain in the local gay community (see Chapter 14). Consequently, police and district attorneys should reach out to their local lesbian and gay communities. For example, they should communicate frequently with community representatives and, when possible, appoint formal liaisons who can respond quickly to requests for assistance from the gay community. Such liaisons might help to develop collaborative programs between police and community groups for directly reducing violence (e.g., through monitoring neighborhoods).

Perhaps the most effective strategy for sensitizing criminal justice personnel to lesbian and gay concerns is to provide them with opportunities for positive interactions with openly gay colleagues. This requires creating a safe environment in which gay personnel know that their sexual orientation will not be used as the basis for harassment or discrimination against them. Police departments in several major cities have adopted antidiscrimination policies and have initiated recruitment efforts within the gay community (e.g., Atlanta, Boston, New York, San Francisco, and Washington, DC).

In recent years, the rights and the needs of crime victims have received greater recognition and attention from lawmakers and the criminal justice system. This trend, while laudable, has not yet benefited those victims who, because of fear and discrimination, never entered the system. Given the barriers that gay people and other groups must overcome to report hate crimes, additional support and advocacy are urgently required if more victims are to step forward. Government at every level should therefore provide funding to community-based programs, such as those that now exist in New York City and San Francisco, that serve victims of anti-gay and other hate crimes.

Community Education

Finally, we must change the cultural climate in which secondary victimization of lesbians and gay men is tolerated. This will require large-scale collaboration of public and private agencies in developing and implementing programs to reduce prejudice against all minority groups, including lesbians and gay men. We discuss four important foci for such programs.

Elementary and secondary schools. Because many perpetrators of anti-gay street crimes are school-age youth, interventions in public and private schools are especially important. To their credit, increasing numbers of schools already are revising their curricula to educate students about prejudice and oppression. Frequently, however, they fail to address anti-gay prejudice and violence. When educators speak out selectively about intolerance, students can easily acquire the notion that some minority groups are acceptable targets for violence and deserve to be victimized.

Schools should begin by enacting clearly stated antidiscrimination policies that will encourage their gay male and lesbian students, faculty, and staff to be visible in the school setting. Institutionally supported contact with openly gay peers, along with training in sensitivity to lesbian and gay issues, will help to reduce anti-gay prejudice among heterosexual teachers, guidance counselors, administrators, and other staff. Such measures also will enable them to promote understanding and reduce conflicts in the school and create a safe environment in which all students can learn without fear.

Because the AIDS epidemic is often associated with anti-gay prejudice (e.g., Herek & Glunt, 1988, 1991), school programs should be instituted to teach students, faculty, and staff alike how to respond appropriately to the social challenges of AIDS. Training in gay and lesbian concerns, as well as in AIDS education, should be reflected in licensing and professional degree requirements.

Colleges and universities. College and university officials must speak out strongly against anti-gay victimization. Formal policies should be established that prohibit harassment, encourage reporting and ongoing monitoring when incidents occur, and assist victims. Staff (including security personnel) should be trained to

recognize anti-gay bias and to act against it. All instances of harassment or other behaviors that violate campus codes and the
law should be penalized, and this response should be publicized
throughout the campus community. Colleges also should create
an atmosphere of tolerance that fosters an appreciation of human diversity. Steps for achieving such an open climate include re-
forming curricula so that course work incorporates diverse
perspectives, adding sexual orientation to antidiscrimination
policies, and actively seeking openly gay and lesbian faculty,
staff, and administrators (see Chapter 16).

Religious organizations. Although no consensus exists among
people of faith on whether homosexual behavior is right or
wrong, anti-gay violence clearly violates religious teachings. Unfortunately, the American religious community largely has
failed to recognize or condemn attacks against lesbians and gay
men. Regardless of their official stance on homosexual behavior
and relationships, clergy of all faiths should consider how their
teachings might be interpreted to justify violence. They should
educate their followers to recognize anti-gay violence not only
as illegal but also as unjust and immoral. Further, a moral commitment to ending violence requires action against the cultural
conditions that foster it. Thus religious leaders who truly oppose anti-gay violence should support legislation to protect the
civil rights of gay people and end secondary victimization, recognizing that tolerance for basic rights in American democracy
does not require agreement with or endorsement of another
group's philosophy or behavior.

Mass media. Until fairly recently, media coverage has focused on
gay people as the perpetrators of crime rather than its victims. Sen-
sational, misleading terms such as "homosexual murder" (when
either the victim or perpetrator is gay identified) and "homosexual
rape" (instead of the more accurate male-male rape) have been employed. Often, gay criminal offenders have been identified by their
sexual orientation in news reports, even though similar identification is not attached to heterosexual offenders.
    Fortunately, print and electronic media have begun to recog-
nize anti-gay hate crimes as a problem deserving attention. In
addition to television coverage on the network news broadcasts

of ABC, CBS, CNN, and NBC, anti-gay hate crimes have received in-depth focus on shows as varied as *Good Morning America* (ABC), *20/20* (ABC), *Nightline* (ABC), the *Oprah Winfrey* show, and the *Donahue* show. Extensive coverage has been provided by National Public Radio and the ABC Radio network as well as by numerous local radio shows. In addition to routine print coverage, several newspapers have printed special articles, such as the *San Francisco Examiner*'s 16-part report, "Gay in America," in June 1989. Additionally, editorials deploring anti-gay violence have been published in the *Boston Globe, Hartford Courant, Kansas City Times, The New York Times*, and the *Philadelphia Inquirer* (NGLTF, 1989b) and, more recently, in the *San Francisco Chronicle* ("Stiff Penalties for Hate Crimes," 1991) and the *San Francisco Examiner* ("Beating Up Minorities," 1991).

Increased attention to anti-gay violence by the mass media is important for at least two reasons. First, it helps set the agenda for policy debate: Identifying the problems of anti-gay violence and secondary victimization as legitimate issues is a necessary prerequisite to formulating a policy response. Second, media attention can help to redefine social norms that currently permit or encourage secondary victimization of lesbians and gay men. This is only possible, of course, when the content of media coverage highlights the unfairness and injustice of the current treatment faced by gay crime victims. Such a message is unlikely to be communicated, for example, in news reports about legislators' attempts to eliminate "sexual orientation" from a hate crimes law. In other words, the media can only report what happens in the larger society; their ability to foster a more adequate response to hate crimes is constrained by the availability of news items portraying such responses.

CONCLUSION

Anti-gay hate crimes and the secondary victimization that follows them are serious problems for American society that require a broad-based response. The current lack of official policy in this area cannot be viewed as benign or even as neutral. Government's failure to institute policies such as those advocated here serves to endorse the continued victimization of lesbians and gay men.

The government's slow response to anti-gay hate crimes recalls its initial slow response to the AIDS epidemic (Panem, 1988). In both cases, the lives and well-being of gay Americans have been accorded less importance than political agendas promoting prejudice. Recognizing the immediate need to end anti-gay violence, some leaders have begun to speak out. They frequently have been met by fierce resistance from those who seek to perpetuate the victimization of gay people, to deny any measure of acceptance or protection to this very vulnerable minority.

We do not dispute the right of any American to believe privately that homosexual behavior is immoral or to refrain from associating with lesbians and gay men. We strongly disagree, however, with those who would codify such a view into statute and policy. The moral high ground belongs to those who oppose violence, victimization, crime, and bigotry, not to those who support it in the name of their personal beliefs or religion.

NOTES

1. *Heterosexism* is defined here as an ideological system that denies, denigrates, and stigmatizes any nonheterosexual form of behavior, identity, relationship, or community (Chapter 5).

2. At the time of this writing, lesbians and gay men have statutory protection from employment discrimination in Wisconsin, Massachusetts, Hawaii, Connecticut, and in several dozen municipalities, including Chicago, New York, and San Francisco. Legislation in California awaits the Governor's signature.

3. Some governmental responses to anti-gay violence have been positive. Statutes against anti-gay crimes have been enacted in at least 11 U.S. cities as well as 20 states and the District of Columbia. State commissions or task forces have been established in California (Attorney General's Commission, 1986) and New York (Governor's Task Force, 1988); in both states, anti-gay hate crimes are included within the scope of the commission or task force. Lesbian and gay male victim assistance programs in Boston, Chicago, Denver, Minneapolis, New York City, and San Francisco currently receive government funding. The Hate Crime Statistics Act, signed into law by President Bush on April 23, 1990, requires the U.S. Department of Justice to collect data on crimes based on sexual orientation as well as race, religion, and ethnicity. Other federal action has included hearings by the House Subcommittee on Criminal Justice (Committee on the Judiciary, 1986), chaired by Representative John Conyers (D-MI); a 1989 research workshop

on anti-gay violence sponsored by the National Institute of Mental Health; and the tracking of anti-gay episodes by a national hate crimes hotline (1-800/347-HATE) operated by the Community Relations Service of the Department of Justice.

4. According to the 1987 National Crime Survey, 65% of victims of personal crime and 51% of violent crime victims never reported to the police (Bureau of Justice Statistics, 1989).

5. Percentages total more than 100% because some respondents had been multiply victimized or gave multiple reasons for not reporting.

6. From a letter titled: "Before the State Commission on Judicial Conduct. Inquiry Concerning a Judge No. 52. Second Amended Notice of Formal Proceedings" (from R. C. Flowers, Executive Director, State Commission on Judicial Conduct, to the Honorable Morris Jackson Hampton; October 11, 1989).

7. Despite widespread prejudice, some lesbian and gay male victims have received fair treatment by the criminal justice system. In 1988, for example, Common Pleas Judge Oscar F. Spicer found Stephen Roy Carr guilty of murdering Rebecca Wight and wounding her lover, Claudia Brenner, as the two women were making love at their secluded campsite near the Appalachian Trail (see the "Survivor's Story" by Brenner in this volume). He also ruled as inadmissible any defense arguments suggesting that the victims "provoked" the defendant's violence by their sexual orientation or behavior. In an Ohio trial involving the beating and strangling death of Michael Kist, a gay man, Common Pleas Judge Norbert Nadel rejected homosexual panic arguments by the defense, describing those claims as "ludicrous." Judge Nadel asserted, "Justice requires that I place the same value on Michael Kist's life as I would on the life of any other unfortunate crime victim, regardless of lifestyle" (NGLTF, 1989a, pp. 26-27). In delivering a 40-year sentence to a defendant convicted of beating a gay man to death, Connecticut Superior Court Judge Raymond R. Norko asserted that "any crime against any person in our society must be treated equally. Otherwise we lose our sense of civilization" (NGLTF, 1990, p. 20).

REFERENCES

Anderson, C. L. (1982). Males as sexual assault victims: Multiple levels of trauma. *Journal of Homosexuality, 7*(2/3), 145-162.

Attorney General's Commission on Racial, Ethnic, Religious, and Minority Violence. (1986). *Final report.* (Available from Office of the California Attorney General, 1515 K Street, Suite 371, Sacramento, CA 95814)

Beating up minorities. (1991, March 8). *San Francisco Examiner*, p. A-22.

Berrill, K. T. (1986). *Anti-gay violence: Causes, consequences, responses.* Washington, DC: National Gay & Lesbian Task Force.

Bureau of Justice Statistics. (1989). *Criminal victimization in the US: 1987* (Ref. No. NCJ-115524). Washington, DC: U.S. Department of Justice.

Cavin, S. (1987). *Rutgers sexual orientation survey: A report on the experiences of lesbian, gay, and bisexual members of the Rutgers community.* Unpublished manuscript.

Chuang, H. T., & Addington, D. (1988). Homosexual panic: A review of its concept. *Canadian Journal of Psychiatry, 33*, 613-617.

Coates, D., Wortman, C. B., & Abbey, A. (1979). Reactions to victims. In I. H. Frieze, D. Bar-Tal, & J. S. Carroll (Eds.), *New approaches to social problems* (pp. 21-52). San Francisco: Jossey-Bass.

Committee on the Judiciary. (1983). *Police misconduct: Hearing before the Subcommittee on Criminal Justice of the Committee on the Judiciary* (Serial No. 98-50). Washington, DC: Government Printing Office.

Committee on the Judiciary. (1986). *Anti-gay violence: Hearing before the Subcommittee on Criminal Justice of the Committee on the Judiciary, House of Representatives* (Serial No. 132). Washington, DC: Government Printing Office.

Committee on the Judiciary. (1988). *Hearing before the Subcommittee on the Constitution of the Committee on the Judiciary on S. 702, S. 797, and S. 2000* (Serial No. J-100-79). Washington, DC: Government Printing Office.

Comstock, G. D. (1989). Victims of anti-gay/lesbian violence. *Journal of Interpersonal Violence, 4,* 101-106.

D'Augelli, A. R. (1989). Lesbians' and gay men's experiences of discrimination and harassment in a university community. *American Journal of Community Psychology, 17,* 317-321.

District of Columbia Lesbian and Gay and Anti-Violence Task Force. (1988). *Violence against lesbians and gay men in the Washington metropolitan area.* Washington, DC: Author.

Finn, P., & McNeil, T. (1987, October 7). *The response of the criminal justice system to bias crime: An exploratory review.* (Available from Abt Associates, Inc., 55 Wheeler Street, Cambridge, MA 02138-1168)

Gonsiorek, J. C. (1982). The use of diagnostic concepts in working with gay and lesbian populations. *Journal of Homosexuality, 7*(2/3), 9-20.

Governor's Task Force on Bias-Related Violence. (1988). *Final report.* (Available from Division of Human Rights, 55 West 125th Street, New York, NY 10027)

Gross, L., Aurand, S. K., & Addessa, R. (1988). *Violence and discrimination against lesbian and gay people in Philadelphia and the Commonwealth of Pennsylvania.* (Available from the Philadelphia Lesbian and Gay Task Force, 1501 Cherry Street, Philadelphia, PA 19102)

Harding, R. (1990, March 27). Capitol gains: A behind-the-scenes look at the passage of the hate-crimes bill. *Advocate,* pp. 8-10.

Harry, J. (1982). Derivative deviance: The cases of extortion, fag-bashing, and shakedown of gay men. *Criminology, 19,* 546-564.

Herek, G. M. (1986). *The Yale Sexual Orientation Survey: A report on the experiences of lesbian, gay, and bisexual members of the Yale community.* Unpublished manuscript.

Herek, G. M. (1991). Stigma, prejudice, and violence against lesbians and gay men. In J. Gonsiorek & J. Weinrich (Eds.), *Homosexuality: Research implicatons for public policy* (pp. 60-80). Newbury Park, CA: Sage.

Herek, G. M., & Glunt, E. K. (1988). An epidemic of stigma: Public reactions to AIDS. *American Psychologist, 43,* 886-891.

Herek, G. M., & Glunt, E. K. (1991). AIDS-related attitudes in the United States: A preliminary conceptualization. *Journal of Sex Research, 28*(1), 99-123.

LeBlanc, S. (1991). *8 in 10: A special report of the Victim Recovery Program of the Fenway Community Health Center.* Boston: Author. (Available from the Fenway Community Health Center, 7 Haviland Street, Boston, MA 02115)

Morgen, K. B., & Grossman, J. L. (1988). *The prevalence of anti-gay/lesbian victimization in Baltimore.* (Available from Dr. Morgen, 28 Allegheny Avenue, Suite 1304, Towson, MD 21205)

National Gay & Lesbian Task Force. (1989a). *Anti-gay violence, victimization, and defamation in 1988.* Washington, DC: Author. (Copies of this and other NGLTF reports [in subsequent references, see "Available from the NGLTF"] may be obtained from the NGLTF, 1734 14th Street N.W., Washington, DC 20009)

National Gay & Lesbian Task Force. (1989b). *Statements on anti-gay violence by religious, political, and law enforcement leaders: An organizing resource.* Washington, DC: Author. (Available from the NGLTF)

National Gay & Lesbian Task Force. (1990). *Anti-gay violence, victimization, and defamation in 1989.* Washington, DC: Author. (Available from the NGLTF)

National Gay & Lesbian Task Force. (1988a). *Lesbian and gay rights in the U.S.* Washington, DC: Author. (Available from the NGLTF)

National Gay & Lesbian Task Force. (1988b). *Anti-gay violence, victimization, and defamation in 1987.* Washington, DC: Author.

New Jersey Lesbian & Gay Coalition. (1984). *Summary of discrimination survey.* Unpublished summary. (Available from the NJLGC, P.O. Box 1431, New Brunswick, NJ 08903)

Norris, W. (1990). *The report to the general faculty of Oberlin College by the ad hoc committee on lesbian, gay, and bisexual concerns.* Unpublished manuscript. (Available from William Norris, Department of Sociology, King Building #305, Oberlin College, Oberlin, OH 44704-1095)

Panem, S. (1988). *The AIDS bureaucracy.* Cambridge, MA: Harvard University Press.

Pierce, R. (1986, February 7). Judge and jury differ in opinions on murder acquittal. *Kalamazoo Gazette,* p. 1 (Kalamazoo, MI)

Platt, L. (1990). [Unpublished data]. Psychology Graduate Program, Graduate School of the City University of New York.

Stiff penalties for hate crimes. (1991, March 12). *San Francisco Chronicle.*

Task Force on Lesbian and Gay Concerns. (1990). *Creating safety, valuing diversity: Lesbians and gay men in the university.* (Available from the Department of Public Safety, 1319 E. 15th Street, University of Oregon, Eugene, OR 97403)

Vermonters for Lesbian and Gay Rights. (1987). *Discrimination and violence survey of lesbians and gay men in Vermont* (Unpublished summary). Burlington, VT: Author.

Winslow, C. L. (1982). *Mayor's survey of victims of violent personal crimes in San Francisco.* San Francisco: Office of the Mayor, Mayor's Criminal Justice Council.

York, M. (1991, March 9). Judge uses epithet for gay man. *Washington Post,* p. B1.

About the Editors

Kevin T. Berrill is Director of the Anti-Violence and Campus Projects of the National Gay & Lesbian Task Force (NGLTF) Policy Institute. An NGLTF staff member since 1982, he has pioneered efforts to document, publicize, and counter violence against lesbians and gay men. He has authored numerous reports on anti-gay violence, and testified before Congress and other government bodies. His work in this area also includes extensive lobbying, organizing, speaking, and training across the United States. Mr. Berrill is a frequent spokesman on anti-gay violence issues in national media and has appeared on such programs as "Nightline," the "Oprah Winfrey Show," and "Larry King Live." He has served on the board of directors of the National Organization for Victim Assistance (NOVA), and is founder of NOVA's Committee on Lesbian and Gay Concerns. He currently serves on the board of the Campus Violence Prevention Center and is writing a book for lesbians and gay men on confronting harassment.

Gregory M. Herek (Ph.D.) is Associate Research Psychologist at the University of California at Davis. He has published numerous scholarly articles on prejudice against lesbians and gay men, anti-gay violence, and AIDS-related stigma. He is past chairperson of the Committee on Lesbian and Gay Concerns of the American Psychological Association. His advocacy work has included testifying on behalf of the APA in congressional hearings on anti-gay violence, assisting the APA in preparing *amicus* briefs for state and federal court cases, speaking on prejudice against lesbians and gay men, and appearing in national and local media on numerous occasions. His current empirical research includes a national survey of public attitudes concerning the AIDS epidemic, sponsored by the National Institute of Mental Health.

About the Contributors

Richard A. Berk (Ph.D.) is Professor at the University of California at Los Angeles in the Department of Sociology and Program in Social Statistics. He has a bachelor's degree from Yale University and a Ph.D. from the Johns Hopkins University. His research interests include criminal justice and research methods.

Elizabeth A. Boyd is completing her doctoral degree in the Sociology Department at the University of California at Los Angeles. Her research interests include interaction in institutional settings, criminal justice, and applied social research.

Claudia Brenner is an architect living in upstate New York. She has made numerous public appearances to speak about anti-gay violence, and is currently writing a book about her experience as a survivor.

Michael Collins is an investigative journalist. His article on the Blue Boys won a Certificate of Excellence for investigative reporting from the Greater Los Angeles Press Club in 1988.

Laura Dean (M.Ed.) is Associate Director of the AIDS Research Unit at the Columbia University School of Public Health, Division of Sociomedical Sciences. Her expertise is in conducting longitudinal mental health studies.

Howard J. Ehrlich (Ph.D.) is the Research Director of the National Institute Against Prejudice and Violence. He is the author of *The Social Psychology of Prejudice, An Examination of Role Theory,* and *Reinventing Anarchy,* among other books and numerous articles in professional journals.

Linda Garnets (Ph.D.) is a lecturer at the University of California at Los Angeles, an organizational consultant, and a psychotherapist. She has presented and written numerous papers and a forthcoming book on gay and lesbian issues in psychology.

Karl M. Hamner is an NIMH predoctoral fellow in the Sociology Department at the University of California at Los Angeles. His interests include the social impact of the AIDS epidemic and intergroup conflict and cooperation.

Joseph Harry (Ph.D.) is Professor of Sociology at Northern Illinois University. His major publications include *Gay Couples, Gay Children Grown Up,* and *The Social Organization of Gay Males* (with William DeVall).

Joyce Hunter (M.S.W.) is the former Director of Social Services at the Hetrick-Martin Institute, Inc., and cofounder of the Harvey Milk High School. She is also President of the National Lesbian and Gay Health Foundation and is a former commissioner on the New York City Commission on Human Rights. She is currently a pre-doctoral fellow at the HIV Center for Clinical and Behavioral Studies/New York State Psychiatric Institute/Columbia Medical Center.

Barrie Levy (L.C.S.W.) is a psychotherapist, consultant, and lecturer in Los Angeles. She is the author of *Skills for Violence-Free Relationships* and *Dating Violence.*

John L. Martin (Ph.D., M.P.H.) is Associate Professor at Columbia University's School of Public Health. He has been studying the effects of the AIDS epidemic on the gay community since 1982. In 1990, Division 44 of the American Psychological Association recognized him for his distinguished theoretical and empirical contributions to research on lesbian and gay psychological issues.

Beatrice von Schulthess (M.P.H.) is completing her doctoral degree in medical sociology in the Department of Social and Behavioral Sciences of the University of California at San Francisco. Her research interests include violence against women, hate crimes, and women's health policy.

David M. Wertheimer (M.Div., M.S.W.) is Social Services Coordinator/Mental Health Liaison for the King County Mental Health Division in Seattle, Washington. He also teaches lesbian and gay studies at Antioch University, Seattle. From 1985 to 1989, he was Executive Director of the New York City Gay and Lesbian Anti-Violence Project.

Shanyu Wu holds an M.D. degree from the Chungking Medical University in the Sichuan Province in China and an M.P.H. in epidemiology from Columbia University. He is Senior Staff Associate in the AIDS Research Unit of the Columbia University School of Public Health, Division of Sociomedical Studies.